About the Book

In *A Full Moon Rising . . . and the Tao of Menopause*, Kimberly Quinn Smith very humorously tells the tale of entering into the new stage of mid-life, while associating hormonal moments with the lunar schedule and her symbolic metamorphosis into a menopausal werewolf. Throughout her journey she flashes back to her colorful 70's childhood, where she grew up in the eclectic town of New Paltz, New York, a small town just an hour outside of Manhattan. She then brings us back through her early motherhood years and lands us where she resides currently, with a house full of teenagers. Throughout her tale, she makes intermittent, contemplative reflections on her *halfway-ness* and explores strategies of how to learn to embrace the *Principles of the Tao of Menopause*.

A Full Moon Rising

… and the Tao of Menopause

A Full Moon Rising

… and the Tao of Menopause

Copyright © 2007 by Kimberly Quinn Smith

All rights reserved. No part of this book may be used or reproduced by any means, graphic, electronic, or mechanical, including photocopying, recording, taping or by any information storage retrieval system without the written permission of the publisher except in the case of brief quotations embodied in critical articles and reviews.

Author's Note:

The stories of my 70's childhood as well as the current stories involving our family are all true as are the characters. The names, however, have been changed to protect the guilty.

Some characters of my current life stories may be composites of more than one person.

Aunt Marla and her immediate family are fictional and meant to be universal composites of the challenging and crazy family members that each of us learn and grow from, and that many of us strive to avoid turning into in our later years.

ISBN: 978-0-6151-4728-4

Printed in the United States of America

Published by Downhill Edge Productions

This book is dedicated
to the *Matriarchs* of our family
Anne Quinn and Nancy Smith
and the *Great Ones* who trod before them
Marion Hall, Grace Cawthorne, Marguerite Kennedy Quinn, and
Helena Smith

winter

January 24th

The *beginning*.

The forties are actually very good so far, other than the occasional psychotic episodes that I have due to what seems to be a fairly severe hormonal imbalance. Every once and a while I take an all out flip over something that I probably normally would not notice, if I were not in a crazed hormonal trance. It's kind of like the werewolf thing. Werewolves can masquerade around as perfectly normal human beings, and then as soon as the full moon rises in the sky it's all over. They instantly become capable of taking out an old lady or very close loved one without hesitation.

Then, as if waking up after a night out on the town and after consuming far too many Long Island Ice Tea's, there is absolutely no memory of what transpired the night before. You wonder if you were doing the chicken dance on someone's table. Or worse, you wonder if you were doing the chicken dance on someone's table naked.

Maybe I got a tattoo. I should do a full-body check when I get in the shower. This is what it feels like to be a woman in menopause. You have to be aware of the moon's schedule. When the moon is about to enter its full phase, it is a good idea to hide, for the sake of your loved ones and the public in general.

A Full Moon Rising…and the Tao of Menopause

January 25th

All of that talk about hormones and werewolves yesterday made me feel as if I must talk about my Aunt Marla as she once again got under my skin. She has this down to a science, getting under people's skin. Basically, my Aunt Marla is a control freak who is not in recovery but very, very, active. She has virtually no appreciation for *The Principles* or mental health in general and therefore she is a walking, breathing life challenge for those around her.

I suppose that the reason we continue to keep her is due to the realization that we are all a mixed bag and we would prefer not to throw the baby out with the bath water. Not only that, but Aunt Marla's mere presence in our family forces us to grow and advance spiritually whether we choose to or not and whether we are aware of it or not, though sometimes I tire of these life lessons to be quite honest.

In order to give you a visual picture for the remainder of my journey, I will describe her for you. Aunt Marla has very dark hair, almost black, and very light skin. She wears dark glasses similar to those that blind people wear, so dark that you cannot see their eyes. They are rather large so they cover much of her cheek area and they lack rims, similar to the *Foster Grant* sunglasses of the 70's.

Aunt Marla has an intense look on her face all of the time as she does not enjoy herself or those around her. Her hands are long and veiny, and her finger tips can have a hint of yellow at times. This is because Aunt Marla is a chain-smoker. After all that the Surgeon General has had to say about smoking, it is a mystery why people continue to do it.

I shouldn't judge her but I do because this is the life stage for judgment.

Aunt Marla is a tough old bird. She is bossy and that is an understatement. Whatever is in her world she assumes is in everyone's world.

Aunt Marla has a fairly severe case of road rage and flips people off constantly. This is a little less of a big deal in Teaneck, New Jersey, because this is the status quo.

I am trying to remember if I have ever seen Aunt Marla smile. No, I don't think that I have.

Not only is Aunt Marla our most toxic family member, but she is a mystery. No one really knows what lies beneath her hard shell and this keeps us interested in her.

Most of all, Aunt Marla has helped me to appreciate *The Principles of the Tao of Menopause* and for this I am and will remain grateful.

January 26th

The *bludgeoning*.

I have to say that I have still not fully recovered from the bludgeoning that I recently received from my Aunt Marla. This is what happened. My cousin was having a baby shower the weekend after New Year's.

In fact, let's go back a bit just so we can fully appreciate the impact of the emotional right hook. Just as every other mother in the United States, I had been running around like an anxious gazelle since the weekend before Thanksgiving, buying, wrapping, sorting, sorting again, writing cards, planning holiday dinners, and baking.

As the room mother for the second grade, it was my job to call every parent and organize who was to bring in what for the class Christmas party. Then there were the teachers' gifts, the preschool teachers' gifts, and the dance teacher, as I certainly could not forget Miss Gabrielle. She has done so much. The bus driver, and oh yes, I have to remember to tip the garbage guys for dealing with all of the extra *Christmas garbage*.

We had the Nutcracker Recital the weekend *right before* Christmas at the Town Hall, the Holiday Concert at the elementary school, and the Christmas party at Church. The little one just had to see Santa. Before long, we were counting down until the big day. The phone was in a perpetual state of ringing with relatives eager to express their holiday joy. I made that one last trip to the grocery store five times. Everyone appreciates fresh produce, and we don't want to run out of coffee. We most certainly do not want to run out of wine when everything is closed as this would be truly catastrophic.

I think I'll get back-up wine just to be safe.

By the day before Christmas Eve, most mothers in America have at least one foot in the grave, and possibly the big toe of the other. We feel like marathoners when they speak of hitting the wall. We know that we have to keep going, just a little more. We can almost taste the finish line. Just put one foot in front of the other, eyes straight ahead.

Now breathe. In with the good air, out with the bad air. Try to forget about that sister-in-law who is overwhelmingly entitled and irritating. I can do anything for one night. If we could all just be like dishwashers the world would be so much easier. Let the good water in and the bad run right through us. Don't internalize. That is the key, not to internalize. This is how people get cancer. They soak up their irritating family members like a sponge. They devour them like a turkey dinner and then it stays with them much into the next day, if not longer, possibly years. When they burp they can taste it. It comes right back up. In fact, the Italians have a word for it.

It's called *agita*.

January 27th

The *bludgeoning* continued.

So, speaking of stomach acid, I was beginning to tell you just one of many Aunt Marla sagas. The reason that there are so many is that Aunt Marla involves herself in everyone's business. Though there is usually no outward benefit to Aunt Marla's sticking her nose in, she continues to do so which would lead us to believe that she must be getting some kind of *payoff* from her behavior.

This is how it works. Whether a behavior is healthy and acceptable or whether it is Aunt Marla sticking her nose in and stirring things up, we will continue to do what we are doing if there is pay off in it. The reason we continue to do what we do is because it makes us feel good on some level even if the good feeling comes from feeling *bad*. In fact, any therapist worth his or her salt will tell you that self punishment is in first place as far as psychological pay off for undesirable behavior. It is all about what reinforces us and what keeps us going.

It is kind of like Aunt Marla's little habit of chain-smoking.

In this day and age, every one knows that smoking is bad, really, really bad. The tar and nicotine cover your lungs with sticky black filth, and then you suffer and die. This is the process for chain-smoking. For an added bonus, your fingers tips and teeth turn yellow, you get *smoker's wrinkles* on your face, and your breath and clothes smell like an ash tray at the bus station. Still, Aunt Marla continues to smoke one death stick after another because she does not value herself and because she is addicted to nicotine.

She is also addicted to black coffee.

Aunt Marla does not drink lattes, espresso, or anything fun or smooth. She does not add cream or sugar to anything because she prefers the bitter taste that black coffee provides. She will even drink the thick, black coffee from the gas station.

She does not add cream or sugar to her coffee, nor does she add cream or sugar to her life.

Of course, the very definition of insanity is to continue to do the same behavior but expecting a *different result*. I think that Ben Franklin said that as he is frequently the mind behind the words of wisdom, though I do not remember exactly.

As I enter the middle stage of life, I am also finding a need to exert less emotional energy, or to *yield* as the Chinese would say, to the circumstances or life experiences that I find challenging. The Chinese and Ben Franklin together pretty much know everything. I have come to this conclusion.

The ability to yield almost comes naturally at this life stage. I am not sure if it is because we start to get tired or if it is due to hormones, but either way it is the natural way of things and to resist the natural way of things only causes friction to the spirit and speed bumps on one's life path. This is why we need to learn the skills of yielding and acceptance so that our journey into our *half-wayness* will be as enjoyable as possible.

By yielding and accepting, our spirits are empowered.

January 28th

Should's and *ought to's*.

Here I sit waiting at the dentist to have a broken molar fixed. Oh yes, this one is good for at least three hours of very valuable life space that could definitely be used for something else. This is also one thing that changes as we get older, and is only further emphasized as we go through *the change* . . . that is, we become very conscious of our invaluable life space. I have become overtly aware that when I am ninety years old and sitting in a rocking chair, with a crocheted afghan on my lap, that I would do pretty much anything to have that three hours of forty years old back. I find myself thinking about this on a daily basis, and have become extremely selective about how I spend my life space.

All of the sudden we sort of have this awakening that our minutes are golden. People now need to be worthy of my minutes. I no longer spend them recklessly or even passively. In essence, we lose our filters, and this will only get worse as we get older, or better, depending on how you look at it. I am thinking it is very definitely a half-full situation.

And speaking of losing our filters, I forgot to finish up the story about the bludgeoning I received from my Aunt Marla, via car phone, as she was on her way up from Teaneck, New Jersey to attend my cousin's baby shower. Where were we . . . oh yes, I was talking about being in the annual holiday blur, familiar to most mothers in America.

On top of the usual 400 activities that conveniently take place all at once during the last two weekends before Christmas, I also turned the big 4-O the weekend before Christmas. It was great, busy, but great. It was the perfect kick off to the big game. There were several parties, out to dinners, pop-ins and drop-bys. There were lots of cards, some with naked guys on them and funny over-the-hill jokes. There were several cakes, the largest one of which must have violated some fire code. In fact, I was facing the other way when they brought it in. When I turned around, it seemed like an edible inferno. The light was nearly blinding, but warm.

It was so very *thoughty* of everyone. That is a word that my grandmother came up with. She had always told me when I was a little girl that I was thoughty, that it was a very good character trait for one to have, and that she was proud of me for it. It was a week or so of festivities, a marathon of scallops wrapped in bacon, little weenies, and delicate treats that looked too pretty to bite into.

In essence, it was a *birthday season*. Everyone should have a birthday season, especially for those milestone birthdays.

It definitely ranked as one of my best birthday seasons ever, especially since my big day is only five days before Christmas, when people are overscheduled and half-crazed with their last minute holiday to-do lists. This made everything even more meaningful simply due to the time of year that I entered the world, and the fact that *my people* made time for me.

I definitely felt the love this year.

I keep straying away from the story of my Aunt Marla, which will more than likely be anti-climatic once I actually put it out there. Maybe it's something deeply Freudian, or possibly an underlying fear that if she reads this that the clouds will part and I will feel her wrath full force. Anyway, Aunt Marla was on her way up from Teaneck, approximately an eight-hour drive from where we live in northern Vermont. It was the weekend after New Year's when I had been going strong to do the whole Martha Stewart thing, *pre-felony* of course, for my husband and five children, as well as for our extended family and friends.

On top of that my sister, her husband, and their three children under the age of six, stayed with us for the weekend to celebrate the New Year together. It was lots of fun, great company, and the cousins got to hang out. This, however, is where the marathon analogy becomes extremely accurate. It was all good, the whole holiday thing, however, I had officially hit the wall. I was done. It was time to recharge and practice good self-care. Unfortunately for me, my Aunt Marla does not value mental health, which is what the cell phone assault was all about.

And yes, we do have caller ID, thank God, which is my primary stress reducing device. There was, however, a snowstorm, so I answered the phone in a good-hearted attempt to make sure that our dear Aunt Marla was safe and sound on her trek up north. What I did not expect was the bludgeoning that I was about to receive as to why I would not be present at my cousin's baby shower which was only a forty-five minute drive (in good weather). I proceeded to explain that I love my cousin. She is adorable, and that I would love nothing more than to be there if I wasn't completely drained and exhausted from six weeks of entertaining.

Even my bone marrow was tired.

It was all about the timing. Had this party been removed from the six weeks of entertaining and crazed holiday momentum, we would have gone for a little while. I felt, however, that I needed to advocate for my kids on this particular occasion. I also needed to model for them how to set boundaries and practice self-care. Self-care does not mean selfish. It means to seek out and embrace balance, and we were out of balance. We were in desperate need of a break, all of us.

Where I am headed with this story is a place of extreme frustration. I say this because you would not believe the resistance I got from my Aunt Marla. She did not care that I was exhausted down to my bone marrow. She didn't care and she didn't understand. Her motto is show up and be miserable. All that matters is that you are at every single family event regardless if it means that you end up on anti-anxiety medication.

In fact, it is fine if you show up as a corpse, as long as you are present and sitting upright.

Many people simply do not value mental health. It is all about *should's* and *ought to's*. For me, it is about balance. It is about acknowledging and embracing limits. When we operate beyond our limits, we get crazy and stressed out, and for the most part are not that much fun to be around.

As mothers, we are certainly not of any use once we allow ourselves to fall apart. Of course, it does take us a while to acquire this wisdom. During the early years, when we are knee-deep in diapers, running from playgroup to play group, feeling enormous amounts of guilt for all we are not doing and being for everyone, we just don't get it. It is a cause and effect relationship. We take on too much, and don't incorporate the word *no* into our vocabulary, we end up as members of club martyr. It is only when we gain the life knowledge of *stage two* that we truly begin to see this cause and effect relationship, and hopefully at this point have gained the strength to make some changes.

This is one huge benefit to being in my forties. I don't care anymore. And, if I am having a particularly hormonal day, not only do I not care, but I could take out your left kneecap if you push me just one more inch. Menopause is actually a good thing, or at least has some good parts to it. One of the benefits is certainly that we no longer keep our super hero suit in the closet.

Young mothers either keep their super hero suit in the closet or wear it underneath their ivory turtle neck sweaters. They only take it out in the middle of the night when they instinctively know that a child is throwing up three bedrooms down the hallway. They put on their super hero suit so they can fly faster. During the day, they wear it underneath, so they can be supermoms in disguise. You see, the whole thing with being a supermom is to not draw attention to yourself. Being a supermom is all about sacrifice. Buying a new pair of jeans or signing up for that West African dance class that you have been wanting to do since you were seven will just have to wait.

January 29th

It is true, that for some unknown reason, personal sacrifice is scripted on the X chromosome. The sacrifice gene remains dormant during the formative years, gaining strength as it takes in all of the information coming at it via verbal and nonverbal gestures of socialization. We are instructed, on a subconscious level how to be female and what it means to be a good wife and mother. This has improved a great deal over the years, however, the residual effects remain, especially for those of us in our mid-life and our mothers before us.

January 30th

Harriet Tubman.

It is amazing to live long enough to actually witness change, not only personal change, but change as a society. Sometimes I think about what it might be like to have been a spirit tossed into a body years ago, as a pilgrim, a pioneer woman in the wild west, or a slave.

I have books on Harriet Tubman, one of the bravest souls God ever created. I think about what it must have been like to be her as a little girl, not being allowed to learn how to read, to watch your siblings being sold like a sack of flour, or to see your dad whipped. I can only imagine the thoughts that went through her mind and the growth that happened.

Such an advanced soul in such a young body.

I wonder what it must have been like to grow into the woman she was, to not give up. I wonder about that split second of revelation when it became clear to her what she was born to do. What clarity of spirit. What strength.

Harriet Tubman, through all of that pain and growth, got to experience and witness enormous change, not only in who she was, but in humanity.

January 31st

The Chinese art of *expulsion.*

I continue to have thoughts of change and personal transformation and this has caused me to purchase red and yellow paper dragons as I am a *dragon* myself in Chinese Astrology.

You should see my house. It is all decorated for Chinese New Year. I ordered it all from a special catalog. I have two twelve foot long dragons hanging from the ceiling and a bright red banner with Chinese characters hanging across the dining room. I have no idea what it says, but I'm sure that it is something cheerful and positive.

Actually, I don't know this for sure, but I also don't speak Chinese or know anyone who speaks Chinese, so I'm thinking that maybe we can just bury our heads in the sand with that one. After all, the Chinese know everything, and have for thousands of years. According to the Chinese Calendar, it is the year of the Phoenix. For us dragons, this means a terrific year of personal transformation. It's amazing how all of the sudden you wake up and you're forty, especially after spending the last decade and a half being pregnant and immersed in the baby/young child stage.

Maybe it's mid-life that attracts people to the ways of the Chinese, when we are ready to break away from conventional ways of doing things and become daring enough to try something different. We are now brave enough to toss away the Tylenol, and try an alternative method of applying pressure to certain parts of the body to make it go away.

For the Chinese, it's all about the pressure points when it comes to medicine. It's too bad that it doesn't work for the irritating individuals in our lives as well. I can only imagine how great it would be to apply pressure between your thumb and index finger and have an irritating individual completely leave our minds, no longer renting a permanent place in our consciousness. There would be no more zoned out mental rehearsals while sitting in traffic of exactly what we will say the next time we see them, or the next time they do whatever it is that irritates us.

They would just instantly vanish, and not in a bad way, but in a wonderfully liberating way. If this were at all possible, the entire nation would be walking around applying pressure to the area between their thumbs and index fingers. People on Wall Street would sit there in their important meetings, dressed in power suits and ties, waiting to get up for that fourth cup of cappuccino, firmly pressing the desired area on their opposite hand until they had completely expelled their family member or colleague from their mind's eye. People would be walking up and down the streets of Manhattan, Boston, San Francisco and everywhere else applying pressure to *the spot*.

Star Bucks go-ers would sip their lattes with a long straw to avoid disrupting the energy flow through their thumbs and forefingers. Stay-at-home moms would sit in the sandbox unable to help their children make a sandcastle until they had successfully completed the process of Chinese expulsion. It could easily become an addiction.

Another spiritual path that I have begun to explore is the resistance of nothing, which is of course the base or the foundation for those studying and practicing Buddhism. This is not easy. In fact, it may be easier to run a marathon backwards in high heels with a twenty pound weight on my back. Carl Jung said something similar when he said *that which we resist will persist*. It seems that the Chinese in general have adopted this way of thinking and did so when time began.

Though this may all seem basic and simple, for me it can be a day to day challenge when dealing with real, day to day issues and people. I therefore do not in any way want to insinuate that I fully grasp this philosophy, but I do think that I get it on some level. It does not mean to cave in and be a wimp at every given opportunity. It does not mean to be *Polly-do-good-for-all*.

It's about *acceptance*.

It may be about accepting that I may never have the approval of Aunt Marla, and that she may get upset each and every time I am not present at a third cousin twice removed's baby shower. I cannot control anyone else, only myself. This should be written into the Constitution or the Gettysburg Address or something. It seems like much too important of a life principle not to be declared by someone on an official document.

The *Live and Let Live* slogan is a brick in the foundation of self-help groups, which is a good thing. It's also a bumper sticker.

Anyway, the part that I need to let go of, to cease resisting, is the part where Aunt Marla gets upset, or anyone else for that matter, because I can't control anyone else's anger. What I can control, however, is how I allow someone else's anger to affect me, and the quality of my day. After all, a person's anger belongs only to them, and not to me. Once I accept this very basic fact, my blood pressure will drop significantly and I will be more at peace with my world. Aunt Marla may be pacing in her living room, or sitting in the front seat of her Saturn stiffly, as she does mental playbacks of our conversation. Each time she plays back, she gets angrier and angrier.

This is how it works with thoughts and feelings. First you think it, then you feel it. Thoughts come first. Thoughts always come first. Without the thought, you can't have the feeling. You would be surprised how many people don't get that. You would be even more surprised at how many control freaks there are out there, spending enormous amounts of energy to control people and situations, yet no effort is made to control their own thinking. Many individuals who feel the need to control or manipulate their surroundings don't understand that if they poured all of that energy inward they would be much better off. They would be happier and their desire to control everyone and everything would diminish. If they had a deeper understanding of *The Principles of the Tao of Menopause*, they would find peace.

This is the *first principle-thought control.*

A Full Moon Rising…and the Tao of Menopause

February 1st

You really would be surprised at how many women enter the stage of mid-life and have no understanding of what it means to be here or of *The Principles of the Tao of Menopause*. Women often enter this stage completely frazzled from the previous life stage. This is especially true for mothers.

For most of us, we enjoyed the stage of young motherhood immensely. We enjoyed saving the first lock of hair and taping it into their scrapbooks along with their first preschool drawing, their kindergarten handprint, and their first report card. Before long we were sitting in the front row of a ballet recital or a soccer game wondering when they began allowing infants to play sports. We realized that this was all happening too fast. Most of us have memories of having moments where we just stared at them while they worked on a fifth grade school project, having interim flashbacks of the same child working on his first wooden puzzle with only four pieces. We watched with adoring eyes as he struggled to find the right place for the giraffe. He would turn it upside down and sideways, then lean on it with all of his weight to get the piece to fit.

After letting him try on his own, we gently reach over and help him slide the giraffe into its rightful position, and smile. He smiles back with eyes that say, "you know everything in the whole world and you are my hero." We cherish these moments.

When we snap out of it, we realize that what we have now are not cheeky little cherubs who worship us, but teenagers. Some may question what the Almighty was thinking when He planned things. To have teenagers *and* be in menopause seems to be ruthlessly cruel, but who are we to question Him. Either that, or it's God's way of expressing his sense of humor. That's it. It's a Divine joke. It must be to allow a household to have so many hormones flying around at once. After all, hormones are life's wildcard. You never know when *a wave* is on its way. We also never know how we will *ride the wave*. Our ability to ride the hormonal wave is dependent on so many variables, that unfortunately for those who live with us, or even those who may be standing in line behind us, it is a dice roll.

Of course, anyone who understands waves and especially tides, knows that they are completely dependent upon the state of the moon.

I was planning to have the family over for our daughter's birthday this weekend, however, according to the lunar schedule the moon will be full and in Scorpio. Having a family party while the moon is full and in Scorpio would involve a high degree of risk and danger, especially for annoying and unwanted family members.

A select few women in the room could end up surrounded by barbed wire and wearing orange suits, but of course, only if they are caught.

This is not their fault as their behavior is controlled by forces outside of themselves. Menopausal behavior is controlled by hormones and the moon.

This is why one must pay attention to the lunar schedule and plan family parties accordingly.

February 3rd

The second principle-let the little stuff go. It's just not that important.

After incorporating the *First Principle of the Tao*, and realizing that thoughts precede feelings, the next step is to use this principle to realize when a wave of *nasties* is upon us and not to resist it. What this means is to accept that this is a *chemical low* and that it will pass. This is not a time to analyze ourselves, why we feel like this, or where our parents went wrong during our early childhood. It is not a time to get *deep*, as these feelings will pass. It may also be a good time to remove all weapons and sharp objects from the house, or at least the ones that are within reach.

Of course, the first principle rolls right into the second and could possibly be the toughest of the Tao principles as the last thing we want to do during a hormonal wave is to let go of anything. What we are inclined to do is *attach*. We want to dive right in and really get into it. In fact, *Darwin's Survival of the Fittest Theory* takes on a whole new meaning . . . as a very powerful and primal urge to rip someone's face off comes right to the surface. Like a lioness on a hunt, we silently sing *I am woman, hear me roar* as we let Polly-do-good-for-all know exactly how we feel about how she keeps her house perfect and free of dust bunnies.

Of course, there can be strength in menopause and in hormones as well. When the darkness fades with the brightness of the full moon as it slowly sinks in the sky, and we begin to recognize our surroundings, we begin to wonder what transpired while we were in our altered state of consciousness. We ponder what happened when we were werewolves last night. What did we say . . . and did he deserve it. We are then overwhelmed with feelings of shame, similar to someone who has just awakened from a drunken episode and shattered a relationship with some very loose lips.

There are moments, however, when a hormonal explosion can be to our advantage, when things spontaneously align with the universe and that person who has been like chronic Chinese water torture for most of our lives makes the unfortunate mistake of glancing in our direction as the full moon rises in the night sky.

Years of built up frustration make their way to the surface as we undergo *the change*. We begin to feel the metamorphosis as our DNA is altered with the gravitational pull of the full moon. We feel the fur grow on our forearms. Our teeth get longer until we feel them touching our bottom lip. Our eyes undergo a burning sensation as they cross over from a gentle hazel to a fiery yellow. The calm mother of five has turned into a hormonal werewolf. Polly-do-good-for-all be warned. She knows not what she does.

February 7th

Be aware of the lunar calendar.

The part where *she knows not what she does* is so real that it has even been used as a legal defense when a woman completely snaps and kills the *other woman* who's phone number she found on the back of a cocktail napkin in her husband's pocket. The reason . . . uncontrollable rage due to a hormonal explosion.

This woman, just an hour previous, may have been walking up and down the isles of the local grocery store squeezing fruit for freshness and stocking up on the cereal that's on sale. She might even chit chat with a few women as she waits in line, while she casually flips through the *Enquirer* she has just pulled off the shelf. She pretends to be completely uninterested in its contents as she reads the captions under each photo, and wonders how the woman in the picture lost 115 pounds in just eight weeks. She begins to think about her own body and her age. Maybe it's time to join a gym before it's too late and gravity completely takes over.

Winter

She wonders if she is attractive anymore.

As she puts her groceries in the car, she thinks about what she is going to make for dinner tonight, and about how much laundry has piled up in the basement. As she thinks about the laundry, she begins to feel a racy sensation all over as the hormones slowly simmer. Then she begins to get irritated at the lack of help she gets with household tasks, especially the laundry. There is no respect. The husband and the kids just assume that she will do it if they forget.

It is the age old *unpaid maid scenario*. Every once and a while she will silently go on strike, refusing to wash so much as a sock, or cook a single grain of rice. After a week goes by and no one in the house has even noticed, she slowly begins to take on her household duties, one at a time, while the resentment builds inside of her like a well-shaken bottle of champagne ready to blow. She feels the hatred molecules running through her veins. She ponders what it is that she hates. As she begins to separate the colors from the whites, she goes through the pockets. One of the teenagers left a pen in one of his pockets. Good interception there.

Then she feels something in her husband's pants pocket. She takes it out and gently unfolds it. It is a napkin from the *Tippity Tap*, a gin mill on the other side of town. It has a woman's name on it and it smells like perfume.

For a brief second she stands there, in shock. A soft glimmer of light gently gleams through the window. It is the moon and it's full. Her eyes begin to burn as if she had just stepped out of a heavily chlorinated hot tub at a cheap hotel. She swipes her sleeve across her mouth. A thick, slimy piece of drewl hangs down from her wrist. Then she notices the fur beneath her sleeve. There is a lot of it. It's thick and bristly. She wonders what is happening to her and where she is. The hatred molecules rise to the surface like foam on boiling water. That woman. She has to find that woman. She searches for her husband's hand gun. It must be here somewhere.

Her glowing yellow eyes rest on the garden clippers hanging above the dryer. These could work if she happens to find her husband also. In a crazed blur, she struggles to find her keys. She hooks them over her claw and climbs in the car, leaving a trail of thick drewl behind her. As she pulls out of her suburban driveway, she rolls down the window and stretches her neck up towards the moon. She lets out a howl that rings through the darkness for miles. She pauses and listens to her own breathing. Off in the distance she can hear the cries of other werewolves. She does not know them but they answer her. They understand.

She knows not what she does.

February 8th

A fine line and the future of medical check-ups.

I think that most of us at this point in life have realized that there is a very fine line between a crazed woman in menopause and someone who crosses over to full-blown psychotic. I know that I am a whole lot less judgmental these days when I read the front-page news.

And, if we were truly honest with ourselves, we would admit that it is not simply a fine line but a thread we are walking on. This is because of the hatred molecules that are produced during menopause. Maybe some day when the doctor orders a routine blood test to check for cholesterol, she will also check our level of hatred molecules. When the lab results come back indicating that our level of hatred molecules is in the dangerous range, she will ask us to step into her office for a private talk.

We will then discuss our habits. The doctor will ask us if we have been setting boundaries with friends and family on a regular basis. She will ask us what our relationship is with the word *no* and how often we use it. She will ask us about our in-laws. She will also want to know if we are having lots of sex as this also helps to regulate hatred molecules and how they are processed in the body. She will then explain that running long distance, playing racquet ball, and enjoying a really active sex life will not only reduce dangerously high levels of hatred molecules, but will add years to our lives.

Physical activity, especially physical activity that involves orgasms is great for a natural endorphin release. It also burns lots of calories. It is your basic win-win situation. She will then tell us that if we eat lots of garlic and avoid fried foods that all will be well.

This is actually the *third principle of the Tao of menopause-have lots and lots of sex*, with your husband, partner, or yourself.

It is interesting that this part of mid-life has not been given the attention it deserves. When we write about or discuss sexuality it is most frequently about teenagers and is often negative. The topics of discussion are usually about how not to get pregnant and how to avoid sexually transmitted disease.

This is important information, however, very little is written about horney women in menopause.

The truth is, that there isn't a twenty-year-old out there who would be able keep up with a menopausal partner. It would be like asking a four-year-old to run the New York City Marathon. They can't do it. For the mid-life lady, however, her sex drive is like rocket fuel. When she gets the urge, the ground below begins to rumble. It is difficult to contain her sexual energy. She is powerful and that power is explosive. She radiates heat from every pore. She is as hot as a white flame, the kind you need special glasses to look at. Her partner can't even look at her directly without causing damage to his retinas. He begins to shake as he gets near her. The ground rumbles like thunder. They countdown. All of the sudden there is more heat, and a feeling so intense that it cannot be put into words. They lift off, together. Before long, they will break through the atmosphere, then float freely through space.

This is what it feels like to have sex when you are a woman in menopause. If it were an Olympic Sport we'd be *bringing home the Gold*.

February 9th

Book stores.

It's worth mentioning also, that the menopausal woman is often liberated from the traditional ways of having sex. And, no, this does not mean farm animals. She does, however, become more willing to try new and exciting things. This is true whether she has been married forever or if she is in a new relationship. She may even buy a book. Menopausal women like books. This is the life stage for personal transformation, so we are all about books. We will buy anything on the shelf if we think it will provide some insight about something, anything.

A Full Moon Rising…and the Tao of Menopause

So, the menopausal woman takes off to a bookstore with her best menopausal girlfriend to buy books on improving their sex lives. In the book, are pictures of new and exciting ways to enhance one's partner and oneself. There are positions, lots of new positions to try.

There is one called *doggie style*, a few that look like you may need to have a background in gymnastics, and a couple that could be considered to be a moderate to heavy aerobic workout. The two women stand there in the isle of the bookstore like schoolgirls getting a glimpse of their first penis. The difference, of course, is that schoolgirls normally hide a copy of *Playgirl* in a bigger Magazine such as *Life* so that they can walk up and down the isle giggling and pointing without being noticed.

Mid-lifers stand in the dead center of the bookstore while people walk around them to get to the cashier. The people excuse themselves as they walk by and wonder what is so funny. Then they notice the cover of the book. Many glare or shake their heads in disgust. Menopausal women don't care whose watching and they don't giggle. They laugh out loud.

Menopausal women are also apt to buy a *toy* or two and make frequent trips to Victoria's Secret. In fact, a bunch of us mid-life ladies went out to dinner a few weeks ago and the conversation caused me to nearly break a rib. I am sure that the rest of the restaurant was laughing along with us or possibly *at* us . . . *like we care*.

Those of us in this wonderful life stage of menopause and plummeting hormones have the world by the ass. It is a confidence that is difficult to explain. We laugh out loud and we are not afraid to get up and dance. We are also quite open about our sex lives, at least within the menopausal community. Of course, if the poor husbands had any idea how well the members of the group knew them they would most likely look for the nearest large boulder to hide beneath.

We talk about everything. There is an implicit trust amongst the members of the menopausal dinner club. Nobody judges anybody else, not that this would happen, as we are far too busy trying to contain ourselves in public. We also do not blab outside of our little dinner club. Just as with any other support group, the premise of *what is said here stays here* applies to us also.

The only difference with the menopausal dinner club is that we have a tendency to get a bit loud on occasion, so what is said often stays between the group members as well as everyone else in the restaurant. Such was the case when one group member brought up her new found friend, the *pocket-rocket*. Feeling somewhat like a twelve-year-old hanging out with a bunch of older teenagers, I was embarrassed to ask what a pocket-rocket was. After the group finally got a grip on itself from laughing so hard, one of the women was able to get the words out to explain to me what it was. Very simply put, a pocket-rocket is a mini-dildo, or better said, a travel-dildo. It is compact like an alarm clock or a tooth brush. Now if they just would have said *dildo*, I would have been saved the embarrassment of asking such a horrid question of my mid-life peers.

Of course, the girls had had a few glasses of wine for themselves at this point so shutting them off was darn near impossible.

Apparently, this particular member was not finding herself satisfied with the mere four times a week that her husband provided his services so she invested in a toy. She can now enjoy self-service and is the master of her own pleasure points. Mid-lifers are all about pleasure points.

It also seems that the more we get the more we want. This is also a Taylor Dane song. I have the CD. It is very true. The more O's we have, the more we *must* have or we cannot go on. It's kind of like having that first potato chip or truffle. If we didn't take that first little nibble we would probably be fine, but once we sink our teeth into that first dark chocolate truffle it's all over. We must have more. The dark side within comes right to the surface as we cave in to carnal temptation. Worse than that, it gets increasingly more difficult to stroll through the produce isle of the grocery store without seeing cucumbers in a whole new light.

This of course, is all due to hormones. Hormones get such a bad wrap. People tend to have sympathy for other people who live with teenagers and hormones are the reason. Hormones are also responsible for postpartum depression as well as a fairly high number of deaths due to crazed menopausal women with handguns.

Very little attention is given to the *benefits* of hormones. In fact, we should appreciate our hormones. If Hallmark came out with a *Hormone Appreciation Day* they would make a fortune, at least from the mid-lifers because *we get it*. We now understand that during the middle of our totally irregular menstrual cycles that our ovaries are kicking out approximately fifteen to twenty eggs instead of just one.

If we got pregnant now there would not only be a huge population explosion, but the suicide hotlines would be ringing off the hook. Thankfully, most of us do not get pregnant, but instead benefit from the intense feeling of horniness that accompanies the ovulation process.

Like alley cats, we are in heat.

February 10th

All of this talk about pleasure points has made me think about *nakedness* and how much it has changed. When I grew up during the 70's, the media was not nearly as saturated with sex. Porn sites did not exist as there was no Internet. Hyper-masculine and hyper-feminine characters on video games did not exist either.

Nakedness in the 70's was healthier and more innocent I guess.

In fact, I remember sun bathing topless with my friend on her roof. We truly thought we were rogues. We also lived in a neighborhood and thought that no one could see us because the roof had a bit of a tilt to it and because of a large oak tree. Well, no one could see us from the street behind us, but we later found out that everyone on Elm street was singing our song. We were just not aware of it.

We used to grow pot in the old field behind her house. It was actually the *New York State Conservation Department*. Our weed was safe.

We never even smoked it. Growing it was enough as this was the stage for rebellion so this is what we did. This is also where my friend hid her stash of *Playgirl* magazines and where my sex education began, in the middle of a field that belonged to the state of New York.

We had another friend in the neighborhood. Her name was Mari and she was a year or two older than we were. Mari knew everything, about sex I mean. She was full of very valuable information and we looked forward to what she had to say as it was mostly all new and we were curious. With the visual aid of the *Playgirl* magazines, she would proceed to describe in detail what *the process* was and variations of *the process*.

We new the basics of course, as they taught us this in school, even in the 70's. Mari, however, was *experienced*. Nobody was ever home at her house and she did a lot of things. Her dad worked about a million hours a week at this company in Manhattan, and her mother took off when she was only eight years old. She had two older sisters and a brother and they did a lot also because nobody watched them either. One of her sisters had already been arrested a bunch of times.

I felt bad for Mari because she didn't have a mother. Her mother had just decided to leave one day. She left a note. Then she went to Europe. I can't imagine how it feels to have your mother leave. It must have felt as if she didn't want Mari. That's how I would have felt. At least I think so.

Mari's mother was never heard from again until Mari was all grown up. I guess she was living in Paris with some guy and decided to become French or something. Who knows. One day she called Mari and just started talking. I can't imagine how Mari must have felt after being abandoned by her mother when she was only eight years old and being without her for her whole childhood. Mari had no mother around to ask questions about boys or sex, or life in general. Each and every birthday and Christmas was motherless. I cannot even imagine being in Mari's shoes.

Mari forgave her mother. It was that fast, too. Though the relationship would obviously be different at this point, Mari did not relish in what could have been or the deep pain she felt when her mother left, nor did she choose to reside in the aftermath of having no mother around for the important moments in her life.

I remember when this happened and I have a clear memory of it as we were grown up. I was in awe of Mari's emotional strength and resilience. Very few would be able to do what she did and with genuine sincerity. I felt that her mother didn't deserve to have a daughter like Mari. She walked out on Mari and missed her whole life. Mari had a really big heart.

I think this is called grace, when we *do get* what we *don't deserve* and we *don't get* what we *do deserve*.

Anyway, the fact that Mari's mother took off is probably why her sister was always getting arrested. The other one got pregnant when she was only a junior in high school. She had an abortion. I am not sure what happened with her brother. He was always really quiet and kept to himself in his room. He had a sword collection.

Anyway, Mari knew a lot of things because she did them with boys even though she wasn't old enough to. It seemed that she did these things because it made her feel good to do them and because she felt loved or something.

She did these things with lots of boys and then she would tell us about them. This was sad, of course, but we were thirteen and looked forward to her stories because we were curious. The things Mari did they didn't tell you about in school.

I guess being a teenager and being in menopause actually have something in common. Hormones for one. As teens, all we talked about was sex and this is true once again. We were also trying to figure out who we were and this is also still true. Sex and self awareness are what it is all about during these life stages.

I reflect on how much the world has changed since the 70's.

As I lay there in bed thinking of the 70's and innocent nakedness, I am startled out of my childhood flashback by a phone call from the seventh grade teacher that it is a snow day.

This is how it works when you have five children. One minute you are in the 70's enjoying a warm memory of sunbathing on a roof, and the next you are making pancakes and coming up with creative art projects to survive a day with five kids stuck inside due to ice and blustery winds.

The kids are not awake yet. The snow is beautiful resting on the railing of the deck, so soft and fluffy. It is a peaceful morning. I embrace this peace. Before long, the kids will be awake and the day will begin with its momentum. I also love the feeling of total solitude that freshly fallen snow brings with it. Snow is from heaven.

This is the *fourth principle of the Tao-embrace spontaneous moments of solitude.* This is true for all of us, but especially for moms in menopause, this is one of the most important principles to master. This means that if the four-year-old falls asleep on the couch, that it is not time to clean the bathroom or return phone calls for work. This time should be embraced and protected. It is invaluable. Our sanity and inner peace depend on having adequate time to ourselves to hear our thoughts and sit with our feelings.

We have much to sort through after all of these years. We have lots to reflect upon and we need silence to do it. Outer silence brings inner silence.

Of course, the woods are best, but even if you are a menopausal woman in the inner city, you can find peace. You can create peace. Candles are good for this. Color is good also. Color can be brought into a living room via fresh cut flowers or seasonally appropriate decorations.

I am big on decorating and it doesn't need to be a party. We have a wood stove in our living room surrounded by brick. We rarely use it so I decorate it with whatever is going on at the time. In the fall it is covered with leaves and ceramic pumpkins. During Christmas, it is happily decorated with a variety of snow people and pink and white poinsettias. Valentine's Day brings with it lots of red, red hearts and cupids on the windows and little ceramic Valentine's decorations on top of the wood stove. In July, it is decorated with a variety of brightly colored gladiolas that stand tall and proud to salute summer's victory after a long, cold winter.

In fact, I usually have at least two vases full of colorful flowers, especially in the dead of winter when there is a drought of color. I also put them in the bathroom. I found an antique porcelain water pitcher that I practically stole for a mere five dollars at a yard sale. I fill it every two weeks with an assortment of fresh cut flowers. Even the ladies at the grocery store know that they are spared wrapping my flowers in the fancy paper as they are *just for me*. They will look at each other and ask me if these are *the ones going in the bathroom*.

This brings us to the *Fifth Principle of the Tao of menopause-keep fresh cut flowers in your bathroom at all times*. They can be pink carnations from the local grocery store or daisies from the backyard. It doesn't matter and long as the bathroom is given the respect it deserves. The reason the bathroom is worthy of so much respect, is that it houses *the tub*. We love bath tubs, all bath tubs. They can be big or small, with jets or without. As long as they can be filled to the top with steamy hot water and lots of bubbles, it really doesn't much matter. In fact, there is not much that a hot bubble bath cannot fix, at least temporarily. Menopausal club members worship *the tub*.

This also happens to be the *sixth principle of the Tao-take lots of bubble baths*. Surround the tub with candles and all things that smell good. These are the simple pleasures of life, the things that make it all worth it. They also happen to be quite inexpensive. My personal favorites are the little gelled bath beads. I like to pull them under water, squish them and watch the gel seep out. I love the smell and it is instant from the time they break open. The other kinds are good, too. It's all good when it comes to infiltrating our senses with wonderful fragrances.

I also enjoy bringing in a book or magazine on occasion. I will admit that I have had a few book casualties, unfortunate victims of slippery fingers that fell to their heated, watery demise, slowly making their way to the bottom before I was able to blindly feel for them beneath the bubbles. Oh well. Thankfully it's not a tumor, only a magazine.

February 11th

Something else I have learned to enjoy is cooking. When I think back to when I first got married, I am not sure I would have envisioned myself sipping a glass of red wine, listening to Miles Davis, and sautéing scallops. I actually enjoy cooking now, but it wasn't always that way.

In fact, my husband saved the spatula that I melted when I attempted my very first pot roast fifteen years ago. From there it became a situation where I had to learn enough things to make in order to fill up the week, not counting Fridays because that's *pizza night.*

Of course some women marry men who cook. I, however, did not. My darling cooked for me once back in 1989 when we were engaged. He made chicken, peas, and mashed potatoes (from a box). This was of course a trick so I would think that we would share the cooking and have a more domestically equal, more cosmopolitan relationship. Little did I know that as soon as we said our wedding vows that I would be destined to turn into Donna Reed.

I have, however, gradually learned to enjoy it, and *gradually* is the key. I think that this is the key with most things actually. We can choose to make something positive if we really want to. In fact, young mothers will rarely complain about going to the dentist to get a filling, because they are so happy just to be able to sit down for a whole half an hour without having to change a diaper or reach for a juice box. It's all in the perspective.

Therefore, as far as the cooking thing, I guess I came to terms with the fact that I was going to spend a good deal of time in the kitchen anyway, since one of us had to feed seven people. It all comes back to resistance. Once we accept something it becomes so much easier and so much more enjoyable, not always, but definitely more often.

So I changed my routine. Several years ago I started having one night, sometimes two, where only one of the kids gets to help make dinner with me in the kitchen. This is certainly not a fast process, but it is nice for each of them to have individual time and nice for me also. The little ones make pasta and easy chicken dishes, and the oldest makes a mean garlic and shrimp dish. He also makes excellent scallops. His younger brother recently told me that he wants to try baked flounder. Sometimes they will sit and flip through cookbooks looking for something new and exciting.

What is also a good thing, is that is pulls me out of my comfy zone. I think most of us have experienced the cooking rut, where we make the same things over and over because we can make them in our sleep or they are quick or both. This is definitely true if we are in the middle of soccer or baseball season when all we are trying to do is survive. In between, however, it is fun to shake things up a little. Even if a recipe totally bombs it was still fun to try and actually most things can be resuscitated somewhat.

The cooking rut is also symbolic of a *life rut*. When we start to spend too much time in sweat pants, it's time to make some changes. It is time to break away from what is comfortable and try something new. The changes don't need to be huge either.

If you are sick of your job, however, and dread getting up to go to work in the morning then now would be the opportune time to jump ship and explore new avenues. Making smaller changes such as buying star fruit instead of the same boring bag of apples every single week at the grocery store is also a good idea. Taking up zydeco dancing or hot air ballooning are also good menopausal activities.

The point is the energy flow. We get out what we put in. Sometimes the toughest part is getting off the couch, making the phone call to sign up for that sculpture class, or buying a shark fillet instead of the usual tenderloin. Having another energetic, menopausal friend can certainly help. She can serve as your own personal set of human jumper cables, taking some of her energy and passing it on to you. Better yet, you can be the jumper cables for someone else. There is strength in numbers, especially within the menopausal community.

February 12th

The mall.

I just have to tell you about my trip to the mall yesterday. I took the baby. Of course I am still calling her the baby even though she will be five in April. That's how it is when you are the mother of five with your youngest. So anyway, the baby and I were strolling through the mall, mainly just to get out in the middle of winter. We had lunch and bought some flip-flops to help us get excited about our upcoming trip to California. Looking in the store windows, I realized that I was experiencing a fairly severe *clothes low*. Ruts take all shapes and forms. We can be in a rut with anything, our jobs, our sex lives, and our clothes.

I realized that I had once again fallen into the habit of subconsciously peeling the same one or two sweaters off the top of the pile, along with the same pair of jeans, alternating with the same other pair of jeans. As far as accessorizing, I had been wearing the same pair of earrings, in the shower and out. I am not much of a purse person either. I like my hands free. I made a decision at that moment walking through the mall that my next trip would be to buy some new and exciting clothes. Not safe clothes. Fun clothes. I also made a mental commitment to buy some fun shoes to wear with my fun clothes. Maybe I'll even buy a purse. I just I hope that I don't set it down somewhere. This could easily happen, as my brain isn't trained to remember to grab a purse out of a booth after having lunch. I usually have a little change purse that stays safely zipped in my jacket pocket. I was never much of a girly girl. I was always more of the outdoorsy type.

So anyway, we were just about to leave, as it was getting late and we had to get back to meet the bus. It was the Friday before Valentine's Day and the window of Victoria's Secret was just blossoming with color, lots of red. In fact, lots of red lace. A little bit of pink, a tiny bit of white, and lots and lots of red. The baby noticed "all of the pretty big girl pants" in the window. She was so taken with the fanciness of the display that her eyes were wide and glistening. She asked me if we could go in and look at all of the pretty things. Anyone who knows me, knows that I do not have a ton of sales resistance when it comes to shopping, but I figured that I was safe in Victoria's Secret surrounded by overpriced and uncomfortable *dental floss*, that I had not a desire in the world to wedge between my slightly dimply rear end.

Boy was I wrong. The baby kept saying, "Mommy look at this pretty one. Don't you like this one. It has hearts all over it." As I watched my four-year-old very gently remove a transparent light pink bra with red hearts on the nipples off the rack, I thought to myself that this must be a sign. The red hearts on the nipples really did it for me. They looked so fun, and they were actually little pockets. Maybe I could tuck some cinnamon candy hearts in there just for effect.

As my four-year-old politely handed me the item, I realized that there was a matching piece of dental floss underneath. On the back, at least I was assuming it was the back, was another heart. The price for the set was fifty-four dollars. That seemed like a lot of cash for something that wasn't going to be on for more than a few seconds. Not only that, but if it were rolled up tightly, it would probably be able to fit in your average travel toothbrush holder. There was not a lot of material there for fifty-four dollars.

It's kind of like over priced appetizers. The shrimp cocktail shouldn't get more attention than the prime rib. The main meal is the focus. Of course, the whole purpose of an appetizer is to enhance the experience of the main course, so there you go. As I happen to be a fan of shrimp cocktail, and appetizers in general, I headed off to the dressing room with my four-year-old in tow, proudly clutching her new found treasure. I put the first one on and my immediate thought was that a membership to the nearest gym may be a better investment.

It did look fun though. I loved the little hearts on the nipples. My four-year-old had also brought one in that caught her eye which was a bit more *matronly* looking, if there was such a thing in Victoria's Secret. It was mostly red, transparent red of course, with white straps and little red hearts along them. It was a slightly padded garment, which was a good thing, as I needed all the help I could get in that particular department. From the bottom of the bra hung two red, transparent *curtains*, also with little red hearts along the edge. This one was possibly more flattering, as it covered what I had stored up to live on for the winter. The other one left not much up to the imagination of my unsuspecting beloved. The matronly lingerie conveniently came with its own pair of dental floss also. I think I'll start a collection.

Of course, a sales lady had been silently circling since we had walked in and had now zoomed in on her target. Before I knew what was happening, my four-year-old and I had been escorted over to the corner of the store where fishnet stockings hung freely on the walls above. There were black ones, red ones, and different black ones with little hearts embroidered up the back. I don't think that I have ever seen more hearts in one place before.

Before long we had put an outfit together, my four-year-old, myself, and our sales lady. I bought the matronly one, and the nippley one, as well as the thigh-highs to match. Now all I needed were some shoes for the show to be complete.

Before I go on about the shoes, I will have to tell you about the men in the store, as I do not know if I have seen anything so funny, at least not recently. The first guys who walked in, were a couple of college kids, probably seniors. They were the real macho types, possibly rugby players. They were looking for an outfit for one of their girlfriends. I could not help but track them with my peripheral vision, trying to be discreet of course, as to remain unnoticed while I listened to every word. They lumbered through the middle of the store tugging on a lingerie here and there, questioning each other about what size they thought she was. They eventually settled on a slinky, burgundy, one-piece lingerie with spaghetti straps. Surprisingly, it was quite tasteful.

My eyes soon caught another man loose in the *all girl* store. This one had his hands in his pockets and was looking down, like a puppy who had just peed on the rug. He was being pulled around on an invisible leash by a well-dressed young woman who appeared to be his fiancé. She had a look of confidence that said *engaged*, that she was about to own her new puppy and bring him home for good. She was quite focused, as if she was on a mission to find the perfect naughty nighty. They were at that age also, so she may have been grabbing several other naughty nighties for girlfriends of hers who would also be getting married sometime in the near future.

That was a fun stage to be in. I remember that stage where we were in and out of bridal shops and *Spencer Gifts* buying obscene things for bachelorette parties. Every other weekend was booked with a shower or a wedding. It was a busy time, a fun time. Now I am forty and the next wedding I will be invited to will be my own children or the friends of my children. I am in between wedding stages, as my oldest is only closing in on fifteen years old, it will be a while. As we have many friends, when the next wedding phase hits, we will be off to the races. I will have to wear conservative mother of bride or groom dresses, or friend of the parents of the kid getting married dresses.

They will be those dresses with the drop waist and matching purse. I may have to rethink that one when it's time. I am not sure I ever want to wear one of those matronly old lady dresses, unless I find myself someday being the *First Lady*. Then maybe I will consider it.

The third man who caught my eye was an older man, wearing a suit and cologne. He was probably in his late fifties. He had a full head of hair and a red tie. This tie announced to all who looked at him that he liked himself very much, and that he was most likely purchasing this lingerie for someone who just barely finished high school. He zoomed in, found the perfect dental floss for his *size one* Barbie, and landed himself at the counter. He then tossed his Visa on top of his chosen items with confidence, as he glanced around at all the women in the store who could only hope to be his someday.

February 13th

Rocket fuel.

Well, I guess you know what we did last night. That's right. We had earth-shattering, menopausal sex, which is the best kind of sex there is. In fact, my legs are still weak.

I, of course, was plotting and planning my delivery silently all day long, as I did laundry, made beds, and cleaned lunch boxes out after the kids got off the bus. My normally active listening skills were temporarily out of order, as I stared blankly at my darling as he told me of the goings on of the day. The kids were full of little ditties also, about who beat whom in capture the flag, and why they felt cheated out of five points on a hard-worked-on book report. So and so didn't want to sit next to somebody else at lunch which caused a minor uprising amongst the fifth grade alpha females. Pass the broccoli please.

A Full Moon Rising…and the Tao of Menopause

All I could think about was how the show could go on with five kids at home. Then I remembered that it was movie night. We normally do not allow television in our house, except on Friday nights when the kids get to rent movies.

On Sunday nights, in an attempt to let the kids wind down from the weekend, we let them watch *I Love Lucy*. Our kids love *I Love Lucy*. We have almost all of them. We even have some episodes of *The Lucy Show*, and *Here's Lucy*. We must have made an impression on them, as they are all excited about going to the Lucy museum when we go to California in April. They have been talking about it a lot.

While my prey was downstairs getting the kids set with their movies, I went into our bedroom and quietly closed the door. I went to work lighting every candle I could find. Fortunately for me, the power goes out frequently up here in northern Vermont, so we are pretty well stocked on candles. I slid into my something totally *uncomfortable*. I opted for the one with the curtains for my first attempt. I'll save the nippley one for Valentine's Day, the *real* day. This was a practice run, as I wouldn't want to be anti-climactic . . . so to speak. I ripped open the package of thigh-highs and pulled them on. They had little rubber strips on the inside, kind of like those things on the bottom of hotel bathtubs to prevent you from slipping when you're in the shower. They were cute though. They were nude with pink and white lace along the top. On went the shoes. I got them at *Payless Shoes*, as for my purposes I figured this didn't need to be such a large investment.

I tip-toed over to the door, stuck my head out and beckoned my prey to come help me with something. As he lumbered up the stairs I felt my heart begin to get racy, almost like a teenager who has made the decision to allow her boyfriend to go to second base if he tries. Whether he does or not, she has crossed the line. She is excited to travel down this path into the unknown territory of her sexual future. I felt this eagerness as I saw the doorknob slowly turn. He had taken the bait.

I glanced up and the first thing I noticed was his smile, not the saliva dripping from his bottom lip, just the smile. His eyes were big, and actually so was something else. Even though he would be kicking forty in the ass himself next year, there was still quite a bit of life left in that horse.

Before fifteen seconds had passed, my new little Valentine's day outfit had been strewn across the room. There was a shoe over by the bay window, and another on the opposite side of the room by my dresser. The dental floss had landed in one of the potted floor plants. Fifteen seconds. Including tax, that's about five dollars per second. No wonder Victoria's Secret does so well. It's a gold mine, and well worth it. I just hope the kids had the volume turned up down there so they didn't hear me as I rounded Jupiter, Venus, and Pluto.

February 15th

And speaking of orbit, I am remembering an experience of one of my menopausal girlfriends that had me laughing so hard that I could have slipped a disk.

My menopausal friend comes from a very large, Italian family. They live in the north end of Boston surrounded by tasteful brownstones and great restaurants. The tasteful brownstones, however, are quite close together as you would expect in a city. Her children were also close together as there were seven of them. Her aging grandmother lived upstairs.

The whole kind of Americanized concept of personal space and boundaries didn't exist in her home. The Rosetti home was always buzzing, especially at dinner time. They were loud about everything. Happy, sad, or mad, they yelled about it. The Italians are passionate people and this is why I must go to Italy someday.

They are passionate about eating and drinking. They do not save the good wine for a day that may never happen. There is always an extra seat at the table just in case a friend or family member stops by. They live, eat, and drink as if this day may be the last one they ever see.

The Rosetti house devours people. It isn't possible to stop by for a minute. For the Rosetti family, *stopping by* is loosely defined.

My friend, Teresa, is the corner stone of the Rosetti Clan. She makes spaghetti sauce from scratch, homemade breads and Italian pastries that could challenge the best of Tuscany bakeries. Teresa is passionate about cooking, eating, drinking, and having a house full of guests.

She is also passionate about her relations with her husband Louie.

Louie is short, with big eyes and thinning, dark brown hair. He is most often seen wearing one of those white tank-top under shirts and sitting in his favorite chair. Louie is surrounded by chaos. The kids run circles around his favorite chair while he reads his newspaper. He doesn't move, but flips over to the sports page. The smell of a smoldering cigar lingers from the coffee table.

At first glance, no one would ever guess that Teresa and Louie had such a passionate *private* life. They would sneak upstairs in the midst of the chaos, with all of the kids home and the sauce simmering on the stove. It was as if no one was supposed to notice or ask, and they never did.

Until one day when eight-year old Anthony went looking for some help with his math homework.

The door was closed but not locked. He walked in carrying his notebook and pencil. There he stood with his mouth hanging open at the sight before him. He turned and walked out, closing the door gently behind him. He wasn't supposed to notice or ask so he didn't.

That night at the dinner table surrounded by his six siblings and his senile grandmother, he began to turn red. His older brother asked him what was the matter. Anthony looked up nervously, not sure if he should expose the pink elephant at the table or continue to eat his pasta peacefully.

He said, "Mom, how could you . . . we're all here."

There was a brief, awkward silence.

Then Teresa stood up, and while shaking the salad tongs wildly at him yelled, "You were all here. You were all here. You are *always* all here. Anthony, you are to excuse yourself after this dinner and go up to your room and get on your knees. You are to get on your knees and give thanks that your parents are still together in this day and age in this crazy world full of divorce. Anthony, and I mean get on your knees and don't forget to say the Rosary."

Teresa then sat down and instructed Maria to pass the bread. The Rosetti family continued to pass the pasta bowl around the table. Mario asked for more meat balls. The buzzing started up again. The senile grandmother began to hum *Somewhere Over the Rainbow* as she did every night and all was well. No one noticed and no one asked.

Anthony excused himself and went upstairs to say the Rosary.

February 16th

Sex is certainly ranked high as an outlet, very high, however, I have to tell you how much I also enjoy dancing around my living room. During that last fifteen minutes or so before the bus drops off the kids, I pop in an *Usher* CD and go to it.

There is something very uplifting and therapeutic about dancing in my living room . . . alone. We have a little sign in the bathroom that says *dance as if no one is watching.* This may be a bit of an overused cliché, but a valid one. Just a few seconds after I crank up the volume on *Usher, MJ Bleige,* or *Aretha,* I find myself sliding around in my socks. On occasion, I will even sing into a spatula when I get really pumped up. It feels so good to let loose, and I would swear that the stress molecules latch right onto the sweat droplets and vacate the body from every pore. Stress molecules have an aversion to music, especially R & B or Motown.

This is why it is so important to incorporate music into your life. If you are just now realizing that you have been in a *music rut,* now is the time to get yourself to the nearest mall and buy some new tunes, specifically ones you can dance to.

As mentioned previously, ruts can surface and express themselves via relationships, jobs, clothes, and yes, even music. If you have been playing it safe with your music, listening to that same old country western radio station or the same old retro station that plays songs from the worst fashion decade in history, then you are in denial as to the seriousness of your music rut. Menopause is a time where our bodies undergo certain changes. These changes also symbolize our need for other changes. Our music habits may be on an IV, sustained only by life support. It is time to pull the plug and let go. Allow yourself to grieve, then head to the mall for a new *Usher* or *Beyonce CD* or whatever else gets you moving and create your own private dance floor. In fact, sound tracks to your favorite Broadway musicals would work well.

This is of course the *seventh principle of the Tao of Menopause-turn up the volume and tear up your living room . . . dance, dance, dance . . .*

The *principles of the Tao*, are to enhance the ability of one to enjoy the self within. This is their purpose, joy enhancement. We need to learn to access this inner joy that is an innate part of our spirits. Often this joy, which very naturally wants to express itself, is being smothered by stress molecules. When we learn how to release these stress molecules, the joy is then able to surface.

It's really very simple.

February 19th

Robert.

Another way to release unwanted stress molecules is to let somebody have it that really deserves it. Yesterday I received a response from a publisher for another project that I am working on that was completely uncalled for. The name of the company was very misleading, and I innocently inquired as to whether this publishing house would be interested in my other project, a book on strategies to maintain or regain a connection with our teenagers. I received a very angry and unprofessional e-mail from *Robert*, the editor, reprimanding me for having the audacity to request a second of his precious time when they do not publish parenting books in the first place.

Robert, whose time is apparently very valuable, far more valuable than the rest of us poor slobs who are not worthy of the publishing persona, wrote four lengthy, condescending paragraphs as to why I was wasting his time. This seemed like a bit of a contradiction coming from Robert, as he could have passed on a simple rejection in one or two sentences, without the venom, and in a fraction of the time that it took him to put together his hostile litany. If fact, publishers as a group, at least the ones that I have experienced, are very kind, nice, and often helpful.

Robert, on the other hand, was an angry individual. I pictured Robert in his little rag wool sweater vest, with lots of plaques on the wall. These are all of his achievements and represent Robert's self esteem. In fact, I am sure that Robert has his own personal wall of awards, not to be confused or mixed with the awards of others in the publishing house. Robert has his own personal *Robert Shrine*. Everyday he must glance up at them to regenerate his self-esteem and self worth, because without them he is empty inside.

Robert is very, very, empty, though he smokes a pipe which sits delicately on his lower lip, slightly off center just as the professors do. This look is important to Robert, the professor look I mean. Wearing his rag wool sweater vest and smoking his pipe make him feel like a true academic. He must present this image to the outside world in order to compensate for what he lacks on the inside. In addition to all of the awards and framed degrees on the wall, there is a picture of his oldest daughter who just graduated from medical school. His daughter's accomplishment also adds to his self worth. There are no other pictures except this one, as Robert's life lacks any depth. He doesn't have any people, not really. He has an ex-wife who moved on years ago, as Robert was too dull for words, and far too angry. He is the king of passive aggression, making little stabs at every one in his life, even the people who work at the Starbucks on the corner because they put too much cream in his latte.

Robert is a thin and pasty looking man. Most *Roberts* are. This only adds to his misery. Robert's father had been a mechanic and his mother stayed home with him, cleaning houses on the side when they needed extra money to get by. In Robert's mind he is better than this. He does not ever want to *be* this. This is why Robert works so hard at this publishing persona that he puts on like a suit each day when he wakes up. It is his uniform. It is the uniform that makes Robert feel important, as he wears who he is on the outside.

It is a sad thing to go through life being a Robert. In his very lengthy e-mail to me, he wrote how I should have done "more research to find a publishing house that would *actually be interested* in my project as his *house* published only books written on law." Robert then went on to say how last year he received more than 1,500 inquiries, only 15 of which *he* accepted, and how all of these *soon to be disappointed writers* would be receiving a response of condemnation by the almighty Robert with his almighty thinking.

In fact, next year maybe there should be a pilgrimage. Writers from all over the world can come in droves to pay homage to almighty Robert. If they cannot afford to make the journey than they can simply face the west at sun down, get down on their knees and bow.

They are to stay in this position until their backs begin to ache as a sacrifice to this man who has done so much for the writing community. They mutter their mantra in unison, the world over . . . *If only we had done our research* . . . They will now, however, meet the unfortunate fate of a letter from Robert.

After reading Robert's lengthy, very hostile, litany, I chose to respond. Normally, in the publishing world, a writer would never consider doing such a thing as it is considered a big *no no* on their planet. Robert's letter, however, deserved a response. The following is what was said to Robert:

Dear Robert,

I realize your frustration, however, I have read your reply and I can honestly say that I have never received a more unprofessional, condescending, offensive, and blatantly rude response to any of my inquiries. For the most part, publishers have been kind and helpful. I will continue my pursuits and spend some additional time researching more professional publishing houses. In the mean time, maybe you can do some work on your personality, especially in the departments of arrogance and anger management. I hope that you find this helpful.

Regards,

Kimberly

It is certainly good to practice *turning the other cheek* most of the time. There are moments, however, when this is not enough and we must *take care of business,* and I must say, Robert had that one coming. It is unfortunate that some people need to be forced to think about others, but a reality. The *Roberts* of the world need to be stopped, and prevented from robbing the joy and self worth of others. Doing so is a service to our community and human kind. Hopefully, our dear Robert will find happiness somewhere down the road, or at least make his way to a spa. Maybe if he could land himself in an herbal mud wrap he would be able to release some of his stress molecules that he holds on to so tightly. I suspect that Robert clings to his stress molecules and attracts even more stress molecules because they make him feel comfortable. Robert finds comfort in being miserable. This is a very sad thing, as Robert's misery has become a habit, much like smoking. He can't stop and he doesn't want to stop, not really.

If only there was a patch for stress molecule addicts.

A Full Moon Rising…and the Tao of Menopause

February 22nd

French women are bad for our self esteem.

Last night we had dinner at our friends' house. We started this *dinner theatre* last fall and so far it has been quite fun. How it works is . . . while we grownups are munching on appetizers and chit chatting, the kids put together a skit. They write it themselves, then act it out with whatever costumes they can piece together. When the kids are ready, we go into the living room and watch, then we clap. Sometimes we videotape them. There are four families in the dinner theatre club, and we take turns hosting. The dinner is usually delightful. Last night, it was turkey, roast pork, spare ribs, blueberries mixed with yogurt, cranberry sauce, and homemade french fries. There is always a tossed salad. It is standard, as is the wine.

Of course, the hens separate from the roosters almost immediately upon entering the room. The roosters head off to the living room, while us hens splice, dice, and catch up on all of the town gossip in the kitchen. It seems that some things have not changed since the 1700's. We are all married to fairly hip, cosmopolitan, socially aware and politically correct roosters, but it doesn't matter. When we go to dinner at someone's house, the roosters go their way and we go ours. It is just how it is, and how it will probably always be.

As the hens were in the kitchen discussing hen issues, the inevitable came up, menopause and weight, menopause and moods, and last but not least, menopause and sex. One of the hens was reading a book called *French Women Don't Get Fat*, which we heard bits and pieces of while I was helping to cut the potatoes for the homemade french fries, and while one of the other hens was mixing blueberries and plain yogurt. I think if we just go out on a limb here, we could probably assume that French women don't eat homemade french fries cooked in gallons of peanut oil.

They smoke large amounts of cigarettes instead. Cigarettes do not have the calories of absolutely delectable carbs, so they therefore do not put on the weight. French women do not suffer the consequences of homemade potatoes, but they also have not fully lived, as they have not experienced what it is like to bite into a homemade fry with kosher salt straight from the deep fryer. They are warm and crispy, heavenly.

What the dinner club hens did have in common with the skinny French women was the red wine. We really like our red wine. Our hostess faithfully refilled our glasses as we chatted, a European tradition. The glasses, however, could comfortably house a small family of goldfish so it was a bit difficult to keep track of the intake. Red wine is good for women, though, so it is o.k. It lowers cholesterol, and therefore reduces the risk of heart attack, another threat of menopause. We are on a crusade against heart disease, all of us.

It does make one wonder how a society where women eat lots of creamy things, smoke like stacks, and dine so late in the evening, stay so thin. Not only do they stay thin, but the French also have one of the highest life expectancies in the world. It just does not make sense. In fact, one of Oprah's top food rules is not to eat a thing after 7:30 p.m., not so much as a grape or a nut. If French women adhered to this food rule they would disappear when they turned sideways.

Everyone knows that the Europeans eat dinner very late at night. They eat late and drink lots of red wine. They talk. They drink more wine. If you ask me, it's not so much what they are eating or when they are eating it. I think that it is in large part due to lifestyle. Europeans in general seem to have more *down time*. They take long holidays to spend with their families. In many European countries they take the whole month of August off. They also take a big chunk of time off in the middle of the day. Being off is good if you can do it without shame.

We Americans have it drilled into our heads that we need to be busy all the time or we are losers. This is especially true of men in the work force. This is very true of stay at home mothers, who feel so guilty for sitting down and reading a magazine when the baby takes a nap, that they will usually hop up and clean the bathroom floor just to quiet the voices.

People in Europe don't seem to have the compulsive drive going on that we Americans do. We need to be doing, moving, talking, and spending all the time. It's what we do.

In our culture, we are groomed to be *human doings* instead of human beings. It's like we are an entire culture stuck on fast forward. We are like this in all parts of our lives. We are like this in our careers, afraid to not be in the right place at the right time just in case we have a chance to zoom in on a possible promotion. We are quick to meet the right people. We shop fast, and are especially competitive if there is a sale going on.

We are fast, fast, fast. Wherever we can cut corners, we do. This is why we invented the drive-through. We can now fill our bodies with crap in the car on the way home or on the way to a basketball game without actually having to take the time to sit and have a conversation. It takes time to prepare a healthy meal, and hopefully it takes at least as much time to eat it. It is all about the process. I think that we forget this, too, sometimes. At our dinner theatre, for instance, it took us roughly an hour and a half just to get it all together. Meanwhile, we chatted as we munched on grapes and cheese. It's all about the conversation, and being with our people.

O.K., maybe it's a little bit about the homemade, crispy fries fresh out of the gallons of boiling hot peanut oil with the kosher salt.

February 23rd

Inner warming.

The hot peanut oil in the kitchen the other night reminded me of another conversation we had that night. This conversation was about the *inner warming* of menopause. The other two hens in the kitchen are a little further down the path of the menopausal journey then I am, so I listened very intently to what is next. I am officially in what is called perimenopause, the precursor to the all out full-blown craziness and hormonal frenzy. Although, according to the women that I have talked with, once a woman makes it through *perimenopause*, it's all over but the shoutin'.

And while you're shoutin', you may experience this inner warming. Often it is referred to as the *hot flash*. Women across the country and the world are excusing themselves to step outside for some air as the inner warming rises within. It is similar to a volcano as it erupts, only we are past the erupting part. We erupt during *perimenopause* when our hormones rise to the surface like hot lava bringing with them every hatred molecule we have stored in our bodies. Our hatred molecules cling to our hormones as they erupt like unwanted lint or dog hair on black pants. They will not separate. They will not go away. This is because, in *perimenopause*, our hatred molecules are part of us. We are one.

What is great about the stage of inner warming, is that we are on our way to becoming normal again. We are almost there. The warming from within signals us that the chronic feelings of wanting to kill someone are leaving us. The inner warming signals us that soon we will be safe when the moon turns full.

February 25th

Until this moment of inner warming, no one is safe when the moon turns full. The next full moon will be in the water sign of Aquarius.

This means that anyone who could possibly have a mid-lifer annoyed with them for any reason should avoid the water at all costs. Avoiding the water would include rivers, lakes, the ocean, and even the bath tub. It would not be beneath the mid-lifer to accidentally bump into an irritating family member or passenger while on a *whale watch excursion* and to send her sailing off the edge of the boat into the deep blue sea.

It is also a good idea to avoid the bath tub, as it would not be unforeseen for the mid-lifer to accidentally trip and drop a blow dryer in, sending the unsuspecting victim to her electric and watery demise.

The sparks would reflect off her glowing yellow eyes while traces of drool land on the edge of the tub and slide down the side to the floor below. There is no remorse. The full moon resides in Aquarius. She knows not what she does.

February 26th

Our oldest daughter is in Boston. This is the first time that she has been away from home other than a sleepover right here in town. She is eleven and a half. I miss her already. Actually, I missed her about ten minutes after she left. All of the sudden we are beginning to *feel* having five children. They are all getting older and taking on schedules and social lives of their own.

The thing is, we expect the early child-rearing years to be overwhelming. This stage is all about basic needs. We go from changing a diaper, to mixing rice cereal with pureed peaches, to the pediatrician. There are all of those well-baby check-ups. It's kind of like getting a puppy. It is every two weeks, then each month, then every two months, then six. It's the puppy schedule.

When we have another baby, we do the puppy schedule all over again only with one in tow. Often when we bring a perfectly healthy infant in for her well-baby checkup, the toddler touches a toy or a doorknob and we leave with a two-week flu virus. This is how it works for young mothers. Then they get to go home and not sleep. When the baby takes a nap the young mother has guilt over not being able to give her toddler enough attention since the new baby arrived. She reads books to him and plays blocks instead of putting her feet up and tipping her head back for that very much needed power nap.

Her iron level is low and her eyes look like road maps to no where. She is walking into walls and unable to retrieve her own name when filling out a form, but she is doing what she needs to do. She is after that *Purple Heart*. We all are after the honor when our kids are little. Just as Canadian Geese fly south for the winter, sacrificing our bone marrow on a daily basis is something that is just in us and the force is a strong one.

We *need* that Purple Heart.

Following the stage of thorough and complete exhaustion, there is a lull, and it is an illusion. The reason that it is an illusion is because this stage is so easy that we get the feeling that we will now coast forever. We have made it. We survived the sleep deprived years with no more damage than a few wrinkles and some small blocks of memory missing. We made scrapbooks, though, of all of the birthday parties, first paintings, height, weight, missing teeth, and first report cards. The fact that some of these moments have been involuntarily deleted from our memory banks due to sleep deprivation is all right because we have scrapbooks.

Thank goodness for the invention of the camera and for scrapbooks.

After this, we are delightfully introduced to *Stage II*. This is the stage of self-sufficiency. We love this stage. We embrace this stage. Our kids can now get dressed, take a shower, and make their own breakfast. If we have done our work early on, they are also at this point able to clean up after making their own breakfast. We can travel with relative ease. They love to be with us, and will still give us a casual hug in public. They are not old enough to have a boyfriend or girlfriend. No worries there. They are not old enough to drive or to know anyone who can drive. Again, no worries.

They come home excited to show us the anti-drug poster that they made for the school contest. It makes no sense to them that anyone would ever smoke, as we all know what it does to our lungs and bodies. They know that smoking takes parents away from their kids. Extended family members who may smoke are now glared at over the holidays for their pure selfishness and stupidity. Every time they slip outside for a butt, our kids delicately glance over the gravy boat and roll their eyes in a loving kind of way. This is a great stage to be in. If only we could stay here forever. Maybe we can shrink-wrap them and hope for the best.

Then all of the sudden, they get *their own people*. Actually, they are often the same people that they had since they were in kindergarten, but now they are making all kinds of plans with their people. Plans,

plans, and more plans. Sports, sports, and more sports. We feel like we want to get a couple of cans of yellow paint to cover our cars with and then stick a big black and yellow taxi sign on the top. The phone number says 1-800-CALL-MOM.

The momentum picks up almost overnight as we shuttle bus the kids off to their first dances, soccer and basketball games, and every where else they are invited. It feels like we have been caught asleep at the wheel. It's as if we were comfortably coasting on cruise control before we were cut off by a little red sports car, forcing us to pay attention to the road and our driving. Basically we were taking it easy, taking it all in, enjoying our kids and watching them grow. Now all of the sudden the horn blows and we are called back to work. Oh well, it was nice while it lasted.

I thought that I had left the land of the overwhelmed behind when I bought my last box of diaper wipes and now here we are again, only in a different way. I realize also that we do have *five* little darlings. Not to blow our own horns, but there are very few such brave souls left in the world. And the thing is, that I wouldn't have it any other way. We love having a high traffic household. It is so much fun and certainly never lonely. It's just that we have both noticed that the pace has picked up lately. In fact, this year when baseball starts, we will have four kids on four different teams. We'll need a well-greased pair of roller blades. We are also a family that does encourage making choices as we value mental health.

Unfortunately for us, they all choose baseball.

Of course the teenager has his group over nearly every weekend. I should take stock in Gatorade and Nestle's chocolate chips as the teenaged boys go through cookies and Gatorade as fast I can stock the house. I used to whine on occasion, but not anymore, as I am so glad that they want to be home where we know where they are. A few extra cases of Gatorade seem like a small price to pay. The next morning when they all arise, the shuttle leaves again to head up to the mountain to go skiing. Like stray cats, they inevitably land back on our doorstep when it is time for dinner. Then they wake up and do it all over again.

I have gotten clever enough to time the whole thing so that I can fit in a quick cross-country ski or snow shoe before I pick them up. It's all about strategy and having a plan. If you don't have a plan, the minutes of the day will swallow you up whole.

February 27th

A plan.

What I mentioned yesterday was very important, about having a plan so as not to let your minutes silently and tragically slide down the drain. Minutes are naturally inclined to slip away so it takes a very conscious effort to prevent this from happening. It doesn't mean that we need to race out and purchase a palm pilot or daily planner. It simply means that when we wake up to take a moment and think about our day and the way that it is headed. The way that it is headed may not be the way that we *want* it to be headed and this can be discouraging as we all need at least part of our day to look forward to or there is not much of a point to carrying on.

This is the *eighth principle of the Tao of Menopause, protect your minutes by visualizing your day*.

We may have a day full of dentist appointments, grocery shopping, and numerous errands. We may have a full day of work ahead before we have to stop on the way home to get a cracked window shield fixed. Minutes can still be salvaged and enjoyed with a strategy and a plan.

For me, this means getting up early in the morning. It was difficult at first, trust me. It feels so nice, especially during the cold, dark months of winter to curl up under the warm covers. However, once I got used to it and got into a bit of a routine, I really began to enjoy the feeling that I got from having that time to myself to get centered. What I do during this time is write. When it gets lighter out I will walk when I am through writing. What feels so good, is that once the momentum of the day begins I feel o.k. with how the day unfolds as I have already had some time for me to do what I enjoy. If I happen to get some more, and I often do, then it is a bonus.

Another way to make valuable use of your minutes is to make good use of those in between blocks of time that seem to get eaten away. These happen all day long for most people. They happen at the dentist, or the doctor. They happen while we are waiting for our oil to be changed.

For us, they often happen while waiting for dance classes to be over. If we added up all of these minutes, they would add up to hours and then days. Our minutes, after all are our lives, and we should do all we can to protect them, enjoy them, and keep them from unknowingly slipping through our finger tips. Our minutes are worthy of our conscious attention.

It is also important to point out that one of the best uses of our minutes is to do nothing, not a bad kind of nothing, but a good kind of nothing. To do nothing and do it *well* is an art form. It takes skill and practice. The reason it takes practice to do the healthy kind of nothing is that the world and its momentum are against it. When we truly do nothing we are still. We are still on the outside and we are still on the inside. The voices in our head are kept at bay and all is quiet.

When we have reached this level of nothingness, the quiet becomes almost loud. Our senses are tuned in and accurate to our feelings. We feel focused and joyful. Eventually, when the world and its momentum pull us out of our transcendental state we feel rested, really rested. It's better than a nap because the rest is deeper and more lasting.

February 28th

I just couldn't help thinking of Aunt Marla after our talk about the art of doing nothing. Aunt Marla resists doing nothing. She has near perfect attendance at work after almost forty years in medical equipment sales. She will go to work sneezing all over everybody with a temperature of 103 degrees because she does not value health, mental or physical. She values dying a slow death and being *a trooper*. It is very important to Aunt Marla that she is on top and that people know that she never misses work even if she is miserable and spreading the flu virus to all that touch the same doorknob as she did when she fell in the door this morning. Poor Aunt Marla's tombstone will eventually read something like this:

> Here lies Aunt Marla.
> She never missed a day of work,
> Nor did she enjoy her life.

How tragic. How very, very, tragic. As far as any of us know, this is the only shot we get. Life is not a dress rehearsal as they say. I just cannot imagine not taking a mental health day once in a while to recharge. It is good for us as well as everyone around us to take care of ourselves, as people who run themselves into the ground are generally not that much fun to be around.

Aunt Marla is not that much fun to be around. She has moments of being fun when she loosens up after a couple of martinis, but mostly she is wrapped up in the demise of our society. She compares what is going on in the world and America with the fall of Rome. In fact, Aunt Marla has been wearing black ever since President Bush got re-elected.

March 1st

I have decided that we should all get down on our knees in gratitude to the heavens above that Aunt Marla has now completed the menopause process. Aunt Marla is now safely in her mid-seventies and free of hormones. Unfortunately, she is still clinging somewhat tightly to the few remaining anger molecules left in her body, but this is more than likely the most healthy Aunt Marla will ever be. The reason is, of course, that Aunt Marla does not *choose* health. She is far more content hanging onto her stress molecules and remaining in a perpetual state of anxiety.

Also unfortunate, is the fact that Aunt Marla never developed an appreciation for *the principles*, nor did she make any effort to incorporate them into her life. To begin with, Aunt Marla is a shower person. She always has been and always will be. How unfortunate.

Showers are all right to get ready for work, but as far as the long, drawn out ritual of the bath . . . one needs a tub for that. One needs very hot water, bubbles, candles, and *time*. The key ingredient is *time*. We need *time* do to nothing no matter where we choose to do it, and there is no better place to do nothing than in a blissfully warm and cozy bubble bath.

Needless to say, you will not find fresh cut flowers in Aunt Marla's bathroom.

Aunt Marla does not have time to do nothing. Rather than rescuing her valuable minutes, Aunt Marla *spends* her minutes, and as quickly as possible. In fact, she cannot spend them fast enough. Aunt Marla even borrows minutes from the next day and the next month, as she wants to be anywhere but the present moment.

Being in the present moment would bring joy and peace, and *human doings* are not interested in this level of living. They prefer to remain in their own level of busy-ness and confusion. This is a stage where thoughts are not controlled and feelings are avoided. What normally happens in order for an individual to advance to the next level, is that they very plain and simply get sick of living that way. Often what causes an individual to advance is a tragedy in her life, such as the loss of a loved one or the end of a long-term relationship that forces them into the moment of *now*. Once they realize what a good place *now* is to be, they choose to return.

This is how it happens.

March 2nd

Drugs are for the weak but my *Cha Cha* is on fire.

Today's topic is heart palpitations. Mild, yet constant heart palpitations are just another one of life's thank yous for being a woman. I was cross-country skiing the other day and they started. Once in a while they will make me cough. Sometimes they happen when I am sitting quietly reading. What happens then, of course, is that I panic that this is it and that I will soon have a full blown heart attack and be hooked up to loads of tubes at the nearest hospital. I think about what a good life it's been but that I am not ready to leave. I think about my kids and if they will remember me. I think about my husband and the new Barbie he will marry after the appropriate amount of grieving time passes. He had better not have *my* kids call *her* mom or I will be throwing plates down from the attic.

This is *menopausal panic* and it is quite common. We experienced the same sort of panic following the birth of our first child when every sniffle or bad freckle we noticed was perceived to be an immediate death sentence. We worried about leaving our baby without a mother. We made frequent phone calls and sometimes trips to the doctor. We went on the Internet and looked things up. We asked our young mother friends if they have ever experienced the same thing. Then we would all talk and convince ourselves that we were fine and pour another cup of coffee.

We would move on with our day until another potentially life threatening illness made its way into our subconscious, then the panic would start all over again. Sometimes it would wake us up. We would nudge our beloved next to us, waking him out of his blissful slumber for some reassurance. We needed to know right then and there that it wasn't a tumor. Half conscious, he would give us the reassurance we needed that he was sure it was nothing. He rolls over. We roll over realizing that he is not a doctor but his news was good.

We'll take it. We roll over again and go to sleep, too.

Young mother panic does not differ all that much from *menopausal panic*. The only real difference is that somewhere in the back of our minds we realize that we are young and that chances are slim that anything huge is wrong. We revert to this thought when our panicked thinking is over the top. What is different with menopausal panic is that we are old now and people really do get these things.

This is the main difference. So when we feel a little irregular or racy heart beat we think immediately that it must be extreme because heart disease is the leading killer of women, mid-life women that is. We compulsively feel our breasts in the shower to make sure that we are free of lumps, as breast cancer is another big one for this life stage.

A Full Moon Rising…and the Tao of Menopause

All of the sudden it seems that there is a real possibility that something could happen.

No wonder we get heart palpitations.

Of course, the worst thing we can do is panic. Breathing is a much better idea. People are always telling women to breathe. I remember being told to breathe in Lamaze class. I had it down, too. It is safe to say that I was the best breather in the whole class. Just bring those contractions on because I was ready. Take no prisoners. I remember them bringing out this horse needle that they called an epidural. It was like show and tell. They wanted us to learn from the visual aid what might happen in the event that we needed medication.

As I was determined to have my baby naturally, I glanced around the room in complete disgust at all of my fellow first-time mothers-to-be who showed even the slightest bit of interest in altering their state of consciousness while in labor. *Real women* can take the pain I thought to myself. Not only that, but real women *want* the pain. You don't earn the *Purple Heart of Motherhood* if you reduce yourself to accepting medication.

Drugs are for the weak.

Shortly thereafter, I was taking a shower one evening when I got my first contraction. It felt like a fleet of Mack trucks had just driven through my uterus, made a couple of loops around my ovaries, then back again. The pain was excruciating and it had only just begun. I stumbled out of the shower and yelled for my husband. We were off to the hospital in no time.

When we got there, we were sent to a make-shift bed in the utility room, as the moon was full (no joke), and so was the labor and delivery floor. I would brace myself every time a wave of intolerable pain came rippling through my body. I thought I must be dying. No one can handle this kind of pain for very long and not pass out. There must be a pass out mechanism that would be triggered any time now. If I could just hang in there, nature would take over and release some endorphins or something. After all, women had been doing this since the beginning of humankind.

Apparently a bed had just opened up, so they wheeled me in this state to one of the pretty birthing rooms, a definite step up from the utility room. Not that I minded being surrounded by paint cans and mops. In fact, I wouldn't have minded if the *New York Giants* paraded right through the birthing room at this point. All dignity was gone. There is no dignity in childbirth. It left with my body fluids. Anyone who has written romanticized little ditties about women bringing life into the world was either a man or psychotic, because no one would go through this willingly if they knew the magnitude of this pain. Like a horse that had just broken her leg in a race, I was waiting to be taken behind a barn and shot.

A Full Moon Rising…and the Tao of Menopause

Just put me out of my misery.

And by the way . . . can I have some drugs please . . . That was *my other self* at the Lamaze class that was so pompous and sure about the whole birthing process. The real me has surfaced now and I really, really want some drugs. I *need* some drugs. Somebody give me some drugs!

After nearly twenty-four hours of labor, my husband was pulled into the hallway by the doctor. They were having a private discussion. I hate private discussions, especially when they are about me. In fact, I hate everything right now. In comes my husband looking at the ground and clutching the patient bill of rights that they had given me upon registration. I had highlighted some areas and written in the margins that no one, and I meant no one was to come anywhere near me or my spine with a horse needle. Thank you very much. Case closed. And I positively wasn't going to have a c-section, the cash cow of the medical world.

I was above c-sections.

He then proceeds to tell me that the baby's heart beat was coming in and out with the contractions and that I would need to have a horse needle and some Pitocin or face the possibility of an emergency c-section. I wanted my eighty-five dollars back that I spent on that stupid Lamaze class. I hope I kept the receipt. I wanted to have my baby naturally even though it was killing me.

I wanted that *Purple Heart*.

In comes Andy the anesthesiologist with his little drug cart. I could hear him clinging and clanging down the hallway. He was probably excited that he had a new victim. He walked in with his friendly smile and introduced himself. I really wish I could pass out now. I felt the sweat droplets congregating along my hairline. I felt dizzy. They rubbed some anesthetic on my back, near my spine, the part of the body that insures that you will be able to walk once you have the baby. Let's hope I don't sneeze in the next few seconds. I took a deep breath and the horse needle was now part of my bone structure. I hate this. I'm scared. I want my mother.

They told me that I couldn't get up as my legs would not work with the horse needle. Great. Before long, I realized that I could breathe again. I stopped hating my husband for doing this to me. I noticed that he had Oprah on the television above my bed. I love Oprah.

The room was pretty. It looked like a room in a New England Bed and Breakfast. How quaint. I felt like I had survived a near-death experience. I had been to the other side and realized that I was not ready to let go. I am back in my body now, thankfully. The contractions were still coming on like the Titans, as I could see them on the little printer thing. It looked like a polygraph hooked up to somebody telling lots of whoppers. It was zigzagging all over the place.

Maybe I should rethink this *au naturale* process. We are a highly technologically advanced country. As far as I am concerned it would be an injustice to all those who sacrificed their valuable life space to do the research that got us to this point, disrespectful actually. After all, childbirth was the leading cause of death for women way back when. I think that I have just developed a new appreciation for pioneer women. As soon as I am able, I will go to the town library and take out every book I can on pioneer women.

My doctor surfaced right in the middle of my pioneer thought. She starts sticking fingers and medical instruments you know where. Lovely. She tells me that I was fully dilated and ready to push. For some reason my new best friend, the horse needle, ceased to work as I suddenly felt like my lower lip had been pulled up over my head. I screamed. I want my mother. The doctor tells me to push. I feel a burning sensation. I was told that she had just preformed an episiotomy. As if my vagina wasn't under enough stress, now she has taken a razor blade to it.

I take a deep breath and hope that I come back as a sea horse in my next life.

They tell me that the baby is crowning. My husband has moved down by my other end now, waiting excitedly for us to become a family. Here comes the burning again. I can't do this for one more second. I can't take it. I can't. I can't.

All of the sudden I feel something sliding fast right through me. In a split second the pain was gone. He's here they tell me. My newborn baby boy was born . . . and I am not pregnant anymore.

Did I mention that . . . I am not pregnant anymore. I am not pregnant anymore. I would get up and do a happy dance if the horse needle would allow it. This was all worth it. He is so beautiful. I would lie down in front of a moving train for him already. I love him so much. They prop me up and rest him against my bare skin. This is what it is all about. This is the part that was very *natural*, a mama and her newborn baby resting skin to skin after the trauma of entering the world. This feeling is something that makes you happy to be a woman.

I want to have four or five more now.

My heavenly minute of peace was briefly interrupted when I felt another contraction. Just a second later, something that resembled a moderately sized jellyfish came sliding out of my vagina. And it was on a leash. Lovely. They had asked my husband if he wanted to cut the cord, but my poor darling was looking a bit pasty so the doctor went ahead and did it.

Out of my peripheral vision, I notice my new best friend Andy the anesthesiologist coming in with his little drug cart. I thought we were all done. This time he had a little sewing kit with him. I was then told that I had a forth degree laceration and needed to be stitched. Maybe this means I will be propped up next to the quilts at the county fair this summer. I feel tugging and pulling. That's it, as the horse needle was still securely stationed next to my spine. The stitching process took quite a while and the grand total of stitches was 147. That must be some kind of record. This alone should insure that I will have outstanding Mother's Days forever and ever.

I'm thinking I deserve it.

March 3rd

I am not sure where that stray brain cell came from. That is called *menopausal flashback*. We mid-lifers do that a lot. We have now lived for four or five decades and there is a lot to reflect upon. Much after the fact, we need to *process*, as this is the life stage of self-awareness. Menopause is where it all comes together. In fact, *we* come together as we get to know who we are on a much deeper level.

March 5th

The origin of quills.

Today I would like to tell you about our discussion on menopausal hedgehogs. Last night, I took our oldest daughter to her first 4H meeting. This is my kid that does her own thing. She is my artist child. She likes art and French. She loves animals, sometimes more than people. I can't blame her there. I feel that way myself sometimes.

The meeting was at the town library. We got there right on time. People were coming from the towns next to ours also. As our town has a mere 992 residents, this is a good thing to invite other towns to join in. Plus, as we do live in northern Vermont, one would assume that farming and agriculture clubs would be quite popular. We recognized almost everybody. There was a grampa with his grandson. There was a woman who said she home-schooled. She had about a million kids. She brought some of the neighbors kids with her as well. She must have driven a bus over the mountain to the 4H meeting. She talked of her sheep and her plans to show them at fairs this summer.

There was another dad from our town who spoke of his angora goats and his wife being a member of the *Spinners' Club*. This is a club that gets together to make mittens and sweaters out of goat hair. They did a presentation at Town Day last summer and one of the women had made mittens out of her Golden Retriever's hair. She said that the dog had shed so much during the heat wave that she had swept up more than enough dog hair during the month of July alone. Just another benefit to global warming I suppose.

Well, my kids got quite a kick out of someone making mittens out of dog hair. As we have dogs also, one of my little darlings got inspired to start a dog mitten business. I had to gently explain that though I admired their entrepreneurial thinking that no time soon would I be purchasing a spinning wheel. I certainly admired these women and their artistic abilities, however, we all have our gifts and spinning wool or Golden Retriever hair is certainly not one of mine.

This is an awful thought, but I couldn't help thinking as they passed around the pieces of different fur and the resulting sweaters, that if you hit LL Bean during their winter clearance sale you can do really well, and without the sweat. I am thinking that maybe I should keep that thought to myself. Again, we all have our gifts.

As my husband and I are originally from the New York and Boston areas, there is a good chance that our family may not be the brightest shining star of the 4H club, but we'll see. One never knows. In fact, just last year when we were skiing with the kids, we noticed a big black animal way up high in a tree. I pointed the little black bear out to the kids in my ski group. We all stood there admiring this little creature. Then one of the children very respectfully reminded me that bear sleep during the winter. One of the other children kind of cleared her throat and softly mentioned that she thought it was a porcupine. The children nodded in unison. It was an intellectual mutiny of eight-year olds. After all, these were Vermont kids and they knew all about wildlife. Boy did I feel like a dumb-dumb.

I didn't even know porcupines could climb.

Apparently, hedgehog is another name for porcupine. As people in the 4H group were discussing sheep, goats, bunnies, and cows, one of the parents mentioned that her son had researched hedgehogs and was thinking of trying to raise one. They were legal in New Hampshire, and had just become legal in Vermont. They are actually a mini-version of the porcupine, pigmy hedgehogs from South Africa.

Now there is something off the beaten path. How cool. This might be a good idea for our youngest son. Up until now he had thought of himself as more of an *Iguana man*, but the hedgehog idea was exciting, too. We could actually feel the hedgehog momentum as more kids got interested in the idea. We exchanged phone numbers on our little green folders that we had been given and headed over to the table where all of the pamphlets were. There were cupcakes because it was the first day. They had the 4H symbol on the top made out of green frosting.

As we were leaving, one of our menopausal dinner club members met me in the doorway and we discussed the idea of getting a hedgehog and their temperament. Hedgehogs apparently make good pets as long as they have a good temperament, otherwise they can bite. I don't think this should be held against the hedgehog as when my temperament is out of sorts I can bite, too. My fellow mid-lifer and I chuckled at the thought of getting a hedgehog in menopause, spontaneously releasing quills when she gets irritated or when the moon turns full.

We can only imagine what life would be like had the good Lord made women with quills. When our level of anger molecules reached a certain level we could release quills in every direction. Or we could learn to focus the energy generated by our dangerously high levels of anger molecules and target the recipient with a missile of menopausal quills.

Advanced quill releasers would teach classes in order to improve on accuracy. They would sell bottles of organic poison next to the organic supplements at the health food stores. We would pour the organic poison on our comb then run it through our quills. It would be good for up to twenty-four hours, however, for best results immediate use is best.

They would work like a prickly stun-gun.

During the holidays, when the very irritating new wife of our brother-in-law does that thing she does that annoys everyone in the family, we would glance over the cranberry sauce with serious eyebrows. This is the warning glance. It is similar to how German Shepards show their teeth and growl. This is a warning to back up or be destroyed. If she so much as thinks about being irritating and entitled, we *release*, as we have no choice. We were forced. If our quills had been combed with organic poison, then our new sister-in-law would simply close her eyes and fall over. We can now feel good about ourselves as we have done the rest of the family a service. They will be grateful to us. Men will envy our quills and fear them at the same time. Younger women will look forward to menopause, the life stage of self-actualization, power, and quills with organic poison.

If menopausal women had quills, we would rule the world.

March 6th

I just have to share with you my day yesterday. I went for yet another blissful cross-country ski deep in the woods at The Winterberry Cross-Country Ski Center. It was incredibly exhilarating. The sun was glistening through the trees and the snow was so sparkly. Before long, I found myself out in the middle of the East Meadow alone. I opened my ears wide to the loudness of the quiet. The mountains in front of me proudly announced their majestic presence.

There I stood in the middle of a snow covered meadow, just me with myself. I turned around and looked at the tracks I had left behind. I couldn't help to think of the symbolism. These tracks were where I had been. They had straight parts and windy parts, but most of all, they brought me to where I was. They brought me to who I am. Then I turned back around and looked in front of me at the tracks that were left by other skiers who were further along the trail. There was a long, straight part, then it wound around a bend and back through the woods. I wondered what was ahead and where this trail would lead.

I hadn't set out that afternoon to contemplate being *half-way* in life, but this is what happened and it was good. It was more than good. It was serene. It was life-giving. I felt the joy of having the awareness of being and a deep appreciation for where I had been, windy parts and all. As I pushed off to continue my journey through the East Meadow, I pondered where this trail may lead and what lies ahead for me on the rest of my life journey.

It felt good to be right where I was, in the middle. I felt grateful to the meadow for the awareness of being, and for returning me to the present moment so that I may appreciate the fullness of now.

March 7th

Isn't it unfortunate when people do not appreciate their *half-wayness*? Some have the perspective that it is half-time and half of the game is over. If they were behind a few points in the first half, they will carry this momentum with them into the second half and probably lose the game, just as they had predicted for themselves.

The reason it is so unfortunate, is that they are missing the whole point and the value of their *half-wayness*. We now have had a whole first half of the big game loaded with exciting plays and life experiences, which can only further enrich the second half. We have wisdom and a more authentic sense of ourselves and life in general. Being *half-way*, we can stand in the middle and see in both directions equally, where we have been and where we hope to be. It is a good place, a very rich, spiritual place.

Aunt Marla never appreciated her half-wayness. She held on to her past like crazy glue, reliving every camping trip or comment made by her kids growing up. She had one boy and one girl, though the girl doesn't speak to her and hasn't for years. No one knows why and no one asks. Aunt Marla has also hung on to everything negative that anyone had ever said to her, some of these issues dating back to the early 1960's.

In fact, I think she has made carbon copies for safe-keeping. Aunt Marla does not want to lose track. During the holidays, she tells these same stories over and over to the point that we have learned to notice the subtle changes that are made with each round of tales. Aunt Marla is a *hanger-on-er*. This is one big reason that she did not embrace or enjoy this wonderful life stage. Mid-life is not a stage for hanging on and being spiritually stuck.

It is a very liberating stage where we spread our wings and soar with confidence.

Aunt Marla did not appreciate her mid-life stage because she did not live it. She resisted it. It must have taken a lot of her energy to resist something so natural and inviting. To resist in general is draining, but of course Aunt Marla prides herself on being drained. It is a medal of honor for her that she wears proudly on her chest for all to see.

March 8th

Blame is a love blocker.

Here I sit staring out the window as the snow falls so gently to the ground. It is early in the morning and it all looks so new, once again. That's what I love so much about snow and winter in general, the newness. Every time there is a snowfall, it feels like starting over. I love to start over as it makes me feel as if I am brand new, too.

This is especially true when it comes to our relationships with our parents. There are very few of us out there who would admit to a completely pain-free childhood. For many of us there was deep pain, and lots of it. As for most, the root of the pain is our parents, and whatever they did or did not do for us. This is where the blame goes. Blame attracts anger molecules like a magnet. Anger molecules attract stress molecules. It is a viscous cycle.

Probably one of the biggest payoffs with blame is that it prevents us from moving on. It is much easier to remain stuck, or at least it may *feel* easier. In reality, of course, once we let go of that pain and the blame that goes along with it, we become lighter. We become free to move on and open to the love of others.

This is because blame is a *love-blocker*.

It serves as a barricade with a barbed wire fence around our spirit. It is a defense mechanism that is trying to protect us, however, by protecting us from further pain, it also protects us from the good trying to make its way in also. Blame is unable to discriminate between intrusive energy. It will block angry energy trying to make its way in as well as loving energy trying to make its way in. On the flip side, blame also keeps what is behind our walls safe and sound. All of those painful memories of childhood that we play back and relive over and over, are kept safely behind the walls. They cannot get out.

That is, until we *decide* to release them.

Often the reason we are unable to let go is that our pain is either the strongest association we have with our parent or caregiver, or the only one. To be emotionally abandoned by them as children was difficult enough, and since we don't want to risk losing our parent twice, we hang on to our pain associated with them. We are emotionally bonded with this pain so much that we become comfortable with it. To take it away or let it go feels far too risky and far too scary for the inner child within.

Some of us worry that if we truly let go that it will invalidate the wrong that was done to us. They think that to forgive means that what was done to us was acceptable. Nothing could be further from the truth. To forgive, at least for me, means simply to *decide* to release my spirit from the pain it has been so desperately hanging on to. We acknowledge that we are valuable, far too valuable to be slaves to incidents and feelings that happened years ago. We acknowledge that the path in front of us is too valuable to spend another minute burdened with these painful thoughts and feelings.

We realize and accept our own self-worth.

By letting go, we rise above being a victim, a position of vulnerability and a position in which we have no control, to a state of being empowered to take charge of our lives. Letting go not only liberates the spirit, but strengthens it as well.

This is the *ninth principle of the Tao of Menopause . . . make peace with your past.*

There is no time like the present to let go and move on, especially for us mid-lifers, as we have the momentum of self-awareness on our side. It is our natural inclination to reflect and figure out where we have been and why we have become who we are. Right, wrong, or indifferent, our past has shaped us. We would not be who we are without it. It is when we are able to accept our past as part of us that we are better able to accept ourselves, defects and all, as being unique and valuable individuals.

This means letting go of our pain, regardless of the wrongness involved. The wrongness, of course, is what we hang onto so tightly because it validates our pain. This is especially true of the woman who was violated as a child. She was an innocent little girl and hanging on to her pain validates this innocence and the wrongness of what happened to her.

March 9th

Granola Woman.

A friend called me last night and informed me that her *quills* had been particularly high that day. She asked me how my quills were. I told her that my quills were in a relaxed state, lying gently and horizontally. My day of high quills had happened earlier in the month, thankfully in the privacy of our own home.

There is a woman who owns the natural food co-op on the other side of the mountain and her very existence on this planet annoys the hell out of me though she is completely oblivious to this fact. It is called *Nature's Way* and the store's name reflects her arrogance.

This woman has always rubbed me the wrong way. She doesn't even need to speak to irritate me. Just her presence on the earth is annoying enough, especially if I am having a day of high quills where I am particularly sensitive to irksome people. Thankfully, *Granola Woman* lives two towns over and I don't have to see her at every single school event.

This woman, for whatever reason thinks that she is better than the rest of us because she eats dried fruit and makes homemade everything without adding any sugar. She also knits and makes quilts as you might guess. She raises her own goats and sheep so that she can spin the wool right there and make sweaters straight from the fur-source. She sells them at her store on a separate shelf next to the dried fruit and essential oils. She also raises turkeys and some strange species of chicken with really bad hair. They look like rock stars of the farm world.

Good for her, I say.

Arrogance is everywhere. People can be arrogant about their careers, their education, their houses, and their ability to dry fruit on the back porch. We all have our gifts. She also grows all of her own vegetables and cans them. She is pretty amazing actually. I would be in awe of her if it wasn't for her attitude. She walks around with this, "We are better than you because we live a wholesome, organic life. We are above owning a television and we are above Spaghettios."

This attitude makes my quills high primarily because it makes other mothers feel badly. Women are champions at comparison. We don't need an ounce of help when it comes to feeling that we don't measure up. It is one thing to be good at something, and to genuinely feel good about our gift or area of expertise. It is another thing entirely to look down our noses at others because we feel that we have really got it all down, living a life of only organic, homegrown vegetables, and sewing quilts that win first place every single year at the county fair. I forgot to mention that she also makes her own honey. Maybe she's printing money in the basement also. Who knows.

My quills get high, because I think about the moms out there who would love to be home and do all of these natural and domestic type things, but who can't afford to. I think about the single moms who may also be against television and do their best to limit it for their children, but who fall in the door after working a double shift and turn it on simply to enable them to sit down and put their feet up.

They don't like processed food either, but they open up a can of Spaghettios because it is quick and easy and because it is all they can afford. They need something quick and easy after working a fourteen-hour day. Especially the single mom who is doing everything she can simply to survive her day and her life certainly does not need a *Susie-can-do-it-all* to rub this in her face. She feels guilty enough for cutting corners just to make it all work.

This is why my quills get high whenever I encounter *Granola Woman*.

March 10th

The irony in the fact that I absolutely despise *Granola Woman* is that I actually admire a lot of what she does. I simply do not like her attitude.

The truth is . . . it is possible that she does not like me either, though I do not know this for sure. She has never said anything but I see it in her eyes whenever I encounter her. She looks at me with arrogance. She looks down her organic nose at me and judges me.

Granola Woman does not own a television. We *do* own a television, actually more than one, but it is very limited. There is no cable access downstairs where the kids' bedrooms are. They are allowed to watch movies on Friday night and then on Sunday night they watch *Amazing*

Race with us, or sometimes *I Love Lucy*. On Tuesday night we all watch *American Idol* together for our oldest daughter as she is infatuated with one of the contestants. We have a teen ahead of her and a preteen behind her and we feel that it is important for them to have something to talk about at school with their friends. This has also morphed into quality family time together. I make a special dessert for us to share during the show and it has turned into a very positive thing for all of us.

Other than that, there is no television watching. In comparison to the amount of screen time that kids get these days, this hardly makes the grid.

I remember growing up in the 70's when things were so much different and television was not as much of an issue as far as sex, violence, or the tendency towards addiction. As my mother was organic, as well as extremely socially and politically conscious, television needed to be limited because it was thought to be the *anti-Christ*. We were sent outside every day after school and all day on the weekend unless it was raining, and a mild drizzle did not count.

In the warm weather, we played baseball and once we were old enough we got to be in *the league*. I remember the year that my dad signed up to be a coach. Just as with anything else, baseball had its in-crowd and we were new to the whole thing so my dad ended up with the *free agents* that no one else wanted.

There was a girl named Jessica. She played in right field and picked dandelions. Not a lot of balls got hit to right field, but when they did everybody had to yell from the bench to catch her attention and chase after the ball. Sometimes Jessica would actually lie down in the grass and count the birds going by. We all loved Jessica.

The name of our team was the *Blazers*. Eventually we were called *The Bad News Blazers* after the *Bad News Bears*, the movie starring Tatum O'Neil and Walter Mathau. The movie was about a beer drinking, cigar smoking coach who takes a team of misfit, foul mouthed, street kids and turns them into a winning team.

We didn't win too much either but we definitely had a lot of fun.

I remember how serious I felt about playing on the *Blazers*. Each game I had to wear my lucky jeans. They were green and they were from *Sears*. Our colors were maroon and yellow. We had uniform shirts made out of some really stiff material that managed to stay creased even after the game was over and we had maroon mesh baseball hats. I collected them at the end of each season and hung them on my bed post.

I felt like royalty having my dad as a coach. He was fair and fun and the kids liked him. He had red hair and a bushy, somewhat un-kept 70's beard. He wore polyester, but when you are nine years old you don't notice things like polyester. Once and a while he would take the team out for ice cream. Mostly teams had to win to get ice cream but he took us anyway because we didn't win that much. We were limited to a single scoop which made the decision an important one as far as which flavor to choose.

What I really wanted was something in the chocolate family, but I would not choose this. The reason I did not choose something that I actually *liked* was because I knew my dad would take a huge bite out of it because he liked chocolate and would never buy one for himself. So instead I would ask for watermelon or black cherry, or something else colorful and fruity because I knew I would be safe as he did not like these flavors.

My little sister got to have an ice cream also which I did not understand as she did not play baseball yet and therefore did not earn the right to get an ice cream. She should be home with my organic mother who did not allow ice cream. The ice cream should have been only for me as I was older and in *the league*.

I was the short-stop and I batted third in the line-up. My best friend was the clean-up hitter. We were proud of where we batted in the line-up and proud to be on the *Bad News Blazers*. This was our world as we knew it.

March 11th

Of course my little sister was part of my world also, though I did not ask for her. In fact, things were going along quite smoothly in my life without her. I was an only child until she arrived and the sun would rise and set on my very existence. I was in Kindergarten.

Then it happened. We were renting a house in the mountains for a short time before my parents saved up enough money to purchase a pre-fab and move to a neighborhood.

This house was all right except for the copperheads. Many people are not aware of copperheads. They are poisonous snakes and they lived in our backyard. I believe they are of the pit viper species though I could be wrong. Off to the side of our house, there was a platform made of cement surrounded by tall grass and wild flowers. It was probably the remnants of a foundation, more than likely for an old barn or shed where copperheads were now free to congregate and sun bathe. They were in the rock garden, too. Our neighbor told us to be careful when we moved in because they could kill a goat or a small child, but she also said not to worry because they had loads of anti-venom at the hospital in Poughkeepsie. She wore rubber boots up to her knees.

My grandparents lived just outside of Chicago. My grandfather was an architect and had designed many of the buildings in Chicago. My grandmother was an artist and she had her own studio at *Brookwood*. *Brookwood* was the name of their estate. I loved to visit them and play with the intercoms in the rooms and go for long walks on the golf course. They had several maids and they were always very nice to me. There was a real King Henry the 8th doll in the maids' quarters and he was in a glass case. He was very fancy so he wasn't to be played with or touched, but it was okay to look at him.

My grandmother had studied art in Paris and they had traveled the world together. Now they were traveling to New Paltz, New York to visit us and whenever they would come, my grandmother would have to pour herself a really tall glass of wine as soon as she walked in. Then she would whisper and say a lot of private stuff to my mother about *Finishing School* and London. I am not sure exactly what all of that meant, but she would make me take off my overalls and put on a dress.

So anyway, life was pretty good, even with the copperheads. Then my sister came along.

March 12th

My little sister.

It is amazing how when you are five and a half years old and your mother's belly is growing and all you can think about is the playmate that will do everything with you. You think about her and dream about her and of all the secrets you will share.

Then she was born.

I remember being at *Barnabee's Bar and Grille* with my dad when we got *the news*. Back then, they didn't allow dads to be involved or cut the cord or anything like that. They were sent to the local bar with their five-year-olds to wait for *the news*.

The second Al came over and told us we headed straight to the hospital.

I had to wait in the car as they didn't allow kids in the maternity ward either. They were strict back then, no fathers and no siblings. So there I sat, completely unattended in the back seat of our car in the parking lot of Vassar Hospital in Poughkeepsie. This was also all right in the 70's, for a five-year old to be unattended in the back seat of a car, as long as she wasn't in the maternity ward.

Then they finally came, with my mother carrying my new little sister in her arms. Mom got in the front seat and held her in a pink blanket. We drove like this all the way back to the snake den. Car seats were not much of a concern back then either, kind of like leaving five-year olds in the back seats of cars so they don't disturb crying infants in nurseries.

Things were much easier in the 70's.

My little sister was, well, little. She was not of any use. She couldn't talk or play or do anything. In fact, she slightly resembled a plucked chicken. It took years before she got old enough or big enough to do anything.

Slowly she grew to be a *toddler*. *Toddler* is a nice word for pain in the ass. My sister had red hair just like our dad and she had a lot of energy. She ran every where she went and at full speed. When it was raining and we were stuck inside, she would do somersaults back and forth on the couch. This went on all day so I had to sit on the floor.

By the time she was three years old she had completely ruined my life.

I remember getting a Brownie Scout camping knife when I was nine years old as a birthday present. We were all settled into our pre-fab by then. It was white and it was in a neighborhood. My room was at the end of the house where my little sister was not supposed to be without my permission.

Anyway, there was a hole behind my door where the door knob would slam against the wall. It didn't have to hit the wall hard to make a mark because the walls were not that thick. I had wall paper on my walls also but the door knob still made a mark and then after a while it had made a hole in the shape of a circle.

My best friend and I, the clean-up hitter, used to drop secret notes into the hole. There they would stay, stuck between the walls of our pre-fab forever. It was our very own time capsule. Someday there would be a highway or a Wal-Mart put there, right where our pre-fab was and they would have to level it. The big trucks and wreckers would have to cease what they were doing and take notice of our secret notes as these would be genuine artifacts of this particular era. They would carefully lift them into special plastic bags and label them with important terminology and put them in the Smithsonian Institution. My friend and I would be famous as we had left our mark on history.

One day when I was not home, my unsupervised, impish little terror of a sister was playing in my room. This was against the law to begin with, and she would have already been severely punished just for trespassing as this was a repeat offense and the court would show no mercy this time. This day, however, she sealed her fate by finding my very special Brownie Scout camping knife that I had gotten as a present for my birthday. She took it and stared at it for a while. More than likely she unfolded it, played with the blades until she got bored and then somehow managed to escape injury.

Soon after, that red-headed three-year-old monster took my special Brownie Scout knife and dropped it down the hole in the wall of our pre-fab. It was gone forever and remains there to this day.

I was beyond angry at this point as I had tolerated this pint sized terror for too long. She would pay this time.

My friend and I tried to get it out by tying a string to a magnet and dropping it down inside the wall but it didn't work. We could feel the knife latch on to the magnet, but then as it journeyed up the inside of the wall it would get knocked off before we could grab it. We tried this for a whole week and then decided to make it an official contribution to our time capsule.

My little sister was my own personal nightmare and very few people understood this.

March 13th

Experiencing operating difficulty. Please stand by.

Though my little sister and I are quite close now, thinking of her as a toddler and this particular stage of my life has caused a vibration in my quills just as it does every time my mind travels to dark places.

A Full Moon Rising…and the Tao of Menopause

My quills were at a moderate level yesterday and I am not sure why. I am thinking that it may have been chemical. My quills were probably at 10 degrees or less, which barely qualifies for a yellow alert for those in our immediate surroundings. A yellow alert is not threatening. It usually signifies a *menopausal funk* and is not normally dangerous. It often happens the day prior to beginning our now very irregular menstrual cycles.

Since we are irregular, we often do not understand why we feel this way until we actually get it. We will probe deeply into our past and explore everything everyone has said to us recently as well in order to find the source of our melancholy. We probe because there must be a reason that we feel this way. Eventually, when our mental search party comes up empty we realize that it is nothing more than a menopausal funk, a day of moderately low quills.

These *sad days* are challenging because they come in waves and are normally quite unexpected. Of course, these days can happen any time and not just in place of the PMS of our old lives. They can arise at any given time and without warning.

In fact, I have a memory of one menopausal dinner club member who was in a menopausal funk and experiencing *operating difficulty*. She walked in the door from work and landed on the couch only to break down in an uncontrollable cry. Hearing the commotion, her teenaged daughter came down the stairs to see what was wrong. There she found her mother, dressed in her business attire sobbing uncontrollably that her entire life had been completely meaningless and without any purpose at all.

The teenager gently rubbed her mother's back and listened to all the reasons why her stay on the planet had been without benefit to anyone, and why the world was not an ounce different because she was born into it. The teenager listened and suggested that her mother breathe deeply as she was beginning to hyperventilate. She listened some more. The teenager then sneaked upstairs to call her mother's best girlfriend who lived only a few blocks away.

Mom's girlfriend raced right over, bearing armloads of self-care products. These included herbal tea, massage oil, bubble bath, and chocolate. By the time Mom's girlfriend emerged from the kitchen with herbal kiwi-strawberry tea, the menopausal wave has subsided. That's right. It was completely gone. She sat and chatted for a minute, then politely excused herself to go change into her sweat suit. It was a beautifully sunny day as she was headed out the door for a good run. She needed to go now as her workout routine had been disrupted this week. She thanked the girlfriend for coming over while she stretched on the floor.

Just as the tide comes in, so it goes out. This is how it is with a menopausal funk. It is like the tide. It comes in and out, just like that.

March 15th

My quills have now lowered and are now lying safely in their horizontal position. Because menopause can be emotionally turbulent, it is good to appreciate when our quills are at rest. When our quills are horizontal we feel like ourselves again, happy and carefree. Horizontal quills are the quiet before the storm, and the quiet in between storms.

This is the *Tenth Principle of the Tao of Menopause-appreciate moments of horizontal quills.*

The reason that this principle is so important, is because during this life stage the degrees and angle of our quills fluctuates so frequently. For some, their quills can go from a mild yellow alert to the highly dangerous red alert very rapidly, causing the automatic quick release to happen almost immediately if some poor unfortunate soul ticks them off. For some this happens daily.

Of course, when we use the word *dangerous*, we are referring to those within our immediate surroundings as well as those who have been programmed into the speed dial list on the telephone. They are at risk as well.

Because the day of the mid-lifer can be one in which she wakes up in a menopausal funk focused on the dark side, it is important to appreciate things when we *do not* wake up feeling like this. There are plenty of days when we do not feel like a piper plane spiraling down to its demise picking up speed as it falls toward a hard and rocky ground below. We need to take notice of these days and be grateful when we feel in harmony with those around us and with life in general.

Of course, we also need to appreciate the crescent moon as it shines brightly in the sky, for the sole reason that it is a moon that is not *full*. The crescent moon is passive and inviting, and does not cause hair to grow on our forearms or fangs to drop from our upper gums. Our eyes don't turn yellow and burn with rage from the anger molecules we have stored up to use for just the right moment, this moment. Menopausal women should take delight in the harmless crescent moon as should their loved ones and anyone who works in customer service.

March 21st

The mud wrap gods.

The sun has finally come out and is shining brightly. It makes us all feel lighter, happier, and more energetic. *Seasonal Affective Disorder* is a very real thing, especially for those who live way up north and for the menopausal crowd in general. Menopausal women need the sun and lots of it.

This is why menopausal women will spontaneously book trips to sunny destinations, sometimes with husbands or partners and sometimes with other menopausal women. The menopausal mid-lifers love to be with each other. They love to travel in groups, much like teenage girls when they head off to the bathroom during the Valentine's Day dance.

They will first cluster. The cluster formation is similar to a football huddle. This is where we gather information. After gathering some initial information, the group moves as a unit in the direction decided upon. This is due to menopausal chemistry as it is strong and very bonding.

Teenagers move in clusters to the bathroom. Menopausal women head in clusters to cruises and spas. I know of one group that travels annually to a spa in Mexico. They save their pennies all year to make their all-female pilgrimage to the sun and mud wrap gods. They even have a self-care schedule, if you can call it a schedule.

In the morning they have their organic breakfast including herbal tea and fruit free of toxins. The afternoon is comprised of Tai-Chi, Yoga, and a guided tour on horseback along the rocky coast. They breathe the fresh salt air. They breathe deeply. Menopausal women love to breathe deeply. They reflect as they stare out at the ocean. They think about their lives past and present. They are grateful and happy. They wonder if the horse they are on will take a wrong turn sending them down two hundred feet of embankment into the shark-infested waters below.

That thought wasn't a pleasant one so they practice the art of thought control and successfully bring themselves back to the present moment, and without the fear of the *what if* type thinking.

They come in for tea, meaning herbal tea as the Spa is a toxin-free zone. There is no caffeine or alcohol offered on the premises. Some of the mid-lifers, of course, smuggle in their red wine as a week is a long time and they would rather not see spiders while on vacation, especially when out of the country. Smuggling red wine in Tupperware is acceptable as long as one does not draw attention to oneself. The thrill of the challenge of sneaking the goods past the *Toxin Police* makes life even more fun.

It kind of feels like when you were a teenager and you went out drinking in the woods, chewing a whole package of bubble gum before you went home. Your parents would greet you at the door and question you as to whether you had a good time. Just like dogs sniffing through coffee grinds on impounded speedboats, they would come closer to discreetly sniff for toxins. They'd sniff and they would ask questions. We would sweat as we tried our best to hold it together. This was not an easy thing to do after mixing Vodka with McDonald's orange soda. We'd sweat some more as the taste from the entire package of grape flavored bubble gum began to fade with our increased swallowing due to nerves.

Finally, they would say that they are glad we had a good time and head back towards the living room. "Good night Dear," they'd say. The sweat droplets would hang on for a second, as they were unsure if this was a false alarm. The sweat droplets were on stand-by just in case they were called back to the forehead for a further assignment. No, it's real. They are sitting down to watch television. We did it. *Operation Teenager Drinking in the Woods Behind McDonalds* was a success. We crawl into bed and fall into a deep slumber.

The mid-lifers have a de ja vous of this feeling when they successfully sneak their red wine and instant coffee past the *Toxin Guards*. It is a small victory in a big world.

Next on the schedule for the menopausal group is an herbal mud wrap treatment. They defrock and are covered from head to toe with mud that serves to cleanse their bodies, not only freeing them from toxins but stress molecules as well. The goal of the herbal mud wrap is to pull stress molecules to the surface. The stress molecules then adhere to the mud and are rinsed away forever in the healing hot spring.

This all comes from the power and influence of the sun.

Just like *Children of the Corn*, with their arms straight out, menopausal women will seek out and follow the sun in an impenetrable trance. They even board airplanes and leave the country in this trance. When they snap out of it, they have arrived with luggage in hand.

March 24th

Peace at last.

I do often wonder why some women dread turning forty or fifty as these are the best years thus far, at least for me. Every life stage seems to have its own lessons to teach, its own benefits, and its own hurdles to jump over. Childhood is fun as long as your spirit was born into a loving family. The childhood life stage is of course the reason that therapists and antidepressants are in existence. This is because the spirit has no control over its own destiny during this life stage and therefore is forced to tolerate whatever it is faced with, regardless of how cruel or harsh the treatment.

For many, this is the life stage where pain is endured and spirits are broken. The spirit survives in any way that it can and hangs on to the hope for a better tomorrow, or a better decade.

A lot happens during childhood that we need to iron out and become at peace with during our menopausal, mid-life stage. This is the natural stage for reflection. Contemplation comes easy to mid-lifers. We look inward for spiritual guidance as we reflect on the footprints we have left behind. We retrace them to look for their meaning and purpose. We ask our footprints why they have brought us here on this particular path as opposed to another we may have taken. We notice the hesitations along the way, where the footprints are deep and slightly off center from the rest of our trail. These are the times that our spirits were challenged, or possibly even stuck for a while.

If we are an injured spirit, and our wounds happened during the childhood stage, we often become supermoms in order to become *that which we did not have*. It becomes our mission in life to be a faultless mother constantly comparing ourselves to others real and imagined. We compare ourselves to other mothers in the neighborhood who talk about all they have done. We compare ourselves to the mothers in magazines standing next to the beautifully decorated Thanksgiving table, with the bronze turkey on the white, pressed linen, surrounded by all the trimmings in the shiny silver dishes.

There is not a thought given to the fact that to create this advertising masterpiece that there was a staff of at least fifteen people including a lighting specialist, a set designer, a wardrobe person, two make-up people, and four chefs from the Culinary Institute. We also, of course, do not take into consideration the touch up photography work after the Thanksgiving photo shoot is complete. Just in case there was some small imperfection, it would be sure to be taken care of in the magazine's photo lab by their very own photo experts.

These things do not so much as cross our minds as we flip through the pages of our favorite magazines, especially during the holidays. Subconsciously, and often consciously we compare ourselves to these fabricated examples of what we feel we *should be*. We are on an undying pursuit for perfection as this yearning stems from deep wounds and unmet needs.

This is especially true for the child that felt unprotected. As a mother, she will never let her guard down. She will be the perfect mom even if it kills her. In fact, the supermom wants to feel the pain on some level. She takes honor in sleep deprivation, and in staying up all night with a child throwing up. She is striving for the *Purple Heart of Motherhood*. When her infant is sleeping, she will not put her feet up and read a good book. She will read to her toddler and build a Lego house. If there is time left over she will bake brownies for the preschool, then maybe scrub the bathroom. She has to deny herself of any time or self-enjoyment, even if only for a few moments. She does this because she was in some way emotionally abandoned when she was a child and over her dead body will she do this to her own children. She confuses healthy self-care with narcissism and abandonment.

Her inner child is soothed by her noble efforts. The little girl within speaks and calls to her. The supermom answers her and reassures her that she is right there and not to be afraid. Someone is there for her. The supermom usually continues this pace until she caves in physically, emotionally, and spiritually. She learns the hard life lesson that we cannot have it all or do it all, at least not for very long.

Something has to give and most often, it is us.

Mothers in general are bred to feel guilty about everything we are unable to do or be for everyone else, but the injured mother feels an intense guilt that most often converts to shame. Most supermoms are emotionally based in shame as this is how messages were conveyed to them as little girls. The message to the inner children inside these grown-up supermoms was not "You *did* something bad," but "You *are* bad."

This is the difference between guilt and shame. Guilt is what keeps us from slashing other people's tires or saying nasty things to our loved ones, as we feel badly when we hurt someone else. Shame is a toxic emotion most often having its roots in childhood that tells us we are bad people. Shame poisons the spirit and prevents personal growth. Shame prevents us from knowing ourselves and from blossoming into the unique individuals we are meant to be.

For the spirit, shame is turpentine.

The saddest thing about this whole dynamic is that turpentine is highly addictive. We take comfort in our own self punishment as this is what we know. If someone looks at us wrong or says harsh words, especially if it is someone close to us, we immediately *personalize and internalize*. This is the routine for a shame-based supermom.

Fortunately, if this mom has not taken steps toward healing thus far, now is the opportune time. She now has the emotional readiness to realize that it is all right to love our children in their own right without having to prove to ourselves and the world at large that we are the perfect mother. We realize that we no longer need to be victims of comparison. We get to a place where we feel all right doing something that makes our heart sing if we have a free fifteen minutes. We realize that it is healthy to take care of ourselves, not only for our own sanity, but for what we are role-modeling for our children. We get it that it is good for them to see us be able to love and like ourselves.

This is also the only way they will learn to love and like themselves as we are their primary teachers. What they see us do, they will most likely emulate. Therefore, if they see a happy, healthy, middle-aged mom dancing around the living room with an optimistic zest for the joy of living, they will most likely adopt this outlook also.

It is during our mid-life, perimenopausal or menopausal life stage that our previous actions begin to make sense. We begin to figure out what our need was to rescue, to over-achieve, to fail, or to hide out and remain invisible. It is almost as if we are able to stop a movie in the middle on one screen, then rewind the same movie on another screen. By watching the beginning over again we catch a lot more of the details. Things become more clear to us.

We realize parts that we had missed or had forgotten entirely.

When we turn that screen off and push play on the screen where we are presently, we view things differently and with more wisdom. The life we are living now makes more sense after watching the beginning again. There is also a certain sense of security in this feeling, the feeling of understanding why we are who we are and why we react in certain ways. We learn to know and understand our *buttons* on a more intimate level. Our buttons are those emotional pressure points that we all have which cause us to act or react in certain ways. They are our built in defense mechanisms that serve to protect our spirits from further harm or irritation. Whether we grew up in a dysfunctional family or in the *Brady Bunch*, we all have at least a couple of buttons as they are what make us human.

Our buttons are our areas of vulnerability.

Once we achieve a deeper understanding of our buttons, we are able to lower our guard with ease, as we no longer carry the underlying fear with us. We have reached a place, a comfortable place where we are able to safely release our fear. Not only have we released our fear, but we have gained emotional wisdom in the process. We realize that there may be certain individuals in our lives who continue to be toxic and are therefore not safe people. We realize that it is healthy under these circumstances to remain guarded, and not some defect of our own character.

We become able to consciously differentiate between these situations.

March 25th

The Chess Tournament.

I have realized that it is never too late to think outside the box or to pursue the *Purple Heart of Motherhood* in a different way. Just a few weeks ago, our oldest son came home with a registration form for the Chess Tournament. Though he talked about wanting to be in the tournament, he left the form in his backpack for a week or so until I finally made him go down to his room and get it. More than likely, it was lying beneath a banana peel or two, as well as school newsletters dating back to the middle of last year.

I read the form and noticed that the tournament was quite a drive from where we live, probably just a hair under two hours one way. As the event was offered to children in grades kindergarten through high school, I figured that it made sense to take a couple more with me.

Our ten-year-old son and our eight-year-old daughter decided to join in on the fun. The little one got shuttled off to a friend, as did the eleven-year-old as one was not old enough and one had no interest in Chess.

The night before, I glanced at the form just to make sure that we knew where we were going. One little detail I didn't notice was that registration was between 8:30 and 9:00 am. The very quick realization came upon me that we had better have all seven of us up and running by 6:45 am if we were going to make it, as we had to drop off two kids in the opposite direction and in different places. This meant that we all had to be up at 6:00 am, dressed, fed and ready to go. For a family of seven, this is a whole lot easier said than done. The teenager moves at one speed in the morning regardless of what he is bribed or blackmailed with. This was beginning to feel stressful.

Before any of us had realized it, we were in the car minus the two we had dropped off and were now on our way to the Chess Tournament. Looking down at the form, just to triple check the date to make sure that it was indeed today and not next weekend, I noticed one other small detail. On the top of the form above the words Chess tournament were some other words. They read, "*State of Vermont Championship* Chess Tournament." There I sat in the front seat, balancing coffee between my knees and wondering how I managed to miss that.

My teenager was in more of a trance than usual. He was staring out the window with a blank stare and his mouth was hanging open. He was either contemplating the essence of being or in desperate need of a sugar fix. We pulled into the nearest convenient store, which is no easy task in northern Vermont. There are often miles in between opportunities to purchase a Pepsi and a bag of chips. This one was a small gas station with a snack section. We seized the opportunity, filling the gas tank and purchasing enough Cherry 7-UP and jumbo chocolate cookies to feed the gang in the back seat. It was the breakfast of champions. If nothing else it would give them an energy boost and hopefully jumpstart the teenager.

March 26th

I could not help but to imagine what the thoughts would have been had we had *Granola Woman* in the back seat when I came out of the Shell station with arm loads of sugar at 6:45 in the morning. She would probably have sat there stoically, gazing ahead and trying not to make any eye contact.

She would be thinking of the organic oatmeal that she gave her own children this morning. The milk that was poured over the top came straight from the goat in the barn. On Easter she allows her children to sprinkle a spoonful of organic brown sugar on the top, but only on Easter and only one spoonful.

Out of her peripheral vision, she would watch my children devour their processed chocolate chip cookies and Cherry 7-up. Silently, *Granola Woman* wonders if this alone is enough to warrant a call to Youth Protective Services.

As she begins to get more worked up thinking about the processed sugar in the car and in the world in general, she may even begin to drool, but just a little bit as *Granola Woman* is a very controlled individual. Even so, the few drops of drool that would gently slide down her thin, defined chin, would be filled with judgment molecules.

Her whole body is filled with judgment molecules, actually, but only a few are released when she salivates only so slightly. A fly might even land on her nose and she would have to tolerate it as it would break her trance of staring out the car window if she were to move. Then everyone in the car would know what she was thinking and that she had leaked some judgment molecules down her chin.

Elite natural food co-op owners such as she have a need to judge privately. No one can know that they are looking down their noses at people, as they are *above* judgment. They are wholesome, organic, and natural. These kind of people don't judge others.

At least this is what they tell themselves.

March 27th

A league of their own.

I have to tell you that the kids did really well in the tournament, especially as there were quite a few kids in the younger age groups, many of whom were involved with Chess clubs. My kids showed up in the t-shirts that they had slept in the night before as we had to wake up so early to get there. Because we live deep in the middle of no where it takes us forever to get anywhere.

So there we were, wrinkled and fueled by processed sugar, surrounded by little brainiacs from all over the state. We were too tired to be intimidated. I led each child to their designated classrooms and then left to find a cup of coffee.

The Chess parents are something that I had never quite experienced, a whole different breed. Each and every one of them did the New York Times crossword puzzle. You knew that much for sure.

So there we sat, waiting. Actually, my husband and I sat waiting. The Chess parents played Chess as they waited, on their very own, wooden, hand carved Chess boards. Some of these Chess boards were works of art. Then, the very second that the results were posted, these calm and quiet Chess parents leapt out of their chairs like Superman on a mission to save Lois Lane from the top of a burning building. I had never seen anything quite like it.

I wonder what *they* had for breakfast.

March 29th

We have been infected by the first grade. Somebody who was up all night throwing up went to school the next day and touched every door knob that he or she possibly could. Thankfully, it appears to be a 24 hour thing thus far, but violent none the less.

I had forgotten what it was like to throw up. I think that it was sometime in the late 70's when I was in middle school. My sister and I were almost never sick, so the once every four or five years or so that we got the pukies it was sort of a big deal. Our dad would come home from work with ginger ale and fudge ripple ice cream. After an entire night of throwing up, followed by an entire morning of dry heaving, the early evening ice cream and ginger ale was a welcome sight. It slid down to an angry tummy with ease and calmed the acids of the savage organ that had been tormented into these violent convulsions by some microscopic alien intruder.

March 30th

My comfort zone.

I miss the comfort of ginger ale and fudge ripple ice cream on the couch under a blanket. As previously mentioned, my sister and I were also products of the anti-T.V. hippy movement, and on the rare occasion that we were sick we got to watch the *Brady Bunch* and *The Munsters*, sometimes *Bewitched*. The shows back then were so much better than the garbage on now.

They were in black and white. There was no bad language, very little sex or violence, and they were funny. I guess that real talent doesn't need all of that to make a person laugh, and no one did this better than Lucille Ball.

I still watch her now when I need a boost. She is guaranteed to lift my spirits. The world was so much different back then. Things were so much simpler.

March 31st

The good life.

What is really weird about life back in *the day*, is that we actually thought that we were rebels.

Spring

April 1st

A decade of bigness and bad clothes.

I think when most people think of the 70's, they think *big*. Hair was big. Cars and collars were big. As horrible as our national taste for fashion was, it seemed to be a decade of extravagance and flamboyance.

The irony of the 70's, is that amidst all of the *bigness* was a time where we did not have a fraction of what we do today. There was a gas crisis, complete with little coupons, so we were not driven to friends' houses on a whim. Our friends were who lived in our neighborhood.

It was the luck of the draw.

We were not driven to ballet, karate, or Irish step dance. We played flash light tag in the yard. Our bikes were our lives. This is how we knew where our friends were after school, by the bikes in the yard. Life seemed easier then in some ways. It wasn't so complicated with stuff and so many activities. Because of this, days seemed longer. The time between getting off the bus and when my mother would scream down the block for dinner seemed like an eternity. To get up and go to school the next day felt good as we felt that we had rest.

We had plenty of *down time*.

Kids today are driven around too much and this takes away from their down time.

April 2nd

My hippy upbringing.

I remember when my mother went through her *Rhoda phase*. She wore head bands almost every day, big wide ones, right across the middle of her forehead. And she had these huge tinted sunglasses. When I look back, I probably should have been embarrassed.

The truth is that I was too busy being embarrassed about the lunches that she packed me. Part of my mother's *hippy phase*, which was quite a long phase actually as it lasted for the majority of my childhood, was *wheat germ*.

We lived in suburban New Paltz, New York, about an hour out of Manhattan. As New Paltz was a college town it was known for its hallucinogens as well as for its concerts. We were actually located just down wind from the birthplace of concerts as New Paltz is only one exit south of the infamous 60's *music Mecca*, Woodstock. The lanes of New Paltz were filled with tie-dyed shirts, sandals, and peace signs. People read poetry on the front steps of bars and picketed and protested with any given opportunity. It was a town where the cars were held together with bumper stickers.

This was the atmosphere of my upbringing.

Our biggest claim to fame was Floyd Patterson, the former heavy weight boxing champ. He had a beautiful house and his own gym. His two girls went to school with my little sister and they were very sweet. Floyd was a very down to earth type of guy and could often be found talking with people in town at the grocery store and at school events. I went to middle school and high school with his later adopted son Tracy, also a regular, very nice person. Years later Tracy invited my children and I to watch him train in New Jersey. He gave them each a signed photo.

Our second biggest claim to fame was the Shawangunk mountain range, nicknamed the gunks. These cliffs surrounded the beautiful, very posh resort, the *Mohonk Mountain House.* It is a beautiful old hotel surrounded by exquisite gardens. It is over two hundred years old and somewhat resembles *Hogwarts.*

These cliffs were ranked among the top in the nation for training cliffs for aspiring young rock climbers. The lanes of New Paltz were filled with climbers young and old, wearing cargo shorts and rag wool socks, talking of the tales of near catastrophes involving pins, ropes, and crevices. Unfortunately, rarely a year went by without the death of a climber.

New Paltz had and still does have a lot of character as it has a tendency to attract colorful, free-spirited individuals. When I was a kid growing up it attracted *Jingles*. *Jingles* was an older man, in his late fifties or early sixties who had very long gray hair. He was draped in silver from head to toe. Pieces of silver hung all over him and made lots of noise as he strolled up and down the lanes, hence his nickname. He wore suede boots with fringe up the back.

Jingles spent his days walking up and down the lanes talking with people on the streets, with himself, and with whomever he imagined was talking with him.

No one ever bothered Jingles and he never bothered anyone else either. His colorfulness was embraced and appreciated.

Today of course, the New Paltz area is developed and somewhat upscale with bistros and cafes on every corner. It has also become a bit of a weekend retreat for some of Manhattan's most successful, artistic, and interesting individuals. When I grew up, however, we lived sort of on the periphery of what would be considered country, bordering on bourgeois/red neck.

There was this place called *The Grain Mill*, and it manufactured all things terrible. We would go on the weekends with my mother's hippy friends and their hippy children to this place where they made organic everything.

One of her hippy friends lived in a purple house, with different shades of the same horrible color and I am not making that up. Her house was next door to *The Grain Mill*.

They had this huge metal machine that made *real* peanut butter. There is not much worse than real peanut butter. It didn't even resemble peanut butter. It was oily and had the consistency of a loose bowl movement following the ingestion of a gallon or so of Metamucil.

It smelled, too, like burnt wax.

April 3rd

I am only now realizing how truly scarred I was by *The Grain Mill* and my organic childhood in general. For a treat, my sister and I got to have these little honey sesame bars, each individually wrapped. I think my mother thought she was fooling us, like it was real candy or something. Even our basset hound wouldn't eat them.

April 4th

Scarred for life.

The worst part of this whole organic thing was that no one would trade with us at lunch. I remember being in the cafeteria, surrounded by kids with *good* mothers who had packed them Hostess cup cakes and chocolate chip cookies. They actually had something to look forward to after working hard all morning in second grade.

Not me. I had real peanut butter slapped onto two pathetic pieces of *melba toast*. Most kids were not aware of melba toast. Melba toast is the obvious compatible partner to oily organic peanut butter. Melba toast is stiff and tasteless and a perfect match for that disgusting stuff as it held it together. For dessert I had my honey sesame treats to look forward to.

No one would ever trade with me. I dreamed of Hostess cupcakes.

April 5th

Wheat germ.

I forgot to further elaborate on the wheat germ. Wheat germ is in the grain family I think, and it can be tossed into anything, even meat loaf. My mother, still donning colorful head bands used to throw wheat germ into everything. She said that it would boost our immune systems and keep bad viruses away. It may even prevent us from entering into future unhealthy relationships.

Wheat germ has loads of uses.

April 6th

The transformation.

After a while, my mother gave up on her *Rhoda infatuation* and she became *Cher* instead. She still wore an occasional headband but they got thinner in their width and shinier. The ponchos and print skirts gave way to hip hugger pants with bell bottoms. She had a shag hair do.

She kind of resembled *Carol Brady*, only as a brunette.

The *Cher phase* lasted even longer than the *Rhoda phase*. I think she actually believed that she had undergone a transformation and become one with Cher's spirit. My mother used to sing. She sang in the car. She sang in the living room, and, as she truly thought she *was* Cher, thought she was good at it.

Eventually she left Cher behind and became Carly Simon instead.

Mom still sang, only with a more *Fleet Wood Mac-ish* kind of style.

April 7th

A different world.

Things were so different back in the 70's. People weren't so full of stress and worry. There was a lot going on also, with the whole Watergate thing going on and that native American man on the commercial talking about litter and how it was destroying Mother Earth. I think that everyone remembers that commercial and the big tear rolling down his cheek.

There was a lot of change going on, but it was *manageable change*. We were sitting in long gas lines with our coupons. People were marching on Washington and debating the whole bussing issue. We weren't worried about terrorists crashing into buildings with airplanes.

People were actively involved with what was going on, just not actively fearful.

April 8th

I woke up thinking about wheat germ and my 70's childhood. I had a big, wide white belt that went with my red and white checkered pants. The bell bottoms were so big and long that I tripped on them once in a while. I had a shirt and a crocheted sweater vest that went with them. The collar was big and pointy. I really loved that outfit.

I also loved *Brownie Scout* meeting day at school because I got to wear my uniform. I had the complete set, the light brown dress with the belt that had the little purse that held my milk money. I had a sash that went from left to right over my shoulder and the very best part, the *Brownie beanie* that I proudly wore on top of my head.

My parents never did replace my knife.

Anyway, the meeting was after school, but I got to strut around the Cherry Hill Elementary School with my nose high in the air and my shoulders back because I was indeed a Brownie Scout. I even had badges on my sash to prove it. I had one for a camp out, and one for building a campfire. There was one for cooking and sewing, and one for knowing what to do in an emergency.

In the summer we got to march in the parade right down the center of Main Street.

April 9th

Clancy.

The only thing better than marching in the parade with my sash that went from left to right, was going to the Town Pool every day in the summer. We had a membership. It was a public place, so this meant that anyone could go, even my family.

It's not that we were that different, but our basset hound had lots of fleas. This didn't bother my sister though because she loved him unconditionally.

His name was Clancy.

He was actually a *Beagle-Basset*, as he was half Beagle and half Basset. Like the rest of my family, Clancy was a hippy also, except for my dad. He's a Republican. Clancy wore a bandana around his neck and paraded around the neighborhood without a worry in the world.

He spent most of his day roaming up and down main street. As we lived in New York, the food was good, the street food I mean. You know, bagels and pizza, stuff like that. Clancy would wander around all day in search of a morsel. Most days, he would return with a burger, a slice of New York style thin crust pizza, or a mouth full of munchkins. There was a *Dunkin Donuts* at the end of the block that was one of Clancy's favorite hang outs.

Lots of times I would go looking for him. Inevitably, I would find him lounging on the front sidewalk giving passers by his best sad Beagle-Basset look with his big brown eyes in an attempt to get tossed the remnants of their breakfast. Of course, anyone who took an actual look at our lovable vagabond would realize that he was most definitely not starving.

He was lovable for certain, however, Clancy chose only to show the love back to *his people* or those who fed him on a regular basis. He had no tolerance for strangers, small children on bicycles, other dogs, or old ladies with metal braces on their legs.

I remember the night our dad got *the call*. Apparently while off roaming the streets of the neighborhood Clancy had gotten irritated by Mrs. Kowalski. Mrs. Kowalski lived over on North Street amongst all of the Italians. The street had about a million kids and was the primary source of players for nightly games of neighborhood flash light tag and street football.

This is because the Italians, along with the Irish, use the rhythm method. I was never quite sure about the rhythm method. I just knew that it meant you went to the same Church.

In fact, every family on that street had at least seven or eight kids and they were all loud, all except Mrs. Kowalski. Mrs. Kowalski did not go to St. Joseph's like the rest of us. In fact, I don't think she left the house much except to get her mail. She would watch out the window, kind of peering through the curtains to wait for the mailman to bring her mail. She would wait until he had closed the mailbox, gotten into his little mail truck and driven away before she would venture outside.

Mrs. Kowalski lived by herself on the corner, wedged in between the Gallos and the Caninos. She had to be a hundred years old. At least it seemed that way as kids. She was old and crabby and got really mad when the ball would land in her yard.

The night we got *the call* I watched our dad turn weird colors as the blood rushed to his face. He was purple and reddish with little white spots in his cheeks.

The call was from Mrs. Kowalski's lawyer and she was pressing charges against Clancy for biting her on the leg when she went out to get her mail that morning. In fact, she was suing us for $10,000. Well, anyone who knew our family would know that we didn't have *ten* dollars forget that amount with a comma and all those zeros. I guess she was *really* mad. My sister and I didn't really get it to be honest. She couldn't have been hurt that badly by Clancy as she wore two metal braces, one on each leg. Also, as she used a walker we couldn't figure out how he even got access to one of her legs. He must have really had to work at it. The worst thing that could have happened would have been Clancy breaking a tooth.

I hoped he had his shots.

It all worked out because the insurance money paid Mrs. Kowalski and we were told never to step foot with our flea ridden mutt near her property again, and we didn't.

Clancy was a good judge of character.

April 10th

The lanes of New Paltz.

Anyway, I was telling you about the fleas. Clancy would return faithfully each night after a long day of roaming around town and land himself on the end of my little sister's bed.

She would look forward to his return, just not the incessant itching that accompanied him.

She had this old comforter that she pretty much had for our entire childhood. It was thinned out in certain places and kind of *thready* in other places. This is where most of the flea colony would congregate.

The threads provided the ideal habitat for the fleas to thrive and reproduce.

Sometimes I would look in and check on my little sister and there she would be fast asleep with our faithful Beagle Basset nestled comfortably at the end of her bed. If you looked closely, you could see a cloud of black specks between them kind of jumping awkwardly looking for a comfortable place to land and be fruitful.

Sometimes I have flashbacks of *Angela's Ashes* and wonder if Frank McCourt did some kind of weird telepathy thing and stole my life story. The lanes of Limerick and lanes of New Paltz weren't all that different.

April 11th

The shame.

I don't think that I finished my story about the fleas or about *the shame*. Shame can emerge from loads of different places such as flea-ridden Beagle-Bassets or from certain racist neighbors who wore polyester as if it were a ceremonial religious robe.

There was this family who lived at the end of our block. The father was a dermatologist and their last name was Rosenburg. They were Jewish. For the most part, our entire town was made up of Italians which could account for why the food was so good, not just the street food, but the diner food also. My family was Irish and everyone knows that the Irish can't cook.

Irish people can't cook. They just drink, and laugh, and tolerate dogs with fleas even if it means certain neighbors won't let you in their house. The Rosenbergs lived on the corner in a brick house with big glass windows. Our neighborhood was very middle class, possibly even lower middle class but of course no one ever wants to admit that, so for the sake of my story let's just say that we were a regular, middle of the road family. As I had mentioned earlier, the houses in our development were all pre-fabricated ranches, or *pre-fabs* for short. A pre-fab means that parts of your house were manufactured in Illinois.

Most of the houses had two or three bedrooms and a little yard. The Rosenbergs had a two story brick house with a little more yard and because of it, they thought they were the Rockefellers. Mr. Rosenberg's office was underneath their pre-fab estate. He had a sign. Mrs. Rosenberg would refer to Mr. Rosenberg as *The Doctor* whenever she spoke of him, kind of like *Little House on the Prairie* when Mrs. Ingall's called Pa to drive Laura into the big city of Mankato to receive medical attention.

As kids, we tried not to laugh as there were at least twenty or thirty other doctors in town, even back then. The Rosenbergs wore polyester. Even worse, they actually thought they looked good. It was kind of like when people say they have champagne taste and a beer budget. The Rosenbergs were *Upper West Side* in their minds and pre-fab suburbia in reality. Same thing.

Then there was Pedro their little ankle biter of a dog. I don't know how people can have those little yips. I felt like saying, "Look, if you want to get a cat, then get a cat." There was an 8 x 10 picture of Pedro on the mantle wearing a yellow raincoat and boots. And no, I am not making it up.

Pedro went for a walk each and every day on his self-retracting leash with Mrs. Rosenberg in her color- coordinated polyester. He would do his daily business and then went back inside. Pedro was basically an *indoor* dog.

Mr. Rosenberg was inside *practicing*. Practicing *what* was sort of up for discussion as Mr. Rosenberg had a reputation for being somewhat *touchy-feely*, with emphasis on the *feely* part. He would have you set your chin on that machine so he could get a good look at your skin cells. As you sat staring into this mechanical face mask without any peripheral vision, he would do a little swipe up against the breast area. The bigger your girls the longer the accidental swipe across the nipples. It's true, too. The whole town knew about it.

April 12th

Super fleas.

The fact that Mr. Rosenberg was a closet perve is only part of the story. Mrs. Rosenberg sent my sister home one day, saying that she could not play with her little Miriam because we had fleas. I was never sure what she meant by *we*, as I hadn't itched in a quite a while, at least since last winter.

In the summer we spent all day at the Town Pool so the chlorine took care of them.

In the winter, things could occasionally flare up. I think that winter is their mating season as this is when *thready* comforters function as the breeding ground for thousands of flea eggs. My dad used a flea bomb once. It didn't work. I think it just made the fleas mad.

We had to leave the house for two hours so we went down the street to *The Diner*. After the toxic fumes had dissipated and we were allowed back in the house again, I remember my sister and I stepping on the rug with a feeling of victory and liberation from the constant itching. There we stood on the living room rug as thousands of black specs jumped onto our socks.

We hadn't killed them. In fact, we hadn't even weakened them. It's kind of like cock roaches. The more they are poisoned the stronger they get. It has been said that if there were to be a nuclear war that the cock roaches would be the only ones still standing. I think the fleas will be right there beside them. Maybe they will evolve and become super fleas.

The most unfortunate part was that we stood there inhaling remnants of the toxic flea bomb and we were still itching.

No matter. Since it was the middle of the summer, no doubt Mrs. Rosenberg was embellishing our flea situation.

April 13th

And the shame continues . . .

O.K. Here is the kicker. Our dad went back to the store and got the biggest, most expensive flea bomb they had and he made us stay outside all day until it was time for dinner. Then he shut every window in the house, set it off, and ran outside.

We did a lot of yard work that day and rearranged the garage.

Later in the afternoon, my little sister went back over to the Rosenbergs, careful not to step on their property. She just sort of stood on the edge of their driveway with the tops of her sneakers lined up against the pavement. The Rosenbergs had black top on their driveway.

You could see Mrs. Rosenberg pacing nervously behind their big, upstairs window with Pedro in her arms. He had a bow in his hair today.

After wearing a hole in her rug from all of that anxious shuffling, she finally came downstairs to talk to my sister who was obediently remaining on Town property.

My sister stuttered as she explained that the fleas were all gone. Our dad used one of those really expensive poison bombs from the *Barkers* department store and killed every bug in the neighborhood, possibly even a couple of cats.

Mrs. Rosenberg just stood there with her little stick body. She must have weighed less than a hundred pounds. She was shaking her head. "The fleas cannot be gone," she said "and besides, your parents are getting a divorce. This is just not the kind of influence we want on Miriam."

My sister turned and walked away, her head hung low.

April 14th

Probably the only consoling factor with the Rosenbergs is that we weren't the only ones banned from their pre-fab brick estate. The little boy across the street was also not allowed over. In fact, he had never been in the house once.

He was black.

April 15th

With all that humanity has been through, with Jewish people and African Americans being treated so terribly, and poor Irish immigrants bringing their fleas over from the lanes of Limerick to work labor jobs for practically nothing, that we could all coexist well together.

I never really understood Mrs. Rosenberg.

April 16th

Pony Boy.

I especially didn't understand her on Halloween. Our neighborhood was the place to be on Halloween. Future delinquents from all over town had carefully hid their assault weapons of shaving cream, toilet paper, and cartons of eggs in gutters all over the neighborhood. There was one kid in particular. Let's just call him *Pony Boy* as he was an original outsider and therefore this name fits very well.

Pony Boy was really, really into Halloween. He waited for it all year. He was the son of my parents' friends and we benefited from this connection. The day after Halloween, when we went out for the bus we would just stand there and see who got nailed the worst by Pony Boy's gang of Halloween hoods. Every house and car would be covered with shaving cream and eggs. Our house would stand proudly in the middle of the neighborhood untouched. Not so much as one egg touched our pre-fab windows.

We had fleas, true, but we had connections.

April 17th

The Rosenburgs, on the other hand, had burnt many bridges and made many enemies. Between banning people for fleas and divorce, and touching many of the women in town inappropriately, they were not very well liked, but they really hammered that last nail in their coffin when they turned off their lights on Halloween.

For Pony Boy and his gang this was like putting a rather large red and black bulls-eye on their big picture window.

Most of the houses in the neighborhood were hit randomly, but not the Rosenbergs. Pony Boy must have used a whole month's allowance just to buy the ammunition.

And what a sight it was the day after. There wasn't a square inch of window left to see out of. There had to be two to three cartons of eggs just on the front window alone. Then, as an annual ritual, Mr. Rosenberg would have to take time away from his scheduled inappropriate touching to clean his windows. He went into his garage and got his ladder, positioning it ever so perfectly, then, from left to right he made clean swipes across his big picture window with lots of glass cleaner. After all, he didn't want streaks.

Of course, it would have been a whole lot easier just to leave the lights on and spring for a couple of bags of candy.

April 18th

Sanuja.

I never finished telling you about that little black boy. His name was Asumpta and his family was from Jamaica. They were very nice. His father was a journalist. His mother stayed home with he and his sister Sanuja. She was so cute. Sanuja always had her hair done so nicely, either in corn rows or in pig tails with colorful ribbons. Asumpta and Sanuja were only about a year apart in age and they played all day together, especially since they were not allowed to play at the Rosenbergs even though they lived across the street.

I remember thinking back then, even at my young age, how much better Asumpta's family was than the Rosenbergs. Their kids were not allowed to play with the Rosenberg children, or step on their property for that matter because of the color of their skin. I was twelve years old and this made me feel sick inside.

It was way worse than being banned for the fleas.

April 19th

I want to tell you about a really bad thing that happened to Asumpta's family. Our town had a recreation program during the summer. When it was a rainy day, they had arts and crafts. The rest of the time they had structured intramural sports and an occasional day trip. For the most part, my little sister and I weren't allowed to go. Though it didn't cost much, it cost something and we didn't have it. Besides that, we had already paid for our family membership to the Town Pool where kids were free to pee as they wish.

For some reason, maybe the stars had lined up in the proper order and we were allowed to go. It was a day trip to Lake Winnipeg. I was excited, especially since my usual melba toast and oily peanut butter sandwich had given way to ham on an actual roll.

A Full Moon Rising…and the Tao of Menopause

This was going to be a good day.

In fact, as I dug farther into my brown paper sack I felt something crinkly. It was a package of chocolate chip cookies. I turned the bag over just to make sure that it had my name on it. There was my name all right, written with a black magic marker on its last leg. Each letter got lighter and lighter as you got towards the end of my name. The last *n* was barely legible, but the lunch was mine. All I could think of was who kidnapped my mother and how much ransom they were asking. I'd give up anything to save her, except my packaged chocolate chip cookies from a real store.

She even gave me a nectarine. I love nectarines. Usually we always got peaches because they were cheaper. Peaches are fuzzy and nectarines are smooth and shiny. Nectarines are an elite fruit.

Things were already going really well and it was only 8:00 am. We boarded the bus. The sun was shining and I had my store bought lunch in my duffle bag, safely wrapped in my towel, just in case anyone noticed my store bought cookies and tried to take them.

April 20th

I still can't get over what happened on that day so many years ago. It was almost lunch time and I was getting really excited to show off my cookies and then to savor each and every one of them.

Spring

It was a day free of wheat germ and sesame honey treats. I felt like a regular kid from a normal family. I mean, other than the fact that my mother thought she was Cher and shopped at the Grain Mill for organic everything and my sister being banned from people's houses for her fleas, we were pretty normal I guess.

Anyway, the lifeguards blew their whistles to call the New Paltz Rec Program out of the lake. Then they called out everybody else. We walked over to the picnic tables to search for our brown paper sacks with our names written in faded black magic marker.

All of the sudden, more whistles went off and then a big horn. Every lifeguard ran to the beach. We watched as they held hands and raked the bottom of the lake. None of us understood what they were doing. Maybe it was a drill that they practiced at lunch time. Maybe it was something that was required by the state of New York.

All of the sudden it felt serious, that it wasn't a drill.

The counselors faces looked serious and they were firm about us staying in the picnic area until they said we could move. Asumpta was pacing back and forth by the edge of the grass. It was almost like he knew.

They were looking for Sanuja.

April 21st

After the rescuers combed the lake three times they found Sanuja's body. She was six years old. This is how old my little sister was and there were only two of us just like Asumpta and Sanuja. I wondered what he would do without his little sister forever and ever. I wondered about his parents. I wondered how this could happen.

After a couple of weeks went by I saw Asumpta outside in his yard. He looked really quiet and sad. Asumpta was only a year older than his sister and he was my sister's friend, too. She went down the street and asked him to play and he did. He didn't say much though.

I couldn't help to wonder if Mrs. Rosenberg was watching out of her big picture window and what her thoughts might be.

April 22nd

It is amazing what people get through, and that they find the strength to carry on when their lives have undergone devastation causing life as they knew it to be completely altered forever. Our spirits are most definitely driven by a Higher Power. We realize this, I think, when life becomes overwhelming and at times unbearable as pain is almost always the motivator.

Beneath the tragedy, a peaceful strength holds us together, and the more we accept the love around us the more love and support we attract.

In my mid-life, I have learned that we attract what we want and what we are accepting of.

April 23rd

Mid-life, of course is an age, or an era, of personal transformation. Like anything, this stage of life can be resisted or embraced. Often people begin by resisting change as it feels new and scary. We are unable to see around the corner or to visualize the big picture, the better place that is calling to us. We cannot see and so we resist. We fold our arms and dig our heels in just to end up further down the road anyway only with a great deal more difficulty, far less joy, and much less change. Forced or resisted change is not of the same quality as accepted change, nor does it bring with it the same degree of joy.

Though it can be difficult, tremendously difficult sometimes, I do try to embrace change. This does not mean that it cannot feel scary at times, but there is an element of trust in the Creator of all things, and that I will evolve and delight in a better place if I am open to going along for the ride.

April 24th

After all, it is all about the ride or the process, and not at all about the end result because there is no end and therefore the result itself keeps changing. For me, this is what keeps life so interesting. I am never finished, but a work in progress.

April 25th

What we think about and thank about, we bring about.

It seems as each and every time I reach some sort of personal plateau that my eyes are opened wide by a new inspiration. For the moment, it is attraction.

My mother gave me a movie called *The Secret*. Many people may have seen it or know of this movie by now as *Oprah* did a show on it as did *Larry King Live*. Basically, the movie talks about the *Law of Attraction* which simply states that we attract what we want, whether our wants are positive or negative.

For example, many people often focus on getting out of debt as a goal not realizing that it is the *debt* part that they are focusing on. It is far more lucrative to focus on abundance and then let the rest fall into place.

We are what we think. I truly believe this.

April 26th

This idea is not a new one. The *Power of Positive Thinking* was written years ago and remained popular for quite a while. The greatest thinkers, inventors, and most financially successful people of our nation's history have known *The Secret* since the beginning.

April 27th

A lot, of course, has to do with one's momentum. It can be difficult to turn one's day around after getting stuck in traffic, being late to a business meeting, and then threatened by a supervisor for being late. Altering the course of one's day and therefore one's life is a skill that can be developed just as with anything else. It takes practice and determination. It takes conscious thought. To control one's thoughts is to control one's feelings and one's life.

We have more power than we think we have.

April 28th

Positive momentum can acquire size and speed much like a snow ball as it rolls down hill adding more to its mass with every inch. Simple laws of physics will tell us that as a snowball gains weight, it gains speed.

When a snowball is positive, there are no limits to what we can achieve.

April 29th

The manifestation.

My positive snowball is to be on the *Oprah Show*. I visualize myself there, sitting next to her on those comfy couches while she asks me about my book. I am smiling and laughing as I am on track with my life and all who I am meant to be. I feel good. This is evident to the millions watching the show. I am engaged in each word she says. The audience asks questions and my heart feels as if it will beat right out of my chest as this is so exciting. It is surreal for me and I am loving it. There is no where else I would rather be at this moment than in my own skin on this stage at Harpo Studios in Chicago.

It is a joyful moment for me.

April 30th

I feel as if I am there and I do not have words to describe these feelings as my real life dream if so full of energy. Being on the *Oprah*

Show feels meant to be for me. It is a picture I carry with me in my mind, a video clip of my destiny that has manifested in reality, my reality. I am truly present in the moment of now and there is no where else I would rather be.

Oprah and I have our picture taken together back stage. I laugh some more with her, and then I go home feeling filled up inside and overflowing with gratitude. The energy of my spirit could light up an entire city. I will relive this day as often as I choose in my mind, pushing the play button on my mental video clip that is now *real*. These joyful thoughts will create joyful feelings and for this I am also grateful.

May 1st

This morning I woke up thinking of egoic thinking and the resulting egoic reaction. What egoic thinking involves is voluntary or involuntary thought energy zipping across the conscious mind. These thoughts can be termed as mental rehearsals and are the source of obsession and mental torment.

For some reason, we are apt to allow these irritating thoughts to run our minds and therefore our feelings. They resemble a sort of cerebral spider web catching any random thoughts that zoom by as if they were flies. The egoic thought gets caught in the web. Upon realizing that it is caught, the thought tries to wrestle its way out of the web and its capture, thereby making more of itself by the attention that it draws to its struggle.

The cerebral web embraces the struggling thought and wraps cerebral fibers around it in an attempt to harness and devour it. The thought struggles more and gains energy, anxious energy. The struggling egoic thought becomes the center of focus for the mind and all other thoughts begin to associate themselves with the thought caught in the web, like a chain. One thought hooks onto another which hooks on to another.

The thoughts play themselves over and over again like pushing *rewind* and *play* again and again. These mental rehearsals begin to take on an involuntary life of their own where the spirit associated with the mind no longer has control over her egoic thoughts and becomes dragged into the web as an unassuming accomplice.

This compulsive pattern of thinking creates an equally disruptive pattern of feelings, a reflection of the insanity within.

May 2nd

The connection.

Thoughts create feelings. I have always found this to be interesting as well as useful as by monitoring my feelings, I can very easily know what the status of my thoughts is.

Many of us continually allow ourselves to replay a situation that happened at work or of an argument we had with someone days ago as if replaying these thoughts over and over will land us in a place of peace with all conflicts resolved.

Nothing could be farther from the truth. By replaying thoughts of situations of the past, we are pulled away from *The Now* which is where we live and reside. *Now* is where *The Power* is.

Feelings serve as a thermometer. They lest us know the temperature of our thoughts and if we are sick.

May 3rd

I am not sure if any of you have read *The Power of Now* by Eckhart Tolle, but if you haven't then you should. I continue to read parts of it over and over as I find myself in a better mental place when I am reminded to control my thinking.

He talks of inner body awareness and of being present in our consciousness. I find this fascinating as well as useful in my day to day life.

May 4th

Today I have a conscious awareness of Aunt Marla, not of any situation in particular, but that she serves as a tool of spiritual growth for me. She is direct contrast as to how I choose to live my life. I am thankful for this contrast as it gives me clarity of my own inner consciousness.

May 5th

California, here we come.

We are preparing to take the kids to California soon and I sense that Aunt Marla will involve herself. I will not waste valuable life minutes thinking about what may happen. I will clear my mind and allow to be what will be.

May 6th

Just as I sensed, good old Aunt Marla has struck again. We had planned to go to California for our family vacation this year, and of course Aunt Marla found a way to interpret our trip as a personal attack on her. She has been fully annoyed for a solid month and a half at this point. It is anybody's guess as to why, but if I had to speculate, I would guess that she is irritated that we are spending so much time to take a vacation as an immediate family when we could be bringing the kids to visit her.

Much of this has to do with her own kids. Last anyone knew, Aunt Marla's daughter had a job in genetics research out in California. She comes back only for Christmas every five or six years. She really hasn't spoken to Aunt Marla for quite some time though no one really knows the inside scoop. It is something pretty intense as there is thick air whenever her name comes up. As Aunt Marla doesn't get much from her own kids, she tries to borrow other people's kids and gets way too involved in their business.

Apparently this is easier than fixing her own life situation.

Basically, we are selfish individuals to not involve Aunt Marla in our vacation plans. There is a word for the Aunt Marlas of the world and they are named after the Greek god *Narcissus*. The Aunt Marlas of the world do not know where they end and another begins, therefore, they perceive everyone and everything to be an extension of themselves. They interpret the actions of others to be a personal reflection of themselves, or in our case, a personal attack on them.

A Full Moon Rising...and the Tao of Menopause

In Aunt Marla's world, by taking our kids to California, we have personally attacked her by ignoring her need to see our children. We have used our valuable life minutes to see other people and to go to Disneyland and this has made Aunt Marla very angry. Poor Aunt Marla. She has been stewing about this one for quite a while and accumulated loads of anger molecules.

Just to add to her misery, she is retiring from her company at the end of July where she has worked for forty years, so she wasn't exactly in a peachy mood to begin with. Working at this company has been Aunt Marla's whole life and her whole identity. I don't think that it is a good idea for her to retire actually, but she seems to want to end this particular chapter in her life.

From what she says, it is the politics. She really liked it there until they hired a Nazi manager from some other state who whipped through the company like a tornado, getting rid of people and ideas and stirring up the whole place. As much as Aunt Marla can be challenging, I have heard that she is excellent at what she does. It is a shame that a control freak can come into a company where people have been working harmoniously for years and turn it upside down. Certain people just shouldn't be in positions of power. I just hope that Aunt Marla being retired will not be our nightmare. She is challenging enough when she has a full schedule and she is two states away.

Aunt Marla called with the date of her party and let us know that her other nieces and nephews would be there regardless if they had to give a bone marrow donation at the door. They are the *good children*, especially the ones who stayed in New Jersey. We black sheep, who dared to move across two borders and seek dual citizenship in Vermont, are the *bad children*. We have fleeting moments of being in Aunt Marla's good graces. When things go her way then all is bright and sunny. When we cannot keep up with her demands and expectations, we get the shaming cell phone assaults, or she goes the other direction and does not speak to us at all. It is a vicious cycle.

It has taken me years to figure out how to ride the wave with our dear Aunt Marla. Sometimes we get in a groove and I feel like I have mastered our family universe, until inevitably a conflict emerges and I am humbled once again. I have come to view my relationship with Aunt Marla as I do my relationship with the weather. I realize that it will rain eventually. It is only a matter of how much and when, so I try my best to enjoy her when she is sunny.

With our dear Aunt Marla, and most families have at least one Aunt Marla, we have to constantly start over. The reason we start over, is because we are all a mixed bag, and the good parts are worth keeping. Aunt Marla has more than her share of moments when I feel the need to close my eyes and resist the anger.

I hear a voice from within telling me to release my anger and use *The Force*.

The voice speaks softly and repeats itself. Don't give in to the anger. Anger leads to fear. Fear leads to hate. Hate leads to suffering, and suffering leads to death. How brilliant. This is a universal truth that has surfaced repeatedly throughout history from the early persecution of Christians to Hitler and the Holocaust.

When we get angry we become afraid. This is because anger covers the face of fear like a mask. When the mask comes off and fear comes forward, we react, often without thinking. We learn to channel this fear towards the individual we feel is violating us, and wish them to know our pain as they have caused it.

We want them to hurt because they have hurt us. We want them to understand our hurt as if they were in our bodies experiencing the same pain. This is the hatred part, to wish someone else ill will even if it does not register on the criminal scale. To make an unconscious or conscious emotional commitment to wish someone ill will is where it all begins. This causes suffering which eventually leads to death, even if this death is a relationship or a part of ourselves or someone else that we cherish.

Yoda was a brilliant creature.

May 7th

Well, we made it. I will be receiving my Congressional Medal of Honor next month for traveling with five young children all the way across the country. We are in California and Aunt Marla is not. She is in Teaneck, New Jersey, and this very thought makes my heart sing on key. We survived the plane flight and so did Aunt Marla. Today we went to the San Diego Zoo and I picked out a post card to send her. It is a picture of an Anaconda, one of the most deadly snakes in the world.

Tomorrow we will go to Disneyland.

The next day we will go to Universal Studios. Then we will fly home. Short and sweet, and a breath of fresh air. Actually, it is air saturated with pollution but we do not care because we are in California and the sun is shining.

May 8th

Re-entry.

Re-entry following a wonderfully relaxing vacation is always difficult and not something I ever look forward to. After leaving the peaceful surface of the moon, we are thrown back through the atmosphere by the violent force of gravity sucking us back into reality. I really hate re-entry.

I will not look forward to this at all.

May 9th

Disney*land* was really fun. It was so retro, kind of stuck in the 50's or something.

It is way smaller than Disney *World*. Disney World has become its own city in a way, possibly its own country. It is vast and overwhelming, with enough rides and shows to keep most families busy for a week. The quality of the shows is pretty incredible also.

Disneyland is small and manageable, almost quaint.

I remember when our parents took us to Disney World. It was fairly new back then. There was only Magic Kingdom and Epcot. Our parents had saved every dime they had to take us on that trip. We stayed at the Polynesian Resort.

I remember the parade across the lake. It was made up of dragons and tropical birds and they were all lit up with colorful paper lanterns. I had never seen anything so beautiful. The beat of the drums in the background kept time with the boats as they crossed the lake.

I was thirteen and my sister was seven and this was a very big deal for the two of us coming from pre-fab suburbia, possibly the biggest deal of our whole lives. We had never even been on a plane before.

In fact, I remember the electric light parade and the fact that we were allowed to still be awake that late at night forget having an ice cream. Disney World is an *organic free zone* and I loved this about Disney World. There was no wheat germ to be found. I wanted to move there.

May 10th

During that same trip, our parents took us to Sea World. I had never seen anything like that place either. There were real whales and manatees. There was a show with water skiers doing stunts and one where the whales circled the tank and splashed us. It was sunny and we got to have ice cream every day. There was no wheat germ at Sea World either, another perfect place.

It was perfect, the whole thing. We were a family and we were together.

Then our parents got a divorce and things weren't perfect anymore.

Sometimes I revisit this place in my mind, where things are perfect, where ice cream is plentiful and wheat germ is prohibited and where parents are still together.

May 11th

Mud Season.

Well, we are back.

Not much else to say about that really, except that in most of the world the sun is shining and people are planting flowers.

I know this is true in California because we were just there. I wish we were still there, but we are not. The plane dropped us off at the North Pole as this is where we live.

Here at the North Pole, people are wading through rather large puddles. The puddles are a bit smaller this year due to the global warming winter we had as there are no snow banks melting, however, it continues to rain.

I have never seen more rain.

I am ready to build an ark.

May 12th

I believe that *Seasonal Affective Disorder* also applies to lots of rain, as it actually refers to a lack of sun light. I cannot remember the last time I saw the sun shine. I believe we were in California.

Spring

You can see why so many people move to California, with its gorgeous weather and grilled chicken wraps with guacamole.

The only thing that would prevent me from living there other than the constant earth quake threat and potential tsunamis, is the over-crowding situation. I have never seen more people, and as you know I am originally from New York, so I have experienced crowded streets.

It is different in California, way more densely populated than Manhattan. No matter what time of day it is you can't move on the freeway. It can be 2:00 in the afternoon or 2:00 in the morning and the traffic is bumper to bumper. I felt as if I couldn't breathe.

I did enjoy the chicken wraps though. In fact, one day we went to *The Getty* art museum. What a spectacular place that is. Our family is comprised of art lovers, and we strongly encourage expressing one's inner artist. Anyway, I sort of assumed that if we decided to have lunch there that it would be processed *museum food*. Nothing could have been farther from the truth. I have never seen so many organic food choices in my entire life and all cooked to order. There were what seemed to be miles of healthy and delectable food stations, from a variety of wraps, to southwestern cuisine, to stone fired pizza. It went on and on. It was a bit pricey, but well worth it.

The bar has been raised on the museum food industry.

May 13th

As I look out the window and notice that it is still raining, I can't help but to visit San Diego in my mind. What a cool city that was. I had wanted to take the kids to Mexico which was right next door, but pretty much everyone we met said that it wasn't safe.

Had it been just the two of us we may have risked it, but not with our five precious gifts. It was cool to see the very large Mexican flag flying in the distance though. It was difficult to fight off the fantasies of enchiladas smothered in green chili.

May 14th

We are now at a steady, but mild drizzle. It is finally slowing down.

May 15th

Well Halleluiah! There is a sun in the sky. It kind of makes me feel like planting something. Here, in the great North Pole area, they will advise you not to plant anything until June 1st as there is a risk of a frost until then.

I, however, enjoy living on the edge and put in all of my annuals at about this time each year. I remember when we lived in our first house next to our two, wonderful farmer neighbors. Even though, we have moved across town, we still consider them to be our neighbors. They are in their late seventies now.

I have a memory of the first year that we moved here. It was an abnormally warm and sunny week at the end of April and I was out filling a barrel in the front yard with petunias. I remember my farmer neighbor coming outside and simply shaking his head in disapproval. *Too early* he was thinking to himself, way too early. She'll learn. And I did. It snowed two feet the next night.

Farmers, together with the Chinese and Ben Franklin, know everything. This much I know for sure.

May 16th

I think that it is important to discuss the farmer's life just a bit more. There is a reason for their wisdom. They are nature based and they embrace simple living. They know what works and what doesn't in life. Farmer's are all about what is real and genuine.

May 17th

Aunt Marla would really benefit from *farm therapy*.

May 18th

I was actually serious about that.

If Aunt Marla were to spend a summer, or preferably a year with a farm family, she would come out a richer, better person for it. Not only that, but we would all benefit from this experience as she would be more focused on what matters in life instead of sticking her nose into everyone's business.

To expect a control addict to go cold turkey and give up her *my way or the high way thinking* completely may be much too high of an expectation, but dollars to donuts she would improve.

May 19th

Simple living.

I actually miss our first house sometimes. The only reason we moved was because the house itself, though quaint and early American, was far too small for a family of seven. It is approximately one hundred and fourteen years old and it has no closets. It is a very small, happy house.

I am assuming that the reason it has no closets is because back then people did not have *stuff*. They had an outfit for during the week and church clothes for Sunday, one pair of shoes or boots and that was it. Slowly, this changed, and we became clutter junkies. This is one thing about Vermont that I absolutely love.

Vermonters are not into *stuff*.

They are all about *being present* and not necessarily about bringing presents. I realize that this is quite a generalization, but it seems that Vermonters remain uninfluenced by the world around them. I like this about Vermont.

May 20th

The glass blower.

I mentioned that the little house we used to live in is happy. It is very happy and I believe that it actually spit out a former tenant we used to have. We rented the house out for a while as we were unable to sell it when we bought the house we are currently living in. My husband and I never intended to be landlords and knew not a thing of what we were doing.

We knew that the whole landlord thing would be temporary, so we figured that we would do the best that we could. We are trusting and do not have a handy gene for eight generations back. This landlord thing would have to be temporary.

A Full Moon Rising...and the Tao of Menopause

We got a call from a single guy in his mid-twenties. He seemed all right and we needed the money so we agreed to take him on as a tenant. He paid cash each month. This should have been our first tip that something was fishy in Denmark, or *Mayberry* shall we say.

We found out that he was a glass blower. Up here in East Slobovia where helicopters fly over head weekly with infrared to detect any crops, the glass blowing career could mean only one thing. The bong pipe industry had a new satellite factory in Mayberry.

From a liability standpoint, this was a basic nightmare. The white flames used to blow these pieces of art work could burn down an old farm house in less than five minutes.

The loud heavy metal music was disturbing our very sweet neighbors. I felt badly about this and went over to ask him to keep it down. He did, at least for the most part.

This guy had dark energy. One day I got a call from the automotive place in town. The man who owns it is very honest and has had his shop there forever. His son also works with him. People come from all over the state of Vermont to have him work on their cars as he has such an outstanding reputation. He is known for his perfectionism and his honesty.

Spring

May 21st

Gustaf.

Anyway, I got a call from Gustaf. He's Austrian. He was wondering if I had a phone number for the tenant renting our house.

Our tenant had apparently split. He left town, and he had left town with four brand new tires put on by Gus. Gus said that our glass blower tenant told him that he would be right back with the money. He trusted this renter guy and got taken. This made me angry. Gus is a good man.

Part of me felt at fault even though I wasn't. This renter guy was staying in our house and for some strange reason I felt as if I was partly responsible. I went over to the house to check it out. He had tried to jimmy the garage door open and damaged the door. He must have used a shovel or something. There was an authentic yoke hanging above the door which was also damaged. I think that's the wooden thing that goes over the shoulder of the cows as they pull a big rake over the corn. Anyway, it was damaged.

I went into the house and walked around to see if there had been anymore damage. I walked out onto the back porch. There is a little enclave off to the side that we used to use for our recycling bins. It was very functional and also out of sight so it wasn't an eyesore. The renter guy had it stuffed floor to ceiling with garbage.

I worried about rats. No one wants to have rats. Mice are sort of a part of life in the country, but rats make me think of the Bronx subway, fleas, and rabies.

We had to hire a sanitation service to come and take all of the garbage away. No rats, thank God.

I went upstairs. For the most part it looked all right. Then I noticed a broken window. As it is an old farm house, these windows are not standard and we could therefore not simply make a trip to Home Depot. We had to purchase a window pane and have it put in. Thankfully our good friend and maker of my annual birthday cake is handy and knew how to do this. He fixed it for us.

Once we got rid of the garbage and fixed the window, we had the house cleaned and decontaminated of the bad energy attached to the dark spirit who had resided there, thankfully for only a short time. The house was happy to be rid of this dark energy.

Our house spit him out and was glad for it.

May 22nd

A day to be worshipped.

I am realizing that I had completely forgotten to tell you about my favorite day of the year, and the only reason to include the month of May on the calendar. It is the *Day of the goddess*, also known as *Mother's Day*.

Each and every year, on this special day, I expect lots of presents and a lovely brunch with my family, as well as rose petals dropped at my feet prior to my each and every step.

May 23rd

It ended up being a gloriously sunny and warm morning. The ground was somewhat dry, though it is all relative. At least I will be able to wear shoes with a bit of a heel without sinking into the mud. This is how we know when it is summer up here in the greater North Pole area. When you can go outside wearing something other than clunky boots and you don't sink or track lots of mud into the house, then it is summer.

Last year, summer fell on a Thursday.

A Full Moon Rising…and the Tao of Menopause

May 24th

My Mother's Day was wonderful, as always. We went to brunch at a local restaurant which has a huge buffet full of just about everything. There was turkey, ham, and shrimp. There was a salad bar and loads of fresh veggies.

The dessert table was to die for. Every year they have a large platter of chocolate covered strawberries. I look forward to this every year.

To even think that out of 365 days in a year, not counting leap year, that only one day is devoted to mothers in nothing short of a sin.

I think, that at the very least, there should be one day quarterly, so that every two and a half months the mothers of the world and therefore the glue of families world wide can be properly worshipped.

May 25th

Shortly following the *Day of the goddess* it was back to reality. They say that December 21st is the longest day of the year, but I beg to differ.

I was right back at it. There was homework to supervise, meetings to attend at school, brownies to bake for the P.T.O.'s annual bake sale, a combined three baseball games to attend with only two parents, grocery shopping, dinner to make, birthday cards to mail, dentist appointments, etc.

P.S.-It is raining again, pouring actually.

May 26th

I wish it was still Mother's Day, and I was sitting at that lovely restaurant sinking my teeth into a chocolate covered strawberry.

Oh well. A year will go by before I know it.

May 27th

May is a bit of a strange month in northern Vermont. It is no longer snowing, usually, though it is not unheard of to see patches of snow here and there in areas not as exposed to the sun and rain. It is also not yet summer. May is in the middle, sort of noncommittal.

May is wishy-washy. I think this is why, with the exception of *Queen's Day*, also known as *Day of the goddess*, I do not particularly care for May.

May is also loaded with obligation, weddings, graduations, Christenings, Communions, and Bar-mitzvahs Perfectly good weekends evaporate one after the other.

Once school is out, the dynamics change as everyone knows that families do their thing in the summer. There are swimming lessons, nature camp, barbecues, and family vacations to the beach. When you have a family, you automatically get a *get out of jail free card* during the summer. May, however, is open season.

As I sit here, with my entrepreneurial gears turning, wondering if it would be a lucrative business to actually print and sell *get out of jail free cards* for people. I would charge extra, possibly double, for a *holiday card*. Getting out of a holiday should cost more as the benefits are far greater. Something to think about.

May 28th

The rain has stopped, but is mushy, very, very, mushy.

May 29th

I think that we should extend the other eleven months of the year by a few days and do away with May all together, except for *Mother's Day* of course. This would only be necessary for those living in states where moose and caribou are the main ingredients in stew.

Tomorrow we have a wedding to go to. It is in Massachusetts, about a four hour drive from here. I am sure that it will be fun as we have not been invited to a wedding for a long time. We are in that in between stage, too old to have a friend getting married and too young to have friends with kids getting married. This is a cousin on my husband's side. As far as obligation, this one does not bother me as these are some of my favorites on my husband's side.

The wedding reception is at an historical society.

May 30th

The *napkin dance*.

Well, the wedding was beautiful. The bride was gorgeous and the couple looked very happy together. They had a rockin' band which made for great dancing. My husband has now developed a reputation for the *napkin dance* and people now actually expect it.

It started a few weddings ago after several cocktails. All of the sudden, he got up with one of the cloth napkins from the table and proceeded to whip it around above his head and with a huge smile on his face, the *party smile* of someone genuinely enjoying himself.

Before long a crowd had gathered and formed a circle around him.

People began to clap in rhythm with the music while party boy danced wildly in the center of the circle. He then danced over to one of the other wedding guests and passed along the *dance napkin*. She then took her rightful place in the center of the circle while my husband took his new place in the crowd and began to clap with the others. The new napkin dancer, the *chosen one*, began whipping the napkin wildly over her head and behind her back . After a few short seconds she passed the napkin along to another guest and so on and so on. Each person danced something different while the circle clapped loudly.

The *napkin dance* has now become as much a part of our family weddings as throwing the bouquet.

May 31st

The added bonus to this weekend is that we still have today off as it is Memorial Day. It is kind of like an adult snow day only with good weather. I have always liked non-holiday holidays, where there is not tons and tons of work to put into them or traveling, yet they are enjoyable.

We usually have a big backyard barbeque to kick off the summer. People bring salads and desserts. We stay out on the back deck as long as possible with candles lit on the tables. It is usually the first time using the grill for the season. Chicken and burgers always taste better in the beginning of the summer. By September it all tastes the same.

This is why we embrace Memorial Day weekend. It is pure enjoyment without all the effort and expectations.

June 1st

Our annual barbeque always goes well. Everybody shows up, young and old. The weather is usually good, relative to northern Vermont. The sun is often shining brightly in the sky. The kids play games in the yard. The adults sprawl out in chairs on the deck solving the world's issues. We eat and drink wine. Then we have dessert.

Life is good.

I remember the month of June back in the 70's when things were slow. As soon as it began to get nice out, we would eat dinner out in the front yard on the picnic table. Not always, but some nights. As we lived in a neighborhood, we had to look up in between bites and passing vegetables in order to wave to people going by.

More than likely, little Vanni would roll by on his big wheel. Vanni, which was short for Giovanni, was my friend's little brother. He was four years old and he rode his big wheel down the center of Elm street each night at this time unless it was raining. Trailing behind him was Nanny. She was not *a* nanny. This was her name, Nanny, and she would yell and wave frantically for little Vanni to get out of the center of the road and move over to the side. They did this every night.

Nanny was from Italy and was the grandmother of my friend and Vanni. My friend's mother worked all day and part of the night as a hair dresser. Her beauty salon was attached to their pre-fab so we would peek our heads in once and a while. Sometimes we used her salon before school. We would pretend that we were hair dressers and do each others hair and nails.

Once my friend gave me a perm. She gave me a trim also just to neaten things up and get rid of any split ends that I may have. It came out really well. At least we thought so. In fact my friend was quite proud of herself. We could not figure out why my mother made me *get in the car immediately* to go somewhere to get it all fixed. I hoped she hadn't hurt my friend's feelings. We were twelve.

So anyway, Nanny was around all the time. She kept my friend's house really, really clean, and would chase us out of the house with a broom after she had cleaned the kitchen floors. I never understood why people cleaned floors anyway as people would just walk on them and get them dirty all over again. Even at twelve years old, this seemed like a waste of valuable life space. My mother must have thought this way also as she never cleaned our floors.

She mostly sun bathed.

Sometimes she would be in the front yard in her bikini with her head tilted to the side to avoid direct rays and possible damage to the retinas. My mother tanned well as she has olive-ish skin. When the school bus would pull up in front of our house to drop me off, all of the teenaged boys would be ogling out the window.

The ogling boys in the school bus weren't nearly as embarrassing as Mr. Donnelly next door. He would mostly stay in his house unless he was mowing the lawn or gazing at my mother over the railing of his deck while he watered his flowers. I have never seen someone water flowers so frequently. It is amazing they didn't turn yellow from root rot.

The neighbors next to Mr. Donnelly, the Macintosh's, had three daughters. We didn't hang out with them too much because they were a little strange and their house smelled of cat pee.

Our neighbors on the other side were the polar opposite of Mr. Donnelly. The Whitmans were outside all day long clipping and weeding and making their yard into a well-manicured putting green. They had little lawn ornaments and wishing wells all over the place and a gazebo in the back. There was a fence that wrapped all the way around the yard. The purpose of this fence was to keep children, dogs, and balls off their yard as this yard was not for walking on. It was only for looking at.

The Whitmans had a pool behind their pre-fab. No one ever saw them use it but it looked nice. I guess the pool was only for looking at also.

Every once and a while they would pick their heads up from their obsessive gardening and lawn work to wave or maybe even say hello as long as the eye contact was minimal and the conversation remained limited to the weather.

This was to avoid an awkward moment of feeling as if they should offer for anyone to use their perfect pool in their perfect yard. Looking back, it would have been fun to organize a neighborhood block party just to see their reaction.

I can only imagine the look on the faces of the Whitmans with my mother in her colorful headband, dark sunglasses and bikini top, showing up with an organic pasta salad. We would trail behind as her little ducklings, headed for the perfect pool free of leaves and bugs with our masks and beach balls. Clancy would follow us and spread himself out on the warm cement as he loved to sun bathe also. He would bring with him his fleas as this is the season for fleas.

We would remember to close the gate behind us as we would plan to stay for a while.

June 2nd

Next to the Whitmans were the Carsons. They were probably the most normal family in the neighborhood. The mother was a teacher and the father had some office job somewhere. They had a daughter, Melinda,

Spring

and she was an old teenager and went to high school. She had blonde hair, blue eyes, and big breasts. The reason I know this is because she often got undressed in front of her window and anyone walking by could see her large breasts whether they wanted to or not.

When our neighborhood street gang would play flash light tag we could see her very well because it was dark outside and she had the light on inside. This made Melinda all lit up like something in a display case. Occasionally this would interrupt our game because the teenaged boys would get distracted.

Then one night when I was walking home, I saw the shadow of someone in the bushes. I stood there for a moment in complete silence so as not to draw attention to my scared breathing. He stood up and was looking in Melinda's window. He did not look like a teenager. He was a man, and he was a big man, though not that tall actually. He was sort of built like a refrigerator. When I saw him creep around to the side of the house I ran home as fast as I could and told my parents.

They believed me but they did not do anything. That is, until a couple of nights later when I heard something outside of our bathroom window. My room was right next door. This is a benefit to pre-fabs as the walls are thin and you know quickly if some creepy prowler is staring at your naked mother in the bath tub. This is where my mother was, in the bath tub. I know this because I could hear the water running. I could hear the rustling of the branches. I got up to look out of my window. I could see the outline of his head and shoulders. It looked like he had short hair and a beard. His hair was a light color. He was stocky, not fat, but solid. When I turned away from the window to go tell my father, I slipped and landed against the wall. The prowler heard the noise and took off.

I saw him run across the street.

I got my dad and we went outside. There was a set of footprints in the mulch directly outside the bathroom window. It had rained that day so we could see them really well as they were pressed in deep. He must have big feet. This felt creepy to me. I wondered if he had been looking at me, too.

A couple of nights later I saw him again outside of Melinda's bedroom. My dad called Mr. Carson and they reported it to the police. The police car came with loud sirens and scared the prowler away. This is no way to catch a prowler I thought to myself.

The next day I came up with a plan. I took some fishing wire and some old cans from the garage and set a trap. I figured that he wouldn't be able to see the wire in the dark and then he would get all caught up in it. I tied the cans to the ends of the wire and hid them in the bushes, out of sight.

Now all I had to do was wait.

He did not come that night, but he did show up the night after that when my mother was in the bath tub again. I had fallen asleep, forgetting that I was on neighborhood creepy prowler watch. It was the cans that woke me up. They were loud because the prowler was all tangled up.

My dad heard him also and bolted out the door. He chased him right through the center of the neighborhood. He ran past the Whitman's perfect yard and then cut across Mr. Donnelly's backyard, through a small field and then to the block below us which had loads of pre-fabs and street lights.

He could see the prowler's blonde hair all lit up in those lights, and his mustache and beard. He could see the color of his t-shirt and that he had jeans on though they were ripped as my dad had chased him through a wire fence that surrounded that small field. Dad knew it was there but the prowler did not and now his clothes were torn and he had cuts on his arms and legs.

The prowler out ran our dad, but the police did catch him later that week based on our description. Apparently, he had been peeping at naked mothers in bath tubs and teenagers dressing in front of well lit windows all over town. The newspaper said that the creepy prowler was suspected of rape and that the police had been looking for him for a few months.

I guess my fishing wire and old can idea worked. I wondered why the newspaper didn't talk about it. It was all right with me though, because at least there was one less creepy prowler in the world.

Someday I will share this story and many others with my children.

As I leave another exciting memory of the 70's behind, another adventure of *the day*, I come back to the here and now and the pleasantness of the month of June.

As the weather continues to stay nice, I begin to lose motivation to be productive.

I bask in the gentleness of the crescent moon.

June 3rd

I go with this feeling of spiritual harmony and sit in the grass in my yard. The sun is shining. I move to the sandbox so that I can wiggle my toes in the sand.

June 4th

This feeling of spiritual harmony fills me up. I sit still in my yard on this day also accepting the warm rays of the sun. I am present in my body and aware of myself. I don't need to move as I am happy where I am.

June 5th

My current Zen state of being is drawing my visual awareness towards the beach. It calls to me. I answer and say yes to the beach.

I will make the plans tomorrow. Never hang up on the beach when it calls.

June 6th

Today I woke up thinking of bone density. Everything you read about us mid-lifers says that we are losing bone density by the second and that we should hold onto every railing we can in order not to slip and break one of our hollow bones. This gets more true the older we get, until the docs suggest not to leave your house at all, especially in the winter.

I think for my 80th birthday I will sky dive or possibly ski the highest mountain that I can find.

A Full Moon Rising...and the Tao of Menopause

June 7th

I have been giving some more thought to how I will celebrate my 80th birthday, as it is after all, less than forty years away. I want to have a solid plan in place in the event I begin to lose my faculties. This will be my living will:

To Whom It May Concern,

As I am born in December, the day I turn eighty I will ski as I have always done. I will ski the mountain of my choice. I will hire a helicopter to bring me to the top so that I may ski the steepest, snowiest terrain I can find. I will ski so fast my eyes will tear. Then I will really pick up some speed.

Do not attempt to stop me as this is what I wish.

When I reach the lodge I will eat birthday cake by a warm, crackling fire.

I wish to live life fully.

The summer after I turn eighty I will sky dive. Do not attempt to stop me as my birthday season should be the longest that it has ever been and celebrated continuously until my 81st year, which will, of course, begin a new birthday season.

Spring

Do not attempt to stop me as this is what I wish.

To live life on the edge, on life's unpredictable terms will be my birthday present to myself.

After a smooth landing on the ground, I will eat birthday cake.

If space travel is an option when I turn eighty, I will request to visit the Space Station so that I may view the moon and this beautiful earth we live on. I will love the part where the space capsule breaks through the atmosphere and catches fire. Do not worry about my eighty year old heart sustaining the plunge into the atmosphere or the hard smack into the ocean's surface. I am quite all right with it.

I am all right with my self, my past, and where I will be going next. Because of this, I am fully here.

Do not worry for me.

Once we land, and the diver's scoop us out of the capsule's cock pit, we will return to NASA where I will eat birthday cake.

When I am ninety, I will travel the world. I will visit the Taj Mahal and eat birthday cake there. If they tell me I can't eat cake there then I will anyway, because no one can tell a ninety-year-old what to do.

When I am one hundred I will take a hot air balloon ride over the beautiful country of Ireland. When we land on the Emerald Isle I will head for a local pub, meet some new and interesting people, and I will eat birthday cake. I will share some birthday cake with my new friends. I will write about my life as a Centenarian.

I will not worry about what I say, as a person can say anything they want to when they are one hundred years old.

My spirit is content.

June 8th

Types of smiles.

My grandmother, the one I am always telling you about, went hot air ballooning for her seventieth birthday. I have a picture of her leaning against the balloon's basket with an enormous smile on her face, as if she was the Wizard of Oz herself returning Dorothy to her Kansas homestead.

It is very easy to tell a smile. A false smile looks false. A forced smile looks, well, forced. A *pose for the camera smile* looks posed, and a genuine smile looks full of joy.

A genuine smile is full of the great *I Am*. It is here, now, and so fully alive as if you want to cling to this moment forever. The joy sits in your chest and the feeling is so intoxicating that it is almost hard to breathe, but you don't think about not breathing because you don't care. You are living and loving that you are truly living. There is no where else your spirit wants to be.

This is the recipe for a genuine smile.

June 9th

Tomorrow I will leave for New York. It is only overnight, but I am looking forward to it as I have been asked to speak on the subject of *Teenage Boys in Crisis*, an area of great interest to me. I am passionate about this particular topic and get all charged up when I talk about it.

June 10th

A night *in*.

When I pulled into the driveway last night my husband realized that one of my headlights was out. As it was Sunday, there was not much we could do as far as having it fixed and it was too late to rent something. Oh well. He suggested that I just drive with my high beams on.

A Full Moon Rising...and the Tao of Menopause

It may tick people off all the way down to New York and back, but it is what it is and I am fine with it.

I am in a good place.

I love days like this when all is right with the universe and with life in general.

Tonight I will stay in the *Holiday Inn Express* and immerse myself in a delightfully hot bubble bath. I will then go over my outline for tomorrow's presentation while watching *Seinfeld* reruns.

I will order take out from a really good Italian restaurant, and then call the front desk for a wake-up call.

I will wear my most favorite jammies, my *New York Yankees* ones. They are navy blue which is my favorite color and they are cotton. I will wear my favorite long sleeve t-shirt from *Rehoboth Beach*. It is worn and comfortable. Some of the letters have faded and it is hard to read what it says. I know that it says *Rehoboth Beach* which is a very cool place that we went. I know that I am comfortable sitting on my king sized bed at the *Holiday Inn Express* in my favorite jammies and long sleeve t-shirt, watching *Seinfeld* with a little aluminum tray of chicken parmesan and a side salad from *Dominick's Restaurant*.

I gave the delivery kid a big tip because I am grateful for this night.

Spring

June 11th

I am as high as a kite and dog tired. I talked with my mother for only a few short minutes while I was in New York, as talking on cell phones while driving is strictly forbidden and I did not want to get nailed by the Feds. It is quite a large fine and not worth losing my *just-earned-check* from my speaking engagement.

This is why people can be seen driving along on the New York State Thruway looking as though they are talking to themselves as they have ear pieces hooked up to their cell phones. It is a smart invention and I may need to look into it in order to avoid future large fines as well as the anticipated stress of fines even if I do not get caught.

I talked with my mother-in-law, however, on my cell phone all the way from Vergennes to Sheldon on the way home as Vermont has no such rule, at least not yet anyway. She and I processed the whole thing.

I told her about what a great day it had been. I had a full house to speak to, not an empty chair in the place. And what a group, so down to earth, and quite chatty actually. To share is to care. This is my philosophy also, so we all hit it off just great.

They were quite a mix, treatment professionals from all over New York, mostly in or around the Syracuse area. As the topic was

Teenaged Boys in Crisis, there was a significant representation from juvenile detention facilities and adolescent residential treatment centers. Very cool people. They had lived. We know this because people are drawn to these jobs to assist in the healing of others. They are no strangers to emotional pain and have now become channels of guidance and healing to kids in crisis. There is no need to ask. You can see it their eyes and feel the warmth they bring into the room.

I was surrounded by Velveteen Rabbits. They had their fur rubbed off as they had really and truly lived.

June 12th

It was so nice to be a channel for other channels. The older I get, the more apparent it is that the key, or one of the keys, is to open oneself up as much as possible to what is, to create a vacuum so to speak. When we clear our minds, our feelings also become clear. When we do this, inspiration flows in from all angles.

June 13th

Fear *constricts*.

I have been working on this lately, clearing my mind and letting the Creator inspire and work through me. It seems that the biggest challenge is getting out of my own way and not resisting what is. I have realized that what works, is to accept what is as therein lies *The Power*.

Acceptance can actually be much easier than resistance, especially with practice, but many of us don't understand this. At least I don't. Acceptance can seem difficult at times. We often let fear get the best of us and we give in to it. When we do this, we constrict and squeeze out all that is truly important.

Fear constricts. We know that for sure. When we are afraid walking around a dark corner and we hear a noise, we constrict. When someone screams at us out of anger we constrict. Even if we are watching a movie that causes us to feel angry or upset for the character, we constrict. Especially if we are physically threatened, our fight or flight response takes over and we tense up all over.

When massage therapists work on tense shoulders that they will describe as *hard as rocks*, they will most often let the person they are working on know where they are tight and ask them if they are having stressful thoughts or if they are preoccupied.

Preoccupied means that one's thoughts are residing somewhere else rather than here and now. The thoughts are residing either in the past or the future and this makes the work for the massage therapist more difficult. Why is this . . . because the shoulders and neck are the closest to the mind which creates the fearful thoughts that cause the body to tighten up.

Fear causes constriction. Period.

In fact, many people grind their teeth at night. Same thing.

Thinking of teeth is causing me to have a menopausal flashback of having my braces tightened when I was a teenager. Very few teens would be able to say that their orthodontist was located next door to one of the biggest, most feared and revered godfathers of New York's underworld. I will not disclose his name as this story is true and I do not wish to became a part of someone's sidewalk in the near future.

Anyway, *the Godfather* lived in a ranch as they all did. I am assuming that this was to avoid paying taxes or drawing attention to the millions of dollars they were laundering. When your income is primarily derived from gambling rings, drug trafficking, and escort services, things get complicated as far as what can be revealed to the IRS as valid income. This is why members of the mob lived in ranches, though these ranches normally had pool tables, gold door knobs, and crystal chandeliers.

It is funny for my sister and I to watch shows like *the Sopranos* as we really lived this. We went to school with mob princesses. They were the true *Untouchables*.

Spring

I remember when one of the princesses had to leave school for a family emergency. Her dad had been busted for a big cocaine heist in Brooklyn and was being sent down the river for ten to twenty. She had to go home to say good-bye. Of course this made the headlines, but the rumor on the street was that he was framed due a *leak*. He was lucky all he got was hard time. The normal protocol for a *leak* is a reservation in the nearest cement mixer.

Strangely, the mob had their own code of honor. If they were going to blow up a house or car, they would always call first to make sure that the wife and kids had a chance to get out. This is true. The mob never hurt women or children, at least not intentionally.

I remember when my friend's mother dated an uncle of one of the princesses we went to school with. He must have crossed somebody as her mother's Cadillac was found somewhere in the south Bronx completely stripped. Again, chivalry was not dead, only the car.

For my 16th birthday, we went to *Umberto's Clam House* in Manhattan. This was a special treat for us as this is where the infamous Joey Gallo got his head blown off at the dinner table. That was a birthday to remember. My dad even had the Italian string quartet serenade me.

Another time, my friend and I were off exploring in the woods and we heard gun shots. Of course we had to check it out so we worked our way up and over the hill as carefully as we could without being seen. We look over the ledge and saw six shiny black limos and men in suits shooting at a target. At least it looked like a target from where we were hiding. We then decided that this was no longer a good idea and headed back home.

Every once and a while an entire family would disappear without a trace. There would be nice kids in our classes whom we became friends with and then all of the sudden they were gone. We just assumed that they had become new members of the witness protection program.

No social security numbers and no finger prints. This was how it worked. It was a fresh start and a much safer existence.

June 14th

Being chased around by the mob would cause most people to constrict I would think.

Of course, the opposite of constriction is *acceptance* and *release* which of course allows for loving, creative, and healing energy to flow freely throughout one's body. For me, when I become open to and reside in what *is* there are no limits to what I can accomplish.

This much I know for sure.

June 15th

Quite frankly, when we stop to think about it, we will arrive at the realization that we are all, in fact, energy. Even our bodies are primarily made up of space.

June 16th

Isaac Newton figured this out ages ago as have many other great thinkers, and of course the Chinese, but as we established earlier, the Chinese have known everything forever.

June 17th

My energy field.

The Japanese have also known everything for quite sometime. As I mentioned earlier, my friend Jonathan occasionally gives me *Reiki* treatments when my sciatica acts up.

At first I didn't know what to expect. I even brought a pair of shorts because I wasn't sure of what it entailed. He told me to lay down and make myself comfortable. He had a blanket spread out and candles.

I already felt better and he hadn't done anything yet.

When he gently laid his hands on me I wasn't sure what to do, so I took a deep breath, then another one, then another one. Before long I could feel the heat radiating from his hands. I felt the heat travel down my leg.

The whole concept of Reiki is quite interesting as it involves the cumulative energy of all of us being channeled to a place in need of healing or wholeness. As I am a Christian person, I had to get things right with my mind and heart, and I realized that it all fit, without contradiction.

For me, I believe that God resides in my body with me in an intimate relationship with my spirit. My spirit is connected to *The Spirit*. This is true for all spirits, and our *connectedness* has a power larger than anything we can possibly wrap our minds around.

June 18th

Sometimes people close their minds to inspiration or information because it does not fit within the narrow parameters of their belief system. This is a huge mistake I think, as inspiration from *The Source* can come from anywhere and work through anyone.

The key is to be open to receiving the love.

I must say that I am feeling the need to give credit where credit is due. My organic hippy mother was always good at receiving the love and acceptance, which means we experienced this also by watching as this is what we knew. We were not brought up in a *narrow* household, even with my dad being a Republican and all.

My parents didn't judge people, either one of them. The people we were surrounded with were colorful. They were good people and we knew this because they were invited to our house. No one had to say it.

One of their friends, Dan O'Shea, had about a million tattoos and had done time in prison. I think he stabbed somebody but I'm not really sure. It had to do with drugs but he was a different person back then and at a different place in his life. At this point, he had been clean and sober for quite sometime and was a counselor at a school near by.

Dan had a thick Brooklyn accent and had been around the block more than once. He really helped a lot with my teenager issues later on. He understood how I felt and he listened to me. I knew that he heard what I had said and that I could trust him. There aren't words to say how cool it was to have an adult other than your parents who you can tell stuff to and who won't think bad things about you for your thoughts or your feelings. He made me feel that I was O.K. on the inside and that I would make it in the world.

A Full Moon Rising…and the Tao of Menopause

This tough ex-con from Brooklyn, covered in tattoos and bearing a scar on the left side of his face was one of the kindest, most loving people I had ever met. If a person were to judge this banana by its peel they would definitely have dropped a diamond in the rough.

Clancy loved him.

I think this was because Clancy could relate to that whole tough guy thing and as well as not having an overwhelming desire to take crap from people. Clancy and Dan had a mutual respect for each other.

Every time Dan came over he would play *rough sock* with Clancy. Maybe I should explain. Clancy had exactly one toy as he was above chasing plastic balls nor did he choose to exert energy in the form of exercise. One day, my resourceful, organic hippy mother took an old sock and stuffed it with other old socks and then tied the end. This was the beginning of rough sock. Of course, back then people wore *tube socks* so Clancy's rough sock was about a foot long.

You had to be strong to play rough sock because Clancy could really get crazy with that thing. Dad loved to swing him around and so did Dan. Clancy would have such a grip on that sock that he would get whipped around in a circle without his little Beagle-Basset paws touching the ground. He would make these horrible, primal, sounds as he swung by his jowls in our living room.

As Clancy was a rogue from the lanes of New Paltz he would fight to the end.

Clancy and Dan understood each other.

June 19th

The *ready position*.

Openness and readiness. Thinking of the rogues of my childhood and how much I gained from knowing them, I can't help to take this with me to another level as inspiration and energy can flow through infinite channels.

A catcher's mitt. Think of a catcher's mitt with a big, wide pocket. This is what we need as spiritual creatures, as energy fields walking around in the infinite energy field of the universe. We need to be clear of mind and heart, open and available to what *is*.

If a ball player isn't paying attention, caught up in the distractions around her with her mitt down, or partially closed than she will not be able to catch the ball when *Spirit* throws it. The ball may contain some brilliant idea for a book or movie, possibly a new invention or business idea worth millions.

What happens . . . either she drops the ball entirely, fumbles it and has to chase after it, or . . . *Spirit* notices that she is not paying attention and throws the ball full of creativity and entrepreneurial wisdom to some one else in the ready position with her mitt open.

The person who is open to catching the ball makes the play. The person who catches the ball creates *Star Wars*, writes the *Harry Potter* novels, or invents the little plastic things on the end of shoe laces. They make the play because they are open and focused. They receive and they believe with complete conviction.

June 20th

After you make the play, say *thank you*.

One other thing. After the player catches the ball she says thank you. She is grateful for her eyesight to see the ball, for her mitt, for her health to be able to be out on the field at all, and most importantly, she is grateful that *Spirit* has chosen her and that she now has the opportunity to use her gift.

June 21st

All of this is really quite important. People don't always get this though, in fact, they usually don't. Instead, they waste their valuable life minutes doing meaningless things and remaining closed. Quite honestly, it doesn't make a whole lot of sense to me.

June 22nd

Circling the drain.

And then there is that whole attraction piece that is also very important. The closed, perpetually *busy-doing-nothing-important* people actually draw more unnecessary *busy-ness* to themselves as well as often unpleasant circumstances.

They get caught in a bad traffic jam. Their *Star Bucks Latte* slips out of the cup holder while they adjust the radio to hear the traffic report. They break a nail reaching over the seat to grab the *Star Bucks* cup to prevent it from leaking latte all over the notes for the afternoon business meeting.

With her head down low in the passenger side, her foot inadvertently slips ever so slightly off the break peddle, and without realizing it she taps the bumper of the car in front of her.

The driver happens to be another *fly-through-life-human-doing* rather than a centered being so his arms start flying around in frustration and rage, not that his meaningless day has been delayed. He then attracts more negative circumstances. The energy of the morning is circling the drain and it is not even 9:00 am.

There is no one to blame, though they both will as they cannot help themselves. It is their momentum.

June 23rd

Of course, just as with anything else, these frustrated human doings could learn the skill of altering the direction of one's day and therefore one's life, but they do not choose this. They are content in their misery as it is all they know.

June 24th

An ancient art form.

And speaking of misery, I woke up with moderately high quills this morning. I am in need of space. It seems that whenever I have a need to lay low, Aunt Marla inevitably calls. It is as if she has some kind of sixth sense. She can annoy people all the way from Teaneck, New Jersey, just by using her brain waves. It is called *agitapathy*, a close cousin of telepathy.

Years ago, women were hung for it in Salem, and occasionally burned at the stake.

June 25th

In case you were wondering, Aunt Marla was born with this special gift. Over time, she developed her gift, and she is now able to use her advanced *agitapathy techniques* from pretty much anywhere in the world.

June 26th

The one frustrating thing about *agitapathy* is that it is difficult, even with advanced menopausal magic, to come up with a counter curse strong enough to block these brain waves. The reason, we can assume, is because *agitapathy* is a gift and not a menopausal spell. On some level, Aunt Marla knows this. She uses this to her advantage when she can predict that she may not be invited to something or she is invited and wants to change the plans in order to have things her own way.

When she even senses resistance to her control she begins eliciting *agitapathy waves* from Teaneck, New Jersey, first at rather long intervals. As her brain waves gain strength, she then shortens the intervals. They are kind of like contractions when giving birth during transition. The waves get shorter and shorter. As they do, they get more intense. Before long, a migraine headache sets in and the unsuspecting individual has no idea what the source of this unforeseen, excruciating headache is. She could be doing the laundry or reading *People Magazine*, then all of the sudden, bang, another contraction.

Before long, it is time to push.

June 27th

There may not be an adequate menopausal counter curse as of yet, but what we do have at our disposal are *menopausal force fields*. *Menopausal force fields* serve to protect a mid-lifer from *agitapathy* and can be a very useful defense mechanism when one is desperate.

June 28th

To use a force field, one must clear one's mind, much like the art of Chinese expulsion is used to rid one's self of irritating family members, only the force field is not an offensive maneuver.

Instead, it is a passive, defensive maneuver, and involves creative visualization.

June 29th

Once the mind is clear and void of unwanted thoughts, one can be open to pleasant thoughts which in turn bring pleasant feelings. For me, my force field manifests itself as a brilliant early morning sunset on the beach. I picture myself sitting there alone on the beach, before anyone else is awake, getting a jump start on my day.

I am full of peace and joy.

Even Aunt Marla can't penetrate this force field.

June 30th

Of course, every mid-lifer is aware that force fields themselves cannot be seen by anyone other than the one who brings them about.

When Aunt Marla is deflected, she has no idea why her *agitapathy* isn't working. She simply bounces off the invisible force field. The bounce feels to her like a brief moment of light-headedness. She stops for a moment, thinks about the last time that she had eaten, then takes a deep breath and continues to annoy others throughout the day.

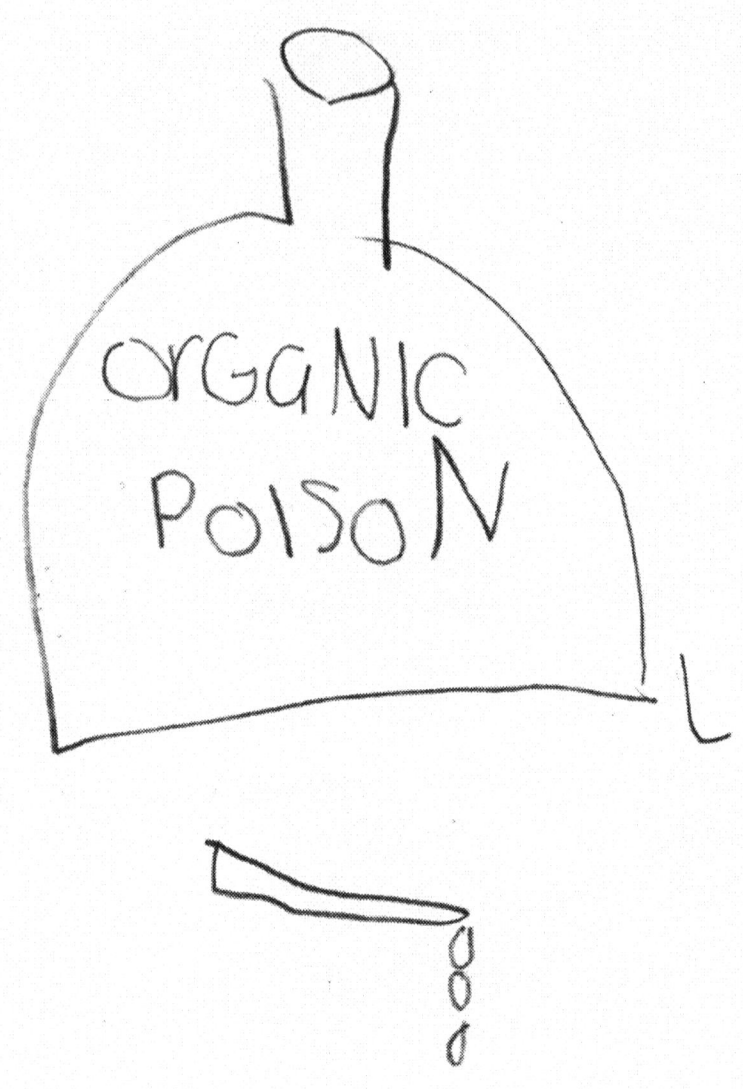

July 1st

The *skunk*.

As we were sitting watching *I Love Lucy* last night, our daughter's dog raced in the door reeking of skunk. The aroma was so intense that it pierced the air as well as our olfactory glands. The smell was actually sobering.

I went from a relaxed, half-asleep state of being to a fully alert state of being in a split second. I had mental clarity. I felt alive and focused.

We chased the dog back out the door and closed it while we could figure out a plan. The horrible aroma lingered behind her and followed her like an invisible kite tail waving in the breeze.

The dog was now outside, probably looking for her new black and white playmate behind the garage. We sat there on the couch deciding upon a strategy. We also couldn't leave our daughter's dog out all night as she is also black and we were afraid that she could get hit by a car.

A black dog belonging to a twelve-year-old girl who is away for a week at summer camp. The dark night. Cars driving too fast on a dark, rural road. What if something happened while she was gone. We would have to tell her as soon as we picked her up. She would be heart-broken. It would ruin the time she had at camp and forever be in her memory bank.

The garbage. Maybe the lids weren't on tight enough. Maybe the garage door was left open. The smell. That horrible smell. Tomato juice. Getting a hyper Border Collie/Black Lab into a bath with the old beagle. They were cohorts in crime. Tomato juice. It's too late. The only store in our tiny town is closed therefore this will all have to wait until tomorrow. What to do with two very offensive dogs who reek of skunk. The skunk is still lurking around the yard somewhere. There is a good sized rip in the screen door. The skunk could get in. Who needs this. Rabies.

July 2nd

The *skunk effect*.

I couldn't help but to think about the *skunk effect*. An outside stimulus had me wide awake and thinking. That skunk has given me clarity and I am grateful for this.

Something else of which I was unaware until this point, the native American totem for the skunk is *respect*. The skunk says without words, "Back up. Approach me carefully and with reverence. Fuck with me and I'll spray you."

This is what the skunk says.

It is very easy for most of us to land in a *couch state of being*. We need the couch. We dream of being able to lay on the couch in a comatose state when we are tired and when life gets to be too much.

The phone rings. We have a cordless phone standing on the coffee table next to us. We have caller ID, so without picking our head off the very comfortable pillow beneath us we can see that it is a telemarketer or someone from the PTO wanting us to bake brownies for the bake sale.

Thank God for Caller ID.

With the most minimal of efforts, we turn our head back towards *I Love Lucy*. We didn't really miss much. The thought enters our head that a book might be nice.

I could really use a good book. I think of my own personal library and realize that I have read everything that I have and that there isn't much to read in the entire house, including magazines as I have read those also. I could use a trip to *Barnes and Noble*. The summer is usually a good time to visit the book store as most of the best selling novels are released then. I think I will plan to go this weekend.

I am so comfortable. I am thinking that I would like to pour myself a second glass of wine but then I would have to get up and it is a long walk to the kitchen. I feel warm. If I shift even the slightest bit my body will land in a spot that has not been warmed up by my body heat so I do not move. If I were to get up there would be an imprint of my body on our very soft and comfy couch. There would be a *couch mold*.

I could stay here forever and not move.

July 3rd

This is what I was saying about the *couch state of being* and how easy it is to stay in this place. The couch state of being is all right in small doses when we really need it, but it is important not to *reside* here as the couch state of being is one of stagnancy and void of any personal growth.

This is also why we need *skunks*. *Skunks* are very important as unwelcome as they may be at times. We will normally resist skunks and will do our best to avoid them. *Skunks*, however, are on their own schedule.

They are hired by the universe, black and white mercenaries sent from above to wake us up. It is the *skunk's* job to shake things up and to catch us off guard. *Skunks* give us mental clarity and force us to find *our way*.

July 4th

Happy Birthday America! I love my country and I love being in menopause. They are delightful places to be, to be in America and to be in menopause.

There is certainly no better place to be a woman than this wonderful country of ours. It just makes things all the better to be able to be in this wonderful life stage here in America with the freedom to figure it all out and at our own pace.

July 5th

A *skunk* came by this morning again. She did not spray the dogs this time, but instead got me and right between the eyes. I was visiting family in New York, just overnight to watch the fireworks with the cousins.

A *skunk* came out of no where and got me.

July 7th

I don't believe that I mentioned that a *skunk* is not always something tragic such as a life threatening situation. A *skunk* can show up in many different ways using different vehicles of awareness. *Skunks* can work through those closest to us, those not so close to us, and *skunks* are known for getting us fired from our jobs. They do this to point us in a new direction and to get us *unstuck*.

Most of us will get angry and resist the *skunk* at first until we look back and realize that it was all for the best.

It is a *skunk's job* to provide spiritual direction.

July 9th

I am sure by now you realize how important it is to appreciate *skunks* as they bring us to a higher level of spiritual existence.

This, of course, is the *eleventh principle of the Tao of Menopause- appreciate skunks*.

July 10th

Captain Plow.

I was remembering my own words this morning when I was reflecting on the retirement party that we attended last night. I was thinking of genuine contentment.

It was a perfect night weather-wise, about seventy degrees, sunny, and with a slight breeze blowing through the air. It was what we think of when we think of Vermont in the summer. There was no where else I would rather be.

I really love it when I feel that way, when I am completely content in my own skin and not preoccupied with any specific thoughts. I was void of thoughts and taking in my atmosphere, the gorgeous evening, and the people around me.

Being in Vermont has been good for my relationship with money for my healing in general. Vermonters are all about being physically present and not as much into gift-giving. There are times, of course when a gift is appropriate, but they are usually small and meaningful, not showy.

To Vermonters, showing up and being part of a celebration *is the gift*. Just being there says that the person whom the gathering is for is worthwhile and important. I love this about Vermont. If the rest of the country were this way, we would have far fewer problems.

In fact, the whole Zen thing has gotten rather trendy, that *less is truly more*. This is not new for Vermonters. They have always been about less is more. They have always been about the people . . . and of course the pot luck.

We have lived in our wonderful, tiny town for almost ten years and have attended many gatherings and I have to say that I would challenge the best restaurant in Manhattan to compete with some of the dishes that show up at these backyard events. When people are asked to bring something, they usually put their best foot forward in the form of a covered casserole dish. I have never seen more decorative desserts and the food is so, well, comfortable.

Anyway, we were invited to this retirement party that was held at our town park. We call it *The Rec Center*, or just *The Rec* for short. It was for a dear friend of ours who had worked as the head of the transportation department for twenty-five years.

The majority of *Mayberry* showed up in his honor. We were all there, the tall and the small, to show our respect for this man who had put in twenty-five years of service keeping our roads safe and clean during the harsh northern winter months.

Summer

There we stood, waiting and drinking from our coolers. For the most part, Vermont gatherings are *byob*, or *bring your own beverage*. This works because you drink what you want to drink and for an added bonus, it is economical. It works. There was a sea of Coleman coolers, some with wheels and some without, lined up like soldiers against the periphery of the town pavilion.

The town pavilion was recently built only a month ago in honor of *Mayberry's* finest, people who were once very much a part of our community that the town had chosen to remember in a permanent kind of way. There is a roof and an upstairs. There are no sides to the pavilion, ideal for the summer months when most of the town functions happen. It has lots of picnic tables underneath.

So there we all were . . . waiting, and talking. I looked around the pavilion and noticed the decorations. Someone had borrowed the town's road signs and hung them up above the picnic tables. There were little construction trucks and plows on top of the tables. They were rusty and lived in. The trucks had been used and loved and were probably borrowed from a grandson's sandbox. In fact, some of them still had sand and mud on them.

Just road signs and sandbox trucks. That was it. No balloons. No confetti. No band. No pomp and circumstance and no need for it.

The people of the town were there. All of us. We watched for *Captain Plow*, the distinguished guest of honor to show up. He was told he was going to a cousin's birthday party. I had just talked with his son, also a good friend of ours, who had said that his dad had no idea that anyone was going to do anything.

There we all stood, around the picnic tables, drinking. My youngest daughter was dipping into everyone else's cooler taking juice boxes because her inadequate mother only brought a jug of Hawaiian Punch. I pretended not to notice.

The smell of steak and barbecued chicken filled the air. Someone shouted, "He's here. He's here." We all looked. We all stared. The pick-up truck pulled in, right next to the pavilion. We stared some more. You could see his face as plain as day. He didn't know what to do. Captain Plow sat there for a moment looking out of the front windshield. Then he turned at us and saw his life.

It seemed like it took him an hour to climb out of that pick-up truck. It was probably about three minutes. I hoped that someone was flipping the steaks.

He walked slowly towards the pavilion and everyone clapped. I was waiting for someone to start singing "For he's a jolly good fellow" but apparently they were going to wait until it was cake time. He just stood there. The town clerk hugged him, then some other lady. I looked around and no one else was hugging so I went up and hugged.

He is a real macho guy, at least on the outside. He has fire red hair, a bit of a friendly temper, and underneath, well, underneath lies a heart of gold. I really love *Captain Plow* and so does the town of Mayberry. This was fairly obvious as we had all taken time out of our days and our lives to be here. To be here shows *Captain Plow* that we do not desire to be anywhere else. We are spending our valuable life minutes on him.

July 11th

Life minutes and how we spend them are very indicative of our self respect. When we value ourselves we value our life minutes and appreciate that they are limited. Our life minutes will eventually run out, especially our healthy life minutes, therefore it is of utmost importance to spend them wisely.

On the flipside of this, when the life minutes of others are *spent* on us there is no greater compliment.

July 12th

I have also been reflecting lately, during these dog days of July when it is so difficult to get motivated, about the mere state of being. July is a good month to appreciate one's state of being as it is much too hot to do anything else.

Even in northern Vermont we have had a month of ninety-five degrees and two hundred percent humidity, a bit unusual for those of us residing just a hair below the artic circle. The air is slow and this makes *us* slow. We are slow and we are sweaty and we can attribute this to global warming.

This means that for those of us in menopause, we have inner warming and outer warming, so we are pretty much, well, warm. Just as with anything else, we must not resist, but yield and pour a nice tall glass of icy cold lemonade and read *People* magazine.

To fantasize about weeding the rock garden or cleaning out the basement will just set us up for failure so it is best not to go there. Instead, we need to realize that it is best to be productive in a more *unproductive* way, to eat cherries and spit the pits in the grass next to us, to read trashy magazines and fall asleep in the sun.

July 13th

I love the lack of a schedule in the summer. We receive countless flyers in the mail advertising this camp and that camp. One is enough. After that, we simply say no to camps.

We say yes to the backyard. Hanging out in the backyard is so underestimated these days. The back deck and the sandbox have so much to offer, yet we race around with our kids in tow pursuing entertainment, structure, and stimulation.

By doing so, we are doing such a disservice to our children. We are teaching them to avoid being in the present moment and therefore they are being brought up not to fully appreciate its value. The children of Today's world have absolutely no concept of the *Power of Now* nor do they realize how much of life they are missing out on. Far worse than all of this is the fact that true joy can only be experienced in the present moment. By choosing to reside somewhere else, one misses out on joy.

July 14th

What I often find to be somewhat ironic is the fact that people have made something that is so simple and so natural into being so difficult. Slowing down and allowing one's self to be still have become skills that very few know or are capable of.

Especially in our country, we are in the habit of *fast* and we are gaining momentum.

Sometimes I have to wonder how we got here, to this fast place. Growing up in the lanes of New Paltz things were much slower, especially during the summer. We played street ball, rode our bikes, and went to the Town Pool.

The Town Pool had quite a high chlorine content. This was necessary, of course, in order to combat the loads of micro-organisms that gleefully resided there. I remember one day when the lifeguards made everybody get out for a moment. They raced over with those long poles that had nets on the end of them. Apparently someone had noticed a brown *floaty* in the lap lane. It looked like a jumbo tootsie roll.

Once they fished it out and threw it over the fence we were free to go back in.

We also spent a lot of time exploring. I remember when my friend and I borrowed her dad's CB radio. We thought we were the beginning and end with that thing and we knew all of the *CB lingo*. We would say, "Breaker 1-9, Breaker 1-9 . . ." and then someone would answer and let us on the channel. We made up names for ourselves and used foul language because we could. After all, we were anonymous, kind of like the 70's version of an internet chat room.

Then one day, we were busy running our potty mouths on the air in one of the alleys behind a store when a red Pontiac Camaro came wheeling around the back and parked right in front of us. Some scary looking guy got out and screamed at us. He had mousy brown hair and pock marks on his face. He looked like a convict.

For a split second I thought my twelve-year-old life was over. He would tie us up and throw us in the trunk never to be seen or heard from again. Front page news. Two children missing. Gone.

In an instant, he squealed out of the parking lot leaving rubber marks on the pavement and we were terrified. We would never touch that radio again. Lesson learned.

We walked back to my friend's pre-fab and climbed up on her roof. We spent a lot of time up there. It was just the two of us and we would talk about everything going on in our world, and not just who said what to whom in the 6th grade cafeteria, but deep stuff. We talked about our families and things going on, stuff that had happened to us. We talked about our fears and about the future. We talked about the possibility of alien life forms.

There were no video games or cell phones back then. There was only the roof. This is what we had.

July 15th

I continue to ponder this thought, about why we are all running at such great speed and what it is exactly that we are running from.

Either we are running *from* something or we are running *towards* something. I am not sure which but we are in a hurry to get there. I wonder what we will do once we arrive.

July 16th

As I ponder this thought about being a society chock full of emotional runners in a hurry to run from somewhere to be somewhere else, avoiding being here, I cannot help to wonder what has happened to make us this way and where we have gone wrong.

Certainly technology has played a role, as prior to television people actually sat and talked with each other. Families ate dinner together. Before the invention of the video game, and in my opinion the *anti-Christ*, kids played board games and actually interacted with each other. They played marbles in the dirt and flash light tag. They read books and went fishing. They laid in the grass staring up at the blue summer sky, finding shapes and pictures in the clouds high above. They daydreamed about being something great someday.

July 17th

Kids don't daydream anymore and I find this to be very, very, sad. It is worse than sad. It is tragic. Instead, their minds are wrapped up in a screen and reinforced by the false sense of accomplishment that video games provide. While their thumbs frantically move up and down, their natural creativity and imagination are diminished.

This is nothing short of a tragedy.

July 18th

Maybe it is best not to get into how we are constantly filling ourselves up with that which we do not need as I could get crazy. The whole topic of parenting in Today's world is one of passion for me as I truly believe that we are headed towards destruction and at a rapid rate. We have allowed ourselves to transform into anxious gazelles, running, running, running, from activity to activity and from event to event. We take numerous digital photos which stay locked up in cyber-prison for a later date so we can remember what a good time we had.

What is worse than all of this, is that we are role modeling this for our children. They are learning that to be worthwhile they need to be on the go and productive. This is very bad news for the future of humanity.

A Full Moon Rising…and the Tao of Menopause

July 19th

Just say no to coffee drive-thru windows.

If we look around, we can also notice that we have capitalized on our anxiety and need to be anywhere but where we are. Fast food chains exist on every street corner across the street from other fast food chains. They are in competition, but they thrive as there are so many of us in need of that *Big Mac* or *Whopper* that both burger establishments seem to have enough consumers to stay afloat.

Even coffee has gotten fast as *Dunkin' Donuts* now has a drive through window. This defeats the entire purpose of coffee. Though caffeine is a stimulant, the essence of coffee is slow. Coffee was invented to be sipped and enjoyed while discussing our most personal issues with close friends while we lean into each other over a small table for two in order to grasp every word. Then the waitress comes by and drops a smidge more in our cups for a warm-up.

We smile gently as a way to say thank you without fully turning our heads as we don't want to miss anything that our woman friend is saying. The words drip from her mouth like chocolate as this is good stuff. We lean in more as this is the only table in the café.

Her neighbor has been sleeping with her personal trainer and had kept it a secret all this time. Who would have known. Had the Cable Guy, who is the brother-in-law of her husband's golf partner's neighbor not walked in on them, well, this would all still be a secret.

Wow. Personally, I'd cancel the cable.

Meanwhile, she has been pulling in and out of her driveway in her powder blue minivan driving her daughter to Girl Scouts and her son to piano lessons. We sit there and try to guess what his reaction must have been, and then what *her* reaction to *his* reaction must have been.

Whoever invented the coffee drive-thru should be shot.

July 20th

Money and its relationship to self respect and personal value.

I read somewhere that people often write of or teach that which they need to work on in their own lives. I know that this is true for me on the subject of money. I also know it to be true that when it is time for us to learn a new life lesson and to incorporate it into our lives, to really undergo a spiritual metamorphosis that inspiration comes from every direction.

It seems that all of the sudden the main theme of whatever it is we need to learn appears everywhere we look and hits us over the head from every angle. We hear things coming from those we love, those we don't love, those we hope to love someday, and strangers. We hear things on the radio, television, and while standing in line at the checkout counter.

Lyrics of songs that were previously hiding beneath a steady, rhythmic beat now come forward and bring with them new meaning. When we dump out our coffee grinds into the garbage, there they will sit on a paper towel spelling out for us that which we need to hear, the message that is trying so hard to captivate our attention and elevate us to a new, more advanced level of existence. The Universe is speaking to us.

The Universe sends *a skunk*.

My particular skunk had a message about money and its relationship to self-respect. Apparently, I had been given enough time to figure things out and make changes on my own. Of course, none of this had worked. Nothing was figured out and no changes were made. The Universe had run out of patience so I got sprayed.

I had been somewhat of an unhealthy relationship with money for most of my life.

Growing up, no one had ever taught me about money or even talked about it. When my parents went through a somewhat turbulent and lengthy divorce, money and what it can do as far as going places and doing things was used as a vehicle to alleviate emotional pain and to *keep busy*. And this is not to place blame. We were all doing the best we could, all of us, however, in the process I did not learn to appreciate or value money. I also learned that money can make you feel better when things are bad.

Basically, what had happened was that I had received incorrect information about money, its value, and its purpose. I was now at a point in my life where I needed to erase this incorrect information and replace it with new and accurate information. I needed to understand that reckless or careless spending is actually a reflection of what is going on inside just as with anything else, such as when we surround ourselves with clutter, or when we spend too much time in sweat pants. The careless use of money was an outward symptom.

I also was beginning to realize that I was, in affect, living in the residual. By this I mean that bills I had accumulated and the resulting guilt and shame were all created by actions that had occurred a very long time ago. I was living and dwelling in the residual of past dysfunction that was no longer a part of me. Once all of this made its way into a clear awareness, I made a conscious choice to expel the incorrect information about money that had been scripted in my subconscious and caused so many problems for me. I then replaced it with newly acquired information that I would now use for my new, healthy relationship with money and myself.

So anyway, I was listening to an audio-seminar of a woman who speaks all over the country on stress reduction, creating the life that you would like to live, and nature-based therapy and treatment for addicted individuals. She spoke of the fact that no one ever talks about money, or being money impaired in the same way that no one talked of sexual abuse back in the 50's. It just wasn't done.

July 21st

Now, each and every time I open my latest issue of *O-The Oprah Magazine*, there is Suze Orman, the money wizard, with her latest financial advice whether I want to hear it or not, and whether I am *ready* to hear it or not.

I could have turned the page and ignored her, a silent rebellion, and a way for me to remain a resident on the *Planet Denial*.

In fact, up until my moment of awareness and clarity I had been quite comfortable on the *Planet Denial*, or at least I thought so. I could spend unconsciously or at times even recklessly. Lots of times. For years I have made trips to the mall on an open-ended hunt for bargains and treasures. I would tuck things away in the closet for Christmas eight months in advance, only to forget about them entirely when Christmas came.

Christmas in general was probably the worst vehicle for my incorrect information about money to manifest, as this is a time when overspending is not only accepted, but *encouraged*. We are bad parents if we do not provide a huge pile of presents for our children, or at least it feels that way. So we buy, buy, and buy some more. Then we wrap, wrap, and wrap some more. We do this in an attempt to fill a hole in our spirit. I believe we all do things to fill up the holes in our spirits.

July 22nd

Soul hole filling.

Alcoholics fill up with alcohol. Over-eaters fill up with food which is often why they are labeled *emotional eaters*. They are looking to soothe and nurture themselves emotionally, and instead fill themselves with guilt and shame and feelings of failure.

There are many of us who fill ourselves up with working and physical fitness. These are even tougher avenues to accept and to hold ourselves accountable for as they are not only socially acceptable, but rewarded. Especially for men, when a husband works 200 hours a week, he is considered a hero and a great provider for his family. He isn't perceived as running from his emotions. He is nothing more than a *human doing* masquerading around as a *human being* as he feels that he himself is not enough.

He must run and do, produce and accomplish. He does all of this to fill a *soul hole*. If a woman is running 80 miles a week, working out on the stair master and the ab-machines on top of raising children while holding down a part-time or full-time job, she is nothing short of a *goddess*. She looks good and people will tell her that.

As women, we often over work also. We rescue. We become care-a-holics, and we pride our selves on doing so. This is because we often feel that we, ourselves, are not enough. We must *do* and *produce* to convince ourselves and the world of our self worth as *being* in and of itself is not enough.

Hearing how good she looks and how people don't know how she does it all is rewarding and therefore reinforces her to continue to be dysfunctional. These vehicles for the *soul hole filling* are much tougher to stop as they are socially acceptable, at least in our country.

July 23rd

I will take a break from my self-loathing cycle, but only for a minute. It is far too rewarding.

Of course, regardless of your poison, the after effect is the same. The guilt and shame are the same.

Summer

For me, I always enjoyed the heroin-type high of being in *The Gap* surrounded by clearance racks, piling my shopping bag higher and higher with mounds of bargain items for whoever's birthday was coming up, Christmas this year, Christmas next year, Christmas five years from now, Ground Hog's Day, or whatever. The rush would last until I was out of the parking lot and heading home.

It was then that the guilt would set in. Following the guilt would be the shame as I would cross over from the feeling of *I did something bad* and stressful to *I am a bad, rotten wife and a bad, rotten person*.

With my self-loathing cycle then in full gear, I was now able to divert my emotional attention to my great feelings of regret as I recounted each and every purchase.

I would think about what was most important to me as far as genuine pleasure. For me this is the beach every summer. I would think about how the money I had spent could have us there for a few more days or possibly an afternoon of deep-sea fishing that the kids love so much. At this point, I would normally be gasping for air wishing for someone to rescue me from myself yet not feeling worthy at the same time.

The very repetitive, circular, self-destructive thinking would then kick in. I continue to do this. I am too old to do this. My reckless behavior is affecting my family. No one should rescue me. I don't deserve to be rescued. These feelings of worthlessness make me feel like shopping again. It is a viscous cycle.

July 24th

So check this out. I had been listening to my inspirational CD in the car on the way home from New York. As soon as I got home I went to the mailbox and what was awaiting me but the latest issue of *O* with some really interesting articles on the cover. The very second that I got the kids settled I would immerse myself into the escapism/personal growth that this magazine provides for me and relax.

I sat myself down in a comfy lawn chair on the back deck with a cold glass of lemonade. I flipped open the magazine sort of randomly just to see where I would like to dive in and where do I land . . . yes, right at the front steps of my dear friend Suze Orman. Now how is that for a message.

The only way a message could be more clear would be if the good Lord Himself parted the clouds and shouted down from above, "It is time to improve your relationship with money and your understanding of its relationship to how you feel about yourself. Once you have this understanding, these old patterns of thinking and behavior will be released from your subconscious and the resulting guilt and shame will be released also."

O.K. All right. I heard you.

July 25th

Financial anorexia.

Speaking of personal growth, I need to divert for only a second to our favorite source of personal growth and life challenges, our very dear Aunt Marla. The reason that I need to bring her up is because she is also *money impaired* only in the opposite way.

Aunt Marla is a *financial anorexic.* It would be easier to remove a limb without anesthesia than it would be to get our dear Aunt Marla to pry open that purse of hers. She deprives herself of life's simple pleasures. She will not buy fresh cut flowers, bath beads, or Godiva chocolate. In short, Aunt Marla is *deprivation- based* and she is miserable. This is not good either.

Just as with anything else and in accordance with the *Principles of the Tao of Menopause*, it is all about balance.

We need to go to the store to buy what we need, no more and no less, because less is truly more. If there is a beautiful dress or a pair of shoes that we cannot live without, well then we must buy it. The drill we need to practice, however, is to leave with just the dress and not the four or five other items simply because they were a good bargain or because buying them is medicating our sad feelings.

Being good to ourselves means that we should indulge ourselves in the simple pleasures. We should buy that dress, eat chocolate, and incorporate fresh flowers into our weekly food budget. When we live in balance we are healthy in every way, and our financial situation reflects this. When we rack up credit card debt, we are not respecting ourselves on some level, possibly all levels depending on the degree of reckless

spending. We are not feeling worthy. We are not feeling as if we ourselves are enough. We are *soul hole filling*.

This is another *principle of the Tao of Menopause-buy only what you need* as our financial health is an outward symptom of our inner health. When we are able to live within our means, we alleviate stress from our lives and achieve a genuine peace of mind.

As my good friend Ben Franklin said, "Lying rides on Debtor's back." We don't feel good about ourselves when we owe people even if the people we owe are working in some high rise building in some city and we will never meet them in this life time. It is the *owing* part that we need to free ourselves from.

July 26th

I have come to realize and with an acute awareness of being, that it is all about the journey and about the *Principles of the Tao of Menopause*. We are all works in progress. Of course, this has been said before and by many, however, it has been heard by only a few.

Certainly, elevating to a more spiritually advanced level of being involves wisdom acquired from one's life experiences as well as our perception of the life experiences of others. After all, our perception is our reality.

In my menopausal life stage, I have reflected on my *half-wayness*. Someday I will reflect on my *three- quarterness*. I will look into the faces of my grandchildren and see my own. I will have flashbacks of being a young parent with all of the rewards as well as the trying times. There will be more footsteps behind me and a shorter path in front of me as I will be closer to wherever it is that I am going. There will be parts of myself that I like and parts of myself that will finish the race rusty and needing oil . . . and I will know them all.

A Full Moon Rising…and the Tao of Menopause

July 27th

Spiritual roadblocks.

I woke up thinking of spiritual roadblocks. Spiritual roadblocks can be a blessing if they lead to transformation, however, if they serve as a crutch by enabling a spirit to avoid being who they are and prevent a spirit from being receptive to all they are meant to be then this can be a very, very, bad thing.

Aunt Marla has at least one, and I would guess probably several fairly large spiritual road blocks, the biggest of which we never mention.

Years ago, at the funeral of Aunt Marla's husband, Reginald, her son told me what happened. Her son had temporarily numbed his loss in numerous glasses of wine after the wake and was slurring his words. We were standing off in the corner of the side parlor where no one could hear us.

Funeral homes are so *museum-ish*. The couches all have that antique *do-not-sit-on-me* look. This is why everyone stands up at a wake. No one feels comfortable sitting down on the funeral home furniture.

Anyway, Aunt Marla's son David stared at the ground for a few, somewhat awkward moments, then looked up. He stuttered as he spoke. Apparently his dad had been an active alcoholic. He had a good job, but he also had developed a gambling problem. It started out with local bookies betting on football games. Then things progressed. Before long, he was making trips to Atlantic City.

Then, one day Aunt Marla came home to a house that was torn apart. It looked as if they had been robbed. There was a series of hang-ups on the answering machine, followed by one message from someone named Carlo. Carlo had a deep, raspy voice and was looking to set up some sort of meeting with Reginald.

Anyway, Reginald disappeared. His body washed up a week later under the Verazzano Bridge.

This happened many years ago and it is not something we are ever allowed to talk about. No one ever has. It is kind of our family's pink elephant. The pink elephant, representing toxic secrets and deep shame sits on the couch with us and has its own chair at the Thanksgiving table, yet we do not acknowledge it. We pass rolls and cranberry sauce back and forth in front of the elephant and tell our stories as if it were not there and as if it cannot hear us. Elephants are funny that way. They can be quite inconspicuous.

A Full Moon Rising…and the Tao of Menopause

July 28th

The cycle continues.

So anyway, no one is really sure if this is why Aunt Marla's daughter doesn't speak to her. She moved across the country years ago and does not come to family events or holidays very often. Her name is Angela. She sends us a Christmas card once a year like clock work which is a bit odd I think. She doesn't write anything in the card. She just signs her name and that's it.

David sort of makes an appearance every few years, but always schedules his plane flights so that there is very little actual visiting time. He always has a reason why he is in some huge hurry to get back. His cell phone goes off constantly and this helps him escape his family and himself. Each time it goes off, David politely excuses himself as if he is the president deciding whether or not to send additional troops into a country.

He smokes, too. You can smell it when he comes back inside.

I think that David arranges every friend and co-worker he has to call at scheduled intervals in order to assist him in avoiding his family and himself. The apple does not fall far from the tree.

July 29th

No matter how you cut it up, secrets are turpentine and corrode the spirit. For us, it was the fleas.

For Aunt Marla, it was addiction.

Her alcoholic husband lost big and in a panic sought Guido the killer loan shark which unfortunately had a tragic ending. Family members floating to the top of the Hudson River with a bullet hole through the side of their head does not exactly bring the family honor.

July 30th

This secret isn't actually a secret since it was plastered all over the news. It is only a secret in our family. It is the dust under our rug, the lint in the refrigerator vent. No one ever goes there.

July 31st

I hope that someday Aunt Marla will be able to free herself from chain-smoking and add cream and sugar to her coffee and her life.

I pray for this release as I love Aunt Marla despite how challenging she can be, and I long to know who she really is.

August 1st

All of this inner-body, spiritual awareness is also drawing my attention to the warmth and *invited-ness* of the outside and of the sun.

August 2nd

I feel the sun on my face. It is warm. It nurtures my spirit.

August 3rd

Here we have another *Principle of the Tao of Menopause-embrace the sun.* Unless you have a family history of melanoma, then get right out there. Find a bench or comfortable place on the grass, close your eyes and lift your face to the sun. Feel the warmth on your cheeks and embrace it. Let the natural heat of the sun's rays warm you up after the short, cold, dark days of winter, and for us northern Vermonters, the long and rainy mud season.

Life is slow in the summer. It is meant to be this way.

The slow part is of utmost importance. There is a very natural rhythm at this time of year, almost like a magnetic force that draws us outside. We desire to sit on a deck or the grass with a nice, cold glass of lemonade.

Do not resist this force but surrender to it as it brings with it rest for the soul.

The naturally slow rhythm of the summer months also brings with it the desire to do monotonous labor, or meditative play. Depending on your perspective, raking the dead remnants from beneath your bushes or weeding your rock garden can either be a chore or a form of meditation.

August 4th

For me, the very natural inclination to do busy work outside is something we should also embrace as this type of meditative play clears our minds of clutter.

August 5th

De-cluttering the mind is certainly very important as it is only when we create a vacuum that new thoughts and ideas can emerge, at least with the full color and detail with which they were intended. Meditation and working with one's hands can help to de-clutter the mind, but it is also important to understand the relationship between inner clutter and outer clutter. Of course, the Chinese have known this since the beginning of time along with everything else.

The name for the de-cluttering of one's atmosphere is called *Feng Shui* and it has become a science, an art form, and a skill for many. *Feng Shui* also involves the re-positioning of furniture in order to enhance the flow of creative energy. *Feng Shui* helps us get out of our own way by freeing up our living space and therefore our mental and spiritual space. Many people don't realize the relationship between the physical and the spiritual. A very definite connection exists and it is important to have an understanding of how one affects the other.

The next *Principle of the Tao of Menopause-get rid of everything that you have not used, worn, or appreciated for the last year.* You can give it away or throw it out, whatever works for you.

And speaking of de-cluttering and rearranging, realize that the full moon will soon be in Virgo. If you know a menopausal Virgo, stay clear. She may be inclined to remove or rearrange certain character traits that she feels are unwanted or just plain irritating. Watch out particularly for quills laced with organic poison and be ready to duck.

August 6th

I so love the month of August as it is slow and the nights are brisk and just right for sleeping. Mostly, there are no graduations, Christenings, wedding or baby showers to attend. Our weekends are our own.

Of course, we got married in August, but it is different when it's *your* wedding.

When I grew up in the 70's, our weekends were always our own as we did not get invited anywhere. I am not sure if we didn't have any friends or if people just didn't make such a fancy fuss about everything. The only wedding we had ever been invited to was our former babysitter and she got married in the woods. It must have been a meaningful place for her.

The traditional bouquet throwing kind of thing with women in really bad dresses was not an experience we had growing up, except for my Uncle Denny. I was a junior bridesmaid in his wedding which took place in Gary, Indiana. They had pink tuxedos with those really frilly 70's collars that had velvet on the edges of the ruffles. My Aunt Sharon looked beautiful though. She had gorgeous dark hair and a nice smile. My Uncle Denny's friend, Tony, had to guard *the church* which was sitting on top of the table as you walked in. *The church* on the table was pink and white and made of cardboard. It housed the cash being dropped in the top as wedding gifts for the new couple. There were four hundred people there and some of the guests were a little sketchy which is why the paper church needed an entourage of inner-city body guards. A couple of them had guns. You could tell by the lumpiness under their jackets.

Anyway, these are the two experiences of weddings from my childhood.

As far as the rest of it all, my parents were in a mixed marriage. My dad was a recovering Catholic from the other side of the tracks and my mother came from a very wealthy, blue-blood type family so we didn't do any of that traditional stuff. I think my dad got smacked around by nuns or something. Anyway, we sort of came in and out of religion like waves on a beach. We would go for a while when the feeling moved them and then a few years would go by.

Then a lot of years went by.

In fact, the one place I remember getting religion was in the car. We had a 1963 Plymouth back then, which at this point was twelve or so years old. It was green, institutional green, *One Flew Over the Cuckoo's Nest* green.

We took it to the Town Pool every day and it burned our bottoms because it had that bumpy plastic stuff on the seats which would heat up wonderfully with the strong summer sun. After my hippy mother would load her favorite lawn chair in the back along with the pool bag we would get in. Sometimes we had to sit on towels because the seats were so hot that you could practically fry an egg on them.

My mother would try the key a few times, then set her head back against the head rest. Her bright red and purple silk head band covered most of her forehead. It was quite long and went half way down her back. She had a shag hair-do and dark sun-glasses and she meditated every day. At first my friends thought she a was a little strange, but then they understood after she explained that it was necessary to purge one's self of stress and all things attracting negative energy from the universe, especially after Vietnam and Watergate. There was loads of toxicity in the air and she was not about to internalize this.

So she tried the key again and the car made a clicking sound followed by a groan. This is the part where we got religion, in the back seat of our pea green Plymouth. My mother would turn to us and instruct us through her large, dark, 70's sunglasses to hold hands. Then she would tell us to close our eyes and pray. We were to visualize the car starting and arriving at the parking lot of the Town Pool safely and without stalling.

We mostly got this religion in the summer because nothing else was as pressing as getting to the Town Pool.

Then, by the time I entered the 8th grade, the clouds parted and my mother decided that I should be confirmed because this was what respectable families did even though I didn't know anything about the Bible or being Christian. Though I started out as a Catholic, she decided that I would be Protestant this time as we were trying something new and so I was dropped off at the Sunday school building along with all of the other teenagers bearing tightly folded arms.

By the third class, we were discussing the Ten Commandments and I was feeling lost and confused so I raised my hand. I proceeded to ask the minister what it meant to commit adultery and he was not at all amused. His face got real tight and his brow sunk over his eyes. Then he pointed to the door.

This was the end of my short-lived career as a Protestant.

This shameful moment would also need to be kept a secret in my later life. Secrets, though toxic, are often necessary, especially if you are dealing with Protestant lineage.

August 7th

Another beautiful day. This makes me feel as if I want to practice the art of *wrong-shui* and get rid of everything in my husband's over stuffed drawers and closets while he is at work.

He wears the same three outfits over and over in an alternating pattern. When I wash them, I place them neatly back on top of the untouched piles beneath. I am quite sure that he does not even know what is in his drawers and therefore would not notice if they were missing. For some reason, he is incapable of parting with anything so I must do the dirty work and create a *clothes vacuum* in his *dresser universe*. This way, once he has been de-cluttered, he will be open to new and different clothes in the future.

With this newly acquired space and openness, he will attract new clothes, or possibly a new wife depending on how angry he gets.

August 8th

The stars were so incredible last night, just another gift of the month of August. There were shooting stars all over the sky. I made about a million wishes.

I wished that my husband would still speak to me after emptying out his drawers and giving them to the Salvation Army.

August 9th

As I was gazing out into space, contemplating the existence of other life forms, I had a thought that female forms of other species must also go through a change of life. They must. I wondered what alien menopause must be like.

I noticed something else. The very bright moon, so high up in the sky . . . was almost full.

August 10th

I woke up with exceptionally high quills this morning. One would not think that summer would be the season for high quills, however, the truth is that quills can rise at anytime. Quills show no mercy.

We should always be aware of the moon's schedule.

August 11th

My quills continue to rise and are reaching dangerously high levels. Anger molecules are beginning to form like armies of soldiers in my veins ready for battle. I *feel* ready for battle.

As I am aware of my present state of consciousness and emotional condition, I do my best to avoid the public as it is not safe. I go to the post office to get the mail at off times in order to avoid the heavy traffic of Mayberry and the daily chit chat that happens at the post office. I wear a wig and dark glasses. I look down as I walk in the door and avoid any possible contact. I turn the key in the box and reach for the mail without looking up. I quickly close the little door with my key and scurry out the door.

Summer

Normally I enjoy going to the post office and I get the mail slowly, but not with high quills and certainly not with the moon simultaneously approaching its full phase. This is a lethal combination for everyone involved. High quills and a full moon.

There is nothing more dangerous in the entire universe.

August 12th

I wake up to start my day hoping that I feel better, but I do not. I realize that this could possibly be my worst period ever. As I am irregular with my cycles at this point, some come and go quickly with little physical or emotional discomfort and some bring with them cramps and high quills. It is a dice roll.

This particular time, I rolled double sixes and I am out for blood. There is no one that I like or feel like tolerating. I will say anything to anyone as I have completely lost my filter. My inner werewolf is so fully alive that I can feel her inside of me. She is waiting for the sun to go down so she can come out to play.

August 13th

There is no way of knowing what may happen when the moon turns full tomorrow night. I must be careful to remain inside my house and off the phone for the safety of my family members, telemarketers, and the citizens of Mayberry.

August 14th

A full moon.

The moon is full and there is the potential for a menopausal murder. I am not a Virgo, but it is a strong and powerful sign and I feel its effects. I like no one and every little noise is annoying me. I am blaming everyone in my mental path for my discomfort. Anyone who crosses me will be the recipient of a menopausal quill saturated with organic poison. I will show no mercy.

August 15th

Today I woke up and the desire to kill people had left me. It has been almost a full week of dangerously high quills. This can happen during menopause. Some periods are worse than others.

The desire to kill people had left, however, the desire to crawl under the largest boulder I could possibly find never to be seen or heard from again had arrived. Just as the tide comes in and out, so it is with the mood swings of menopause and the level of one's quills.

I was worthless. I knew this for sure as this is the way I woke up. Worthless. Lacking any value what so ever. I had never done anything truly meaningful in my life and no one liked me anymore. Not only was I not liked, but I was not appreciated either. I knew this because this is what my feelings were.

My ability to block or control my thoughts was impaired, at least for today.

I dropped our oldest son off for his high school soccer tryouts and I saw my life flash before my eyes. Today he left for high school, tomorrow he would leave for college, then graduate school. By Sunday he would be married. By the following Tuesday I would be a grandmother. I cried so hard that I couldn't breathe and then I took the garbage out.

I look forward to the arrival of the crescent moon, with its mild gravitational pull and low quills.

August 16th

Like a plane coming in for a landing and lowering its flaps, my quills have lowered, thank God. It had been almost an entire week of being on red alert and avoiding the public for fear of being front page news. Once the menopausal fog had cleared and my fangs retreated beneath my gums, I realized that I had not undergone a complete personality change, nor did I need shock therapy. I had just had a really, really bad period. Since it had taken so long to arrive, the anger molecules had built up and reached dangerously high levels possibly setting the stage for a menopausal murderess to do her thing and put an end to Polly-do-good-for-all who is constantly calling about doing my share for the hockey team's bake sales.

I could have been the reason that her children were left motherless and the hockey team without brownies.

And the worst part would have been our lack of remorse, because when our quills get high and the moon is full we don't care. When the moon shines on our yellow eyes and our fur grows beneath our ivory summer tops and khaki Capri pants we are not aware of what we are doing. There is no awareness of who we are. We just stretch our necks up towards the moon's glow and howl from the core of our existence. We unite our spirits and our energy with those around the world. We feel the power and we feel the universal hatred for brownie-baking PTO suck-ups and irritating *hockey people*.

August 17th

Our son made the soccer team and it is Division I. We are so proud and happy that it is difficult to contain ourselves. I am glad that he did not have to relay this wonderful news through plexy glass during visiting hours.

I have lowered the bar as far as expectations for myself, at least for the time being.

August 18th

Happy Anniversary to us!

Today is our 16th wedding anniversary. It is amazing how times goes by so quickly. It seems like just yesterday that I walked down the isle, only about 35 pounds thinner . . . glowing and very much living in the moment . . . overwhelmed with the exhilarating experience of having all of our people in one room just for us, watching our every move. The day went by so quickly, yet it seemed as if it were in slow motion at the same time.

All five senses were maxed out, taking mental snapshots of every detail. One thing I remember the most was the band. They were this rockin' band from Long Island that played all 50's and 60's music, the best music for dancing in my opinion. In fact, as I remember, very few people sat down through the whole reception. The music was way too good. If I had it to do over again, I wouldn't change one thing. I would gladly eat pasta for the first four years of my marriage in order to have a great band for my wedding. It was that worth it. A party is only as good as its band. That's all I have to say about that.

Of course, Aunt Marla was around sixteen years ago also, doing all of the same manipulating and controlling behavior that she does now, only worse, as she had not yet experienced the mellowing effects of the aging process. She tried her best to have a say in everything even though we were paying for the whole thing. She had numerous issues with the seating chart. This one had to sit next to that one or she would be devastated. This one could *not* sit next to that one because they hadn't spoken in over twenty years.

Aunt Maggie's son made the radically rebellious move of marrying a Protestant girl and she had never gotten over it. In fact she refused to go to her own son's wedding because of it. Entire families can be broken up over marrying Protestants. If nothing else, it can greatly affect future seating charts at other people's weddings. It's kind of like a chain reaction or dominoes or something. As previously mentioned, Protestants can cause all sorts of problems.

In fact, I remember when my darling brought me to the first event with the in-laws. It was his Nana's 70th birthday party at a fancy restaurant. He sat me down with the "Over-Eighty Club," which was primarily comprised of the great-aunts. Of course, at my naïve age of twenty-three, I had no idea of the interrogation that I was in for. I wasn't just questioned. I was grilled, much like a murder suspect on *Law and Order* before they narrow things down to the most likely killer.

The first question, of course, was whether I was Catholic. They all leaned in, looking over the rims of their bifocals waiting for my response. I felt the sweat droplets start to emerge from my hairline as I tried to speak. There was a lot of pressure here. I really liked this guy. What if I said the wrong thing and I flunked the in-law quiz. Would there be a make-up quiz for those wishing to improve their grade, or was this it.

This felt like sudden-death on the dodge ball court in fourth grade. If you get hit, that's it. It's all over. Have a seat on the hot pavement and wait for the next game to start, and expect to be the last kid picked next time. Loser. That's how sudden death feels. It's instant pain. There is no time to process what is happening to you.

So I looked up and muttered to the CEO of the *Over-Eighty Club*, who is currently ninety-eight and one of my favorites, that yes, I was Catholic. They all breathed a heavy sigh of relief, sat back in their chairs, and ordered another round of martinis. I sat back also, realizing that my answer was correct, and silently gloated in my victory.

After the ladies took a sip of their fresh cocktails we got back to business. I could tell there was more to come as they were still staring at me as if I was on the witness stand. On my end, I thought the fat lady had sung her final note, but this was not the case at all though I passed the biggest part of the exam. She came out for an encore, and with the encore came another question. I could tell that this was serious as well, though not quite as much was at stake as the possibility of their great-nephew entering into a mixed marriage by marrying a Protestant.

They took another swig of their martinis in a very synchronized fashion, leaned in once again, and peering over their spectacles asked me if I was Irish. This time I was the one who took a deep breath. With a surname of *Quinn* it was tough to go wrong with this one. I felt the confidence run through me as if I had checked off my last answer on the test knowing that it was right. When I looked up and saw their faces I realized that it was even better than answering the last question correctly. It was the bonus question and it was worth double the points. I did it. I got the extra-credit. Instead of getting a 100, I got 110. This meant that I had room to mess up later and I could still keep my "A." It was my cushion, my insurance.

August 19th

Salute your *hate club*.

It does feel good to be liked and accepted and it is human nature to have such desires, however, it is also important to remember that everyone cannot like everyone and this is a plain and simple truth. *People- pleasers* and *care-a-holics* have a difficult time with this and continue to try to gain the approval of others in order to maintain a 100% approval rating.

Not only is this impossible and setting one's self up for failure, but it is insincere and an illusion even if this occurs for only a brief moment. People can pretend to like other people simply to avoid any issues which is actually a grown up way to be and very much all right as long as it is not over done.

What is also important to remember, is that people who do not like us can also play a role in *defining* us. In other words, there are certain people that we do not *want* to like us, as if they did something would be drastically wrong either because something is very right and good about us, or because something is wrong and defective in them.

To realize that having some people who do not like or accept us is not only o.k., but a good thing, and a giant step toward emotional health for most of us. In fact, for those of us who may wrestle with codependency, this is nothing short of a spiritual revelation.

When we take a look at who doesn't like us and why, we can hold our heads up high and be proud that we are who we are and that they can't stand the sight of us. We salute the members of our *hate club* as we are thrilled that we do not meet their criteria.

I am remembering a time back in *the day*, when my father recruited someone for our hate club, and well-deserved it was. I had just gotten my first job at a local ice cream parlor in the mini-mall next to Shop-Rite. It was new and a little out of the way so we didn't get many customers. The family who owned it was from Egypt and spoke very little English. They had a son who was probably in his early twenties. I was sixteen as this was the rule in New York to get a job if you were going to be on the books.

The son's name Sharyck. He was tall and thin and made the hair on my arms stand on end. After only a month or so they let me close the store. In this day and age, I cannot imagine allowing a sixteen year old girl to be in a store late at night with little or no traffic, but people didn't think that way back then. At least we didn't.

There was a walk-in cooler in the back of the store and it was my job to put everything away that had not been used that day. One night I went in the cooler to do what I was supposed to do and I saw the door handle turn. There was no way out, no windows, and no way to scream. I was surrounded by boxes and ice cream cakes.

The door opened and in walked Sharyck. I would have been relieved as this was not a stranger walking in from the streets, but my instincts told me otherwise. He had a weird look in his eyes. He moved closer and tried to grab my arms forcefully.

Without thinking I shoved him with all I had in me and he fell backwards over the boxes stacked behind him. I ran out of the cooler, out the front door of the store, through a dark alley, and then home where my father was in the middle of his Friday night poker game with the guys.

The living room was filled with cigar smoke and beer drinking.

I just stood there out of breath, struggling to get the words out of what happened to me.

Dad told me to get in the car and I did. He drove me to the ice cream store and walked in with me. There was no one there, only Sharyck. All of the sudden Dad grabbed Sharyck by the back of the neck and put his face in the steel sink. He said a few choice words and then pulled Sharyck out of the sink. Then he shook him and threatened him some more. Then Sharyck went back in the sink. Then he landed on the floor. Then we got in the car and went home.

The guys dealt Dad a new hand and all was well in my world once again.

I said goodnight to the poker guys and then went down the hall to check on my little sister. She looked so sweet sleeping with Clancy nestled on the end of her bed. She was still a little girl and I hoped that she got to stay this way for a very long time.

I remember how strange it felt for me that someone could want to hurt me and force himself on me. Thinking the whole thing over the next day made me realize how vulnerable I was in that store and that horrible things could have happened to me. It felt adult and I was still a girl. I became aware of how the world was different for girls.

I never did go back to get my paycheck.

August 20th

High School.

Our oldest child is nearly the age of this memory of my first job at the ice cream store and this feels different for me.

As I sit here very early in the morning waiting for our oldest to emerge from the shower, I can't help but to be grateful as the tears well up in my eyes. He starts high school today and I am having a tougher time with this one than I did when he started Kindergarten. It all seems to be going so fast.

The part that I am so grateful for is that his spirit has been loaned to us and that we have enjoyed him so much. Especially as parents, we can get caught up in our children being *ours* and it is times such as this when we are reminded differently. Our son is merely passing through on his own journey to somewhere else and we are only a part of this experience.

For this, I am both sad and grateful.

August 21st

It is amazing how having our own children turn a certain age brings back memories of being that age ourselves. The day Ryan started high school made me think of the New Paltz High School and what it was like to start all over at the bottom of the food chain.

I remember being nervous and excited at the same time. I remember feeling academic pressure as from here on in everything mattered. College was next so there was not a lot of room for error. No more fooling around. It was time to get serious and grow up.

There was a part of me that did not want to grow up and stop fooling around. I was noticing the football players and how cute they looked in their uniforms, and they were older. I liked this. Some of them had cars. Just being in this new school made me feel so much older than I did last year in eighth grade.

I got recruited for the basketball team. To this day I am not sure why, as baseball and skiing were what I was into and good at. Anyway, I agreed to try out and I made the team. As there was a series of cuts, I sort of assumed that I may not make it as a freshman. I approached the locker room door and there was my name. I made the Varsity and I was the only freshman. I still didn't get this as basketball was not really my sport but I would have fun and meet some new friends.

The coach's name was Vince and he touched girls inappropriately. I found this out fairly soon as kids talk. At first I was nervous that he might try to touch me but I didn't feel any *vibrations* coming from him so I stopped being nervous. We were a good team, undefeated actually, until we met up with the Papelli sisters from Highland. Highland was our rival high school. One of the Papelli sisters was six feet tall and the other one was a few inches taller more than that. Their team would pass the ball to one of those tall girls who would be conveniently located beneath the basket and toss it in with minimal effort. They could make baskets without interference because no one could reach the ball when they held it over their heads. I had never seen girls so tall. I wondered what their dating life was like.

I had time to wonder a lot of things because I spent most of the game on the bench. This was all right with me because quite honestly I was nervous out there on the court, especially as I was all of five feet and a couple of inches.

I was far more comfortable on a ski slope as this was natural for me, as natural as breathing or walking.

Basketball felt awkward, but I was the only freshman on the Varsity team and for this I was proud, even if I was experiencing this pride from the bench.

Vince was proud, too. He was especially proud of one of the girls on the team because he spent a lot of extra time with her. It felt squirmish to watch him with her. Those vibrations were in the air when they were in close proximity to each other. We all felt it but we didn't talk about it. I felt badly for that girl because I don't think she knew how to get out of it. She didn't have the strength on the inside.

The vibrations bothered me. She was fifteen years old and Vince was the age of my dad. This made my stomach feel sick.

August 22nd

At a certain point, I began to wonder if my high school was the national center for inappropriate touching or if this happened in high schools everywhere. I say this because my *Humanities* teacher was also liberal with his affection. After class each day he would keep only a few of us afterwards and only for a few seconds after the bell rang. He would say, "Girls, now before you leave, you must give Mr. Chase *some candy* . . . or I cannot go on with my day. Common girls, give Mr. Chase *some candy* . . ."

There he would stand between us and the door, the only way out, with his cheek tilted to the side in the waiting position like a teenage boy saying good night at the door step of his first girlfriend. We would take turns, one after the other, kissing Mr. Chase on the cheek before we were allowed to leave and continue on to our next class.

As this was the late 70's, teachers kissing freshman girls was acceptable.

August 23rd

From there, we would cross the hall and go to gym class. We had gym class twice each week as this was the law for public high schools.

Our gym teacher's name was Pat and she wore men's clothes. She even wore tighty-whities. We knew this because we could see them when she bent over to put the balls and equipment away. The waist band said *Fruit of the Loom.*

Pat took teaching gym very seriously. She even went through this phase where she made us write reports about the origins of volleyball and golf. Maybe she wanted to feel like a *real* teacher. I understood this in a way. Gym is important, but most kids don't consider it to be a real class like math or science or something. It is a requirement of the state of New York and a nice break in between the real classes to have fun and let off steam.

Some of the kids made fun of her. I didn't understand this because she was nice and gym class was fun. Not only that, but my mother had a woman friend who wore men's clothes. Her name was Louise and she was a friend of Dan's also. They worked together.

This truly did not bother me and this was because my hippy mother and my Republican father had all sorts of people over to our house. I learned early on that it was all about the love, and not about tattoos or women wearing men's underwear.

Not only this, but Pat the gym teacher didn't position herself between us and the door and force us to kiss her on the way to our next class.

For this I was grateful.

August 24th

High School was a whole new experience for lots of reasons other than the inappropriate kissing of students by the faculty, or gym teachers wearing men's underwear. It was a huge step from little kid to big kid. All of the sudden I knew people with jobs and cars and this made me like an adult.

I also started to think older thoughts and about what I wanted to do. I thought about driving and the freedom that it would bring. I thought about making money of my own and the freedom that would bring also. Not just baby-sitting, but real money.

I remember our guidance counselor, Mr. Schwartz. He was so cool and all of the kids liked him. He had this big, comfortable office with pictures of places all over the country, like the Grand Canyon and other far away places. There were pictures of colleges and up-lifting quotes all over the walls such as *You are who you choose to be* and *Be your best self each and every day*.

Kids loved to hang out in Mr. Schwartz's office because he was fun and he listened to us. He understood us, and we always felt better leaving than we had when we had first walked in with the heaviness that often accompanies adolescence.

Kids were drawn to Mr. Schwartz.

Then one day Mr. Schwartz was fired. It happened all of the sudden. Just like that. No one understood why, but the rumor was that the principal felt threatened by him because the kids liked him so much. They were afraid that he had too much influence over us and no one should have influence except the principal. This was a by-law of the student handbook.

We were all taken by surprise and very upset. We needed Mr. Schwartz and we needed his office. There were couches in his office and they went along each wall. The couches were comfortable and Mr. Schwartz was comfortable and it was not all right with us that he was fired.

We thought about what we could do about this injustice.

We brainstormed and came up with the idea of staging a walk-out, complete with banners and picket signs. This was my idea and I felt good about it. My gut was telling me that this was the right thing to do and I listened to my gut. Back then it never would have crossed my mind not to listen. When my gut spoke, the truth was heard by my spirit and the voice was crystal clear.

We made colorful signs. I wore my feather earrings for good luck.

We had chosen 9:00 am on the dot to walk out of the building. I wondered if people would wimp out at the last minute. I anxiously watched the clock as the moment got closer. I looked out the window at the parking lot that would soon be filled with eight hundred students. The clock ticked and it was time. I got up and look around the classroom. I signaled everyone towards the door. They stood up also and followed me.

Part of me felt as if I was going to throw up. Part of me was proud of my *chutzpa*. This is a Yiddish word for guts, only it's deeper and more meaningful. *Chutzpa* is a great word, very New York, very strong.

As we marched down the hallway, the other classroom doors opened and kids joined us in large numbers. We walked out the side doors and headed for the parking lot. We were almost all there.

Then the principal came out and he had a very mad look on his face and was a bit red in the cheek area.

I climbed up on the hood of a friend's station wagon. This is because I am short and I wanted people to hear me. I hadn't planned to talk in front of this crowd that I had just led out the front doors of our high school, but I felt the words rising to the surface. I felt strong about this feeling. My words had conviction.

I proceeded to talk about Mr. Schwartz and how important he was to all of us. I talked about his character and about how he was wronged. I explained that the bigger injustice was to those of us without a voice and that we had joined together to be that voice.

We were the students of New Paltz High School.

What I didn't know was that Mr. Schwartz was in his office cleaning out his desk. We thought he was gone.

He walked out with his box of stuff, not knowing that we were all out there for him. He turned and looked at us. He saw the signs. The crowd went wild. Then the police and reporters showed up. As this was a non-violent protest, we began to chant and wave our arms. We got louder. Mr. Schwartz stood their and waved to all of us. Then he blew a big kiss to all of us, nodded at the principal who was now a deep shade of purple and got in his car.

The reporter took a picture of me standing on the hood of the station wagon wearing my feather earrings and holding a megaphone.

The next day it was on the front page of the *New Paltz News*.

August 25th

I woke up to the sounds of both parents beckoning from the living room with firmness. I contemplated climbing out the window and then decided against it as this would only prolong the inevitable. I must face the music like the true rebel that I was becoming.

Women had starved themselves to gain the vote. People had marched on Washington. I had organized a walk-out in my high school parking lot donning purple feather earrings as a response to a local injustice.

I pulled my shoulders back, took a deep breath, and headed into the living room.

There they stood with my Republican father clutching the *New Paltz News* tightly. My picture was large and took up most of the front page. I saw my hippy mother's face. She grabbed the paper away from my Republican father and welled up with tears. Then she smiled and walked over to give me a hug. "My baby," she said, "My baby is all grown up and organizing walk-outs. I don't know what to say. I am so proud of you Honey."

My Republican father did not look quite as happy, though he commented on Mr. Schwartz's abrupt dismissal with disapproval and said, "He was a nice man. It will be tough to replace him." Then he said something about hoping it wasn't a permanent mark on my school records.

My hippy mother then turned with a bit of an indignant look and said something about bringing honor to the town and to the family.

As I stood there not sure about what I should do or say, I heard my hippy mother rummaging through the junk door in the kitchen for a pair of scissors. She cut out my picture that was on the front page of the *New Paltz News* as she shook her head from side to side, bursting with pride. She smoothed out the picture and then tacked it up on the wall. The next day she made copies for all of the relatives.

I was suspended from high school for a few days and was forced to write a letter of apology to the principal. My hippy mother explained that this was bureaucratic bullshit and that such injustice created by authoritarian bastards breeds smaller injustices, kind of like dominos and the government.

She bragged about me all summer at the Town Pool.

August 26th

A couple of years later I graduated and my mother invited Mr. Schwartz to my party. He was working in another school district and he looked happy. It was good to see him and he was glad to be there and to see *his kids* again after such a long time.

Clancy didn't try to bite Mr. Schwartz. He didn't even growl.

That's all I need to say about that as Clancy was a true character barometer.

August 27th

Though I was not yet aware of the moon or of the lunar schedule at this point in time, it is possible that is was full and that my inner, youthful Sagittarian had come out to play. I was being controlled by outside forces and this was not my fault, nor my concern.

I can only imagine what could have come about had my powers reached maturity.

August 28th

When I think of this menopausal flashback from the early 80's, it was all about respect. There was respect of self and respect of others. One stems from the other and I was beginning to learn this on a conscious level.

The fact that is, what had happened was deeply rooted in wrongness and wrongness does not sit with the spirit well. It is expunged like a bad shrimp or piece of pepperoni. The spirit picks up on this wrongness with sensitive radar and then makes the move to throw it up in order to bring balance back and return to health.

This is the lesson I learned. Walk-outs are like throwing up. They cleanse our systems of unwanted bacteria and toxins.

August 29th

Granny's wake.

Last night, again, we were reminded that life as we know it is not on our terms but on the terms of He who created us. My husband and I attended the wake of a very dear friend's grandmother. She was ninety nine years old and eight months.

When we pulled into the funeral home, we were greeted by seasoned looking gentlemen wearing suits and warm smiles. There were so many people there that they had to direct people to park up ahead on the front lawn.

We all walked in together, the *inner circle* as we call ourselves, to go through the receiving line. Granny looked beautiful lying there so peacefully. As always, she looked like a million dollars in her red dress and pearls. Red was her color.

As people stood talking and remembering Granny, I contemplated the thought of how she had almost made it to one hundred and why she was taken only four months short of this monumental milestone birthday. Our five children had been wondering this ever since we received the initial phone call. "She almost made it," they said, one after the other. And, "Imagine telling people that you are one hundred. That is so cool."

As I looked at her dressed so beautifully I realized that she had had a full life and she was simply *done* even if she had a mere four months to go on our very earthly time watch. There were old pictures on the wall to help people know her. My favorite one was the one in the middle. It was a picture of Granny and her husband, circa 1927, complete with the 20's dress, glasses, and hair do's. Her husband's *do* was tall and rippled, a signature of the times. They had their whole lives ahead of them as well as the Great Depression, Television, Roosevelt, Harry Truman, the Polio vaccine, World War II, Poodle Skirts and Chevy's, racial riots and walks on Washington, Martin Luther King, Jr., a walk on the moon, Vietnam, Watergate, an AIDs epidemic, terrorist attacks on September 11th and the Internet.

I wondered what it was like back then in rural Vermont where indoor plumbing and electricity were luxuries. How difficult things must have been as a young mother. I could only imagine.

The many pictures, however, showed a rich and happy life. They were full of people and events.

Looking at her wedding picture taken back in 1927, I couldn't help but to wonder what she was thinking. I wondered if she was having thoughts about her future and about how many kids she may have. I wondered if she was worried about the state of the world and if life for women would ever change.

Looking at her sitting there in her black and white wedding photo at twenty years old, I wondered if she knew she'd live to be ninety nine and eight months.

August 30th

Our perspective is our reality.

I awakened this morning still caught up in thoughts about Granny's wake and of our funeral ritual in general. I think for most people attending funerals is not enjoyable, yet necessary for our own closure. They are also very much about respect and value for the person's life and of life in general. This, to me, is why wakes and funerals are so important as difficult as they may be.

I looked around at a room full of people all sharing fond memories they had with Granny and of how much she meant to them. Each individual's experience and memory was different as Granny filled a different need in each and every one of them. Each person in Granny's life had respect for her and valued her in their own way. Each had a different perception of what she meant to them. The Granny in one person's world was unique and known only to them in a way that is so intimate and spiritual that it could be known by no other.

This is true of all of us and our relationships with those we love. We live in our own world with that person and this no one else could possibly understand, nor can we understand their world. What we share is the person herself and the deep value and respect we had for her. This is what we have in common, value and respect for the person we loved and will now be without for a while. This is why we go to funerals and why they are important.

August 31st

One thing I have always questioned when at a funeral is if the one who has moved on is present at this ritual in some way and if they are aware of those who are there. I think about this and believe that we must be aware in some way of those who have spent valuable life minutes on our behalf. I personally believe that we know who is there and that we receive their private, personal expressions of value and reverence with an open and grateful heart.

September 1st

This month the full moon will be in the very gentle sign of Aquarius once again. Most people who know an Aquarius will agree that they are very likable and genuine people. They will do anything for you, some times too much as they can tend to be *care-a-holics* and *people pleasers*.

As this is a gentle sign, a menopausal mid-lifer who happens to be an Aquarius may not be quite as dangerous as her menopausal sisters of different astrological signs, however, never let your guard down as a full moon is still a full moon and its gravitational pull should never be underestimated.

It would be far more likely to have an encounter with a menopausal Sagittarian, who, while under the hypnotic power of the lunar force may seek out and destroy these people pleasers. Nothing agitates a menopausal Sagittarian more than a *kiss-ass*. As they are inherently strong and of robust health, they have little if any tolerance for people who whine, complain, or suck up to others as a weak attempt at a means to an end.

Sagittarians have no respect for these people.

Therefore, when the full moon lands in the sign of Aquarius and these types of people become more visible, the Sagittarian cannot help but to be inclined to have their way with these pathetic *polly-do-good-for-alls*. It is their mission. In fact, in certain communities, P.T.O. meetings are prohibited when the full moon is in Aquarius.

As previously mentioned, the Sagittarian is easily irritated to begin with and emotionally speaking, the strongest of the menopausal community members. When they get annoyed they do not care, nor take into consideration the effects on others as they are all considered to be inferior. Sagittarians are born leaders and at the top of the menopausal food chain.

Members of the menopausal community who commit heinous verbal acts against community do-gooders are of course given a *menopausal pardon* as they are being controlled by an outside force and therefore *know not what they do*. The much revered and feared Sagittarians are also given a menopausal pardon though they are fully aware of what they have done.

They just don't care.

September 2nd

It may be good to know some strategies just in case you encounter a menopausal Sagittarian when the moon is full, especially if you happen to be an Aquarius yourself or if the full moon has landed in this sign simply to prevent your complete demise. In fact, the only night all year that is more threatening to humanity than the full moon sliding into Aquarius is when the full moon lands in the sign of Sagittarius itself. As the menopausal power of the Sagittarian takes on full lunar force from within. When this is the case, it is really best to run for cover and remain there until the sun comes up.

September 3rd

Speaking of gentleness, there is another sign that would qualify as mild and this is the sign of Pisces. The menopausal Pisces loves the water and the sun. As the Sagittarian has an insatiable wander lust, if you have made plans to go somewhere warm and beautiful with gorgeous beaches and palm tress, it is best not to mention this to a menopausal Sagittarian as they will not be happy for you. They will want to kill you and then transfer your plane ticket to themselves.

September 4th

On a more positive note, when all is well with the Sagittarian there is no limit to what she can do especially when the moon is full. If no one she knows is traveling to somewhere wonderful and there are no P.T.O. meetings scheduled that are loaded with *people pleasers* doing nice things for external approval, her energy is free to do other things, great things.

The Sagittarian is born to do great things.

The Sagittarian is full of passion. She may write a best seller. She may run for a political office and win by a land slide. The menopausal Sagittarian knows her potential. Her inner voice speaks to her with clarity, especially when the moon is full.

September 5th

The Sagittarian has an innate desire to become famous. She feels famous on the inside. Now this inner famous feeling needs to manifest into her reality. This is her destiny.

The Sagittarian can write and become famous for an award winning screen play, or she can make the front page of every newspaper in the country for being the primary suspect in the disappearance of the P.T.O. chair person. It can go either way depending on how her energy is channeled.

The Sagittarian enjoys and thrives on living on the edge.

This makes her feel alive.

September 6th

For the most part, the gentle month of September soothes the often tempestuous Sagittarian. September is the calm before the storm as when they enter their own astrological zone in late November and early December, very complex anger molecules begin to develop and flow wildly through their veins.

With the holidays happening at the same time, things can get a bit volatile for those related to the Sagittarian, especially those seated at her Thanksgiving table as this is the peak of her cycle.

It is always best to say a Novena or two before visiting a Sagittarian for the holidays and remember to savor the gentle month of September and the delightfully mild crescent moon.

In addition to September being warm and gentle, the air is dry and heavenly. The mornings and evenings ask for a light sweater or jacket, just the right weather for an autumn walk. It is the ideal weather to do pretty much anything.

I also have always enjoyed September as it is still somewhat *slow*. We embrace *slow*. In fact, on any given summer day, we can be found in the backyard hanging around in the sandbox or on the swings. We make an occasional jaunt to the local bike trail, then to the *Pine Cone* snack stand for an ice cream cone. This is the extent of our movement during the summer.

In the evenings we can be found on our deck cooking on the grill and savoring the sweet taste of all things seasonal . . . garden ripe tomatoes, summer squash, cucumbers, peppers, as well as volumes of marinated chicken and hamburgers. We savor September, as we hang on for dear life to the gorgeous weather, the grill, and our flip-flops.

We dig our heels in as we cling to the rest and rejuvenation that the summer brings before she politely bows and concedes her position to the very dominating season of winter. Of course, in between, we have the breath-taking season of autumn with the fall foliage bringing some of nature's most colorful and brilliant artwork. Autumn allows us to transition to the inevitable ice and cold with grace.

The reason for all of this seasonal drama and description, is due to the fact that we live closer to Santa than anyone else in the United States. It is possible that there may be a few poor souls clinging to the northern border of Maine, but basically we can reach out and grab the North Pole with relative ease. The winters are at least eight months long which is why we can still be found grilling hamburgers on our back deck at the end of September, even if we are bundled up in fleece pullovers.

As mentioned, many are aware of the DSM diagnosis of *Seasonal Affective Disorder* which was born in northern Vermont. This disorder affects people who become sensitive to the lack of sunlight during the cold and dark winter months. It can cause people to become depressed, to drink heavily, or to become compulsive Internet shoppers. Some may resort to cross-dressing and trying out alternate personas. Many of us will do whatever it takes to feel alive and part of the world that exists in the sunlight.

Though our family does embrace the winter in that we are avid skiers and snowshoers, it does get dark rather early on our planet, which is why we hang on for dear life to the lovely, very warm and gentle month of September. It also happens to be one of the few months where the temperature is above zero. We do not suffer from *Seasonal Affective Disorder*, however, we do choose to remain in *seasonal denial* as long as possible.

September 7th

It is amazing how in the midst of the beautiful weather and gentle reflection that things can turn around in an instant. My husband and I were sitting on the couch reading together late in the evening when we received a phone call that Aunt Marla had had a heart attack. The news was that she was going to be all right and didn't have any lasting damage. They kept her for six days before she was sent home.

Apparently, she was delivering a motivational speech for her department while under pressure from the *powers-that-be* that had been very focused on meeting this year's quota when all of the sudden she stopped talking and sat down in her chair. People stared at her wondering what was happening as she tried to speak. No words left her lips.

Finally someone realized what was happening and called 911. The ambulance got there within minutes and took Aunt Marla to the nearest hospital.

Thank God she was not driving. Our dear Aunt Marla actually has somewhat of a lead foot and can be seen whizzing up and down through Teaneck at any given time. More than likely she would be wearing her dark sunglasses and making gestures to all those who in her opinion could use a driving lesson. Yes, our dear Aunt Marla is known to have a slight case of road rage. Of course, the truth is that she is irritated with the state of humanity in general and not just those on the interstate. Occasionally her fellow motorists get a hand gesture, but usually they get the horn followed by a loud explanation from behind the driver's side window of just why the state of New Jersey needs to tighten things up as far as who they give licenses to.

Anyway, hearing this news of what happened to Aunt Marla was sad, but not surprising. She holds on tightly, to everything. For Aunt Marla, there is nothing more important than proving points and teaching lessons to those in her life. She has a tremendous need to call the shots and be *top dog* as they say. Aunt Marla is a control addict, and just as with any other addiction she will strive for that fix, or emotional pay off without regard to the cost. Aunt Marla enters into a blind blur not unlike a heroin addict, each time she feels as if someone else is trying to tell her what to do or how to be. She must let them know who is in charge.

She feels this control surge rumble through her veins like white-water rapids making their way through a narrow gorge. The rapids have a powerful momentum that takes on a life of its own, capable of swallowing a kayak whole without resistance or mercy. This is how it is with control addicts. They are forceful and powerful.

September 8th

A junction of choice.

The news on the street is that Aunt Marla is going to be fine. She is still somewhat shaken emotionally, and will be for quite some time, but thank God she has no lasting damage. If we give a moment's thought to what could have been, it is frightening.

What we now have here is a junction, a junction of choice. This is what happens with life's *skunks*. They have a very definite purpose, though we often cannot see it when we are in the midst of it. When we are in the eye of the storm, with swirling, high intensity winds whipping all around us, we are unable to focus on the new direction we are being pointed in.

At this point, what is important is to simply *acknowledge* that we are being pointed in a new direction even if we have no idea what that new direction is or where we are headed. We need to acknowledge the junction or fork in the road. By doing so, we humbly accept that a power higher than all of us is at the reins of our lives. We cease to resist and let go. We open our hearts and minds to the possibility that we may, in fact, not know what is best for us, and that our own will may have gotten in our way. This is why we may have been derailed from the path we were on and forced to take a different one. In a way, it is a form of *Divine tough love*.

It is not unlike a parent attempting to steer his teenager in the right direction. Our Creator gives us all of the free choice and slack *we think we can handle*. Then, when the freedom to choose turns into frequently made bad choices, or choices not made for the benefit of our spiritual growth, we often find ourselves being scooched over from the driver's seat into the passenger side. Things may stay this way, at least for a while, until we can prove that we are trustworthy and responsible to drive again. Our Creator wants us to have all of the slack we would like, but not so much that we hang ourselves.

This leads us to the *Fourteenth Principle of the Tao of Menopause- acknowledge the junctions of choice.*

Even if we do not actually make any immediate changes, it is all right, as long as we sit with the idea that change is imminent. Of course, this is especially true if the junctions are health-related junctions, as our bodies are crystal clear indicators of what is going on in our emotional lives. We need to acknowledge that our bodies manifest *dis-ease* in a variety of ways and that we need to pay attention to what our bodies are saying to us.

We need to fully understand that stress kills. It is the number one disease in the United States. Stress is deadly. We know this to be true, yet we ignore all those little warning signs that tell us that something is not right with our internal world. We stick our heads in the sand and pretend that all is well, that we love our careers, our partners, that things are fine at home, that the teenager is at the library when he sneaks out at night.

Why do we do this . . . because the *Planet Denial* is a seemingly safe and comfortable place. When we live on this planet, we have the *illusion* that all is well with the universe and with our lives. It is only when we are forced by life's *skunks* to return back to the planet where there is only one moon in the sky, that we are forced to really look at ourselves and the direction our lives are taking us.

For Aunt Marla, what happened had the potential to be a blessing. Her heart was full of shame from what happened with her alcoholic husband who ran from the mob and ended up floating in the Hudson River with a bullet hole in the side of his head. Her heart was full of guilt, real and imagined, as she wondered what she could have done to prevent such a catastrophe.

The rumor that ran around the block after the mob incident was that Reginald got so desperate that he put the house up for one hand on the Black Jack table. Had he won he would have won big. But he did not win. He lost.

He lost his home and himself.

I can only imagine what it must have been like to sit there at that black jack table for the few short seconds after losing everything you own, knowing that you will have to face your wife and two young children. The shame must have been so intense that Reginald would have liked to be anywhere but in his own skin and this is why he did what he did.

Because the autopsy showed that Reginald had taken his own life, the insurance company wouldn't pay out for his life insurance.

Aunt Marla, who had worked so hard her whole life, was now left with nothing. She had no husband, no house, and two kids to take care of. She was starting over.

Her only inheritance was shame.

September 9th

It is interesting how shame can be passed down through generations much like diabetes. Aunt Marla's son David is well on his way to becoming an alcoholic if he has not arrived at this place already. He runs from himself daily and drinks to numb his pain and his shame. He also drinks to numb the pain of his mother.

Angela runs from her pain by not communicating with anyone in the family. Her tool is avoidance. By staying away from her mother and brother, she removes herself from her own pain and shameful memories. Of course this does not work, but instead works to create anger molecules which ride on the back of the blame she carries around with her every day.

Angela blames her mother for what happened to her father.

I think this is what lies behind the chain-smoking and road rage.

This is most definitely what lies beneath her need to control everyone and everything. Aunt Marla is afraid. She is afraid of more pain and more shame.

I wonder what her spirit is like, beneath all of that.

I wonder what her dreams are.

September 10th

After thinking about life's *skunks* last night, I couldn't help but to ponder where I would like to be in ten years. For me, this means the seasoned stage of my fifties as I am presently in my forties. Thinking about Aunt Marla makes me know for sure what I do *not* want to be, but as far as what I *do* want to be will take some active thought and effort. The following is a list of what I would like to be at fifty years old, just shy of one decade from now:

- I will have the charisma that accompanies genuine self-acceptance and self-love.
- I will wear a smile well, so that people can see in my eyes that a seasoned spirit resides behind them, a spirit that has seen and experienced many things, and through all has maintained the zest for life.
- I will be taking even more walks, praying along the way.
- I will learn Italian and then make a trip to Tuscany.
- Even if I do not learn Italian, I will still make a trip to Tuscany.
- I will accept my body the way it is and enjoy every bite I put in my mouth as if it is my last.
- I will more fully explore and appreciate the art of Chinese medicine.
- I will stretch often.
- I will listen more actively and become a better observer of life.
- I will watch *I love Lucy* reruns whenever I want to.
- I will order a delicious seafood dish from a gourmet restaurant and bring it home to eat on my couch.
- I will buy new jammies often.
- I will wear a bikini if the feeling moves me to.
- On certain beaches, I will wear only the bottom half.
- Hot bubble baths will continue to happen every night as if they were part of some religious ritual.

- I will explore new books to read, possibly biographies of incredible women.
- I will cease to allow people to irritate me who are unworthy of my life space.
- I will stop at every yard sale I see whether I am going to be late somewhere or not.
- I will be grateful every day that I am alive and healthy.
- I will reside in the present moment.
- I will appreciate my mother.

Well, that pretty much sums it all up for me. I believe that it is very important to consciously think about the direction that our life is going. Otherwise, we tend to steer our spirits on autopilot, living very much in a passive, almost lazy and apathetic way. It is only when we make a conscious choice to live deliberately that things get done.

We are who we choose to be. We are a culmination of our thoughts.

What happened to Aunt Marla really affected me as far as making me think about the direction of my own life, as well as the fact that stress kills. Worrying and *what if* type thinking kill people. We know this, as it is a medically established fact even in the world of western medicine.

Therefore, if the result of being all worked up, proving points, hanging on to old issues and anger results in incapacitating, debilitating, or fatal medical situations such as strokes, heart attacks, and cancer then why do we continue to do these things? I am not sure that I know the answer to that one, however, it is a very clear and basic cause and effect relationship. Letting go of old issues, accepting ourselves, our life circumstances, and making peace with our past so we can more fully live in the present lead to a long and healthy life. Not doing so leads one down a much bumpier path.

September 11th

Mothers and daughters.

I would like to return to the goals that I have set for myself as far as where I would like to be a decade from now, and focus specifically on the part where I will desire to appreciate my mother. Appreciating one's mother is not merely a goal but a life long process, and just as with most everything else it is all about the process.

As most of us are aware, it is different with mothers and daughters than it is with mothers and sons. Sons are easier for mothers because they are eager to please and rarely confront them with their own opinions. Having a son is like having a golden retriever.

They worship and adore you, will do anything you ask of them, and follow you from room to room expecting nothing in return other than some attention and affection. Sons are honest, direct, and sensitive.

Daughters, on the other hand, are not only completely uninterested in pleasing their mothers, especially during adolescence and early adulthood, but actually go out of their way to make their point known. They have minds of their own and they will fight to the end in order to have the last word.

Both genders challenge us as parents, however, it is no secret that the mother-daughter relationship is a complicated one. This is also evident by the volumes of books written on the subject. We start out life gazing into our mother's eyes while she feeds us and holds us against her warm, cozy body. We hear her heart beating and it comforts us. Nothing can harm us and there is no where else we would rather be. She is everything, and on some level we understand that her survival is *our* survival. Our beings are one and we cannot live without her. There is no one more beautiful. She is a goddess.

So ends stage one of the very complex mother-daughter relationship. During stage two, the young daughter still enjoys being around her mother and beams with pride when her mom is the one who surprised the soccer team by bringing homemade brownies to the game. Her mom is the best mom there is.

While the daughter's feelings of worship are still there, they are slowly and gradually deteriorating. She begins to notice faults in her goddess. The young daughter begins to have ideas of her own. She no longer believes that everything her mother says is true or right, especially if it is affecting her social life. These thoughts are only on simmer at this point, as the young daughter has not acquired enough ego-strength or *female-ness* yet to fully separate or to be confrontational.

This will not happen until her estrogen levels have increased enough to activate the *confrontational molecules*. This normally occurs around the age of twelve, but may happen sooner depending on genetics and family history.

Once the estrogen is flowing freely through the teenage daughter's veins, and in bountiful quantities, the goddess is removed from her throne where she is sure never to return again.

This is stage three of the mother-daughter relationship and it will last for a very long time. To the former goddess, it may feel as if it will never end. Her sweet daughter has been possessed by the demons of adolescence. There is not so much as a trace of her former self. On a good day all the former goddess gets are heavy sighs and a few eye-rolls. The rest of the time she is getting opinions, lots of opinions, and they are opinions with conviction.

The former goddess, during moments of vulnerability walks into her teenager's trap with no way out but to lose yet another battle. The goddess, then digs deep into her reservoir of argumentative energy and retaliates. No one gets anywhere. Hurt feelings and anger fill the air. It stays this way for years and years. The former goddess knows nothing except how to ruin a perfectly happy teenage life, and the daughter doesn't realize how much easier things would be for her if she would just listen.

September 12th

As my thoughts are still with the whole mother-daughter relationship issue, I will choose to remain there for the time being. The fourth stage happens during the late teenage and early years of adulthood, where the former goddess sinks even lower to the status of what the daughter would term the *I never want to be like her stage*. This is stage four of the very complicated mother-daughter relationship, and it is the stage where carbon copies of every conversation and interaction are filed in alphabetical order and made in triplicate for safekeeping. The daughter decides that if there is one thing that she knows for sure is that she is determined *not* to turn into her mother when she becomes a mother.

She cannot stand that her mother could possibly think that she could know or understand what she is going through much less offer advice. It is downright arrogant and to do so is just plain aggravating. The young adult daughter has graduated from the heavy sigh and eye-roll stage, as she has now developed enough ego strength and *female-ness* to get ugly and confrontational. In fact, the daughter not only enjoys confronting her mother, but actually looks forward to it. Butting heads is a sport for girls and they will fight to the end whether they are right or not, and whether she can even remember the reason for the argument or not. It is the sport of the game, kind of like modern hunters with their high-tech rifles. It is no longer about the meat and the bearskin rugs. It is the thrill of the chase and taking down their prey.

Of course, on the other side, the mother's *female-ness* kicks into gear just like riding a bike. She suits up with her emotional armor and heads into battle against her young adult daughter. The mother has an air of confidence about her as she is heading into battle from a place of *seasoned female-ness*, as her estrogen levels have been flowing for many more years. The mother knows full well that her daughter's new boyfriend is no good and will never amount to anything. If only her daughter could see it. If only her daughter would appreciate her lifetime of wisdom and experience things would be so much easier for her. She is so stubborn.

The daughter, who had realized at this point that she was no longer interested in this young man anyway, continues to date him for the sole purpose of aggravating her mother as the pay-off is huge. It just feels so good to be defiant and to finally have control of her life that she can hardly contain herself. The daughter perceives her mother to be on a mission to ruin her life. She has daily thoughts that her mother is just plain evil, and she has all of the evidence in the world to support her theory.

As her friends' mothers are all cut of the same evil cloth, the teenage or young adult daughter receives enormous amounts of validation about her issues with her mother. Like other species of wolves, teenage girls travel in packs. They travel in packs to the women's restroom and they travel in packs to discuss their evil mothers.

September 13th

Stage five of the mother-daughter relationship usually occurs when the daughter becomes a mother herself, as it is not until then that she is able to appreciate anything that her mother has done for her. This, of course, is because of the nature of being a mother. A mother, when she becomes a mother, immediately rises to the exalted status of being a life source. She is the source of milk and warmth. She is our lifeline. She has to love us unconditionally.

This means that if later in life we kill someone in cold blood and in broad daylight that she still has to love us. She doesn't have to agree with what we did but she has to visit us in prison and write every day.

We are born with these expectations of our mothers. We do not like it when dads mess up either, but it is a crime worthy of capital punishment if a mom falls short. As she is only a couple of notches below God in our eyes, when there is pain it runs deep. It is just they way it is.

It is usually not until we are gazing into the eyes of our own infant that we truly get this. There is not a creature on the earth that is more defenseless and vulnerable then a baby human being. We instinctively know this as we felt those little fingers wrap around our heart at birth. Their very existence depends on us. Their health and happiness depend on us.

We must teach them every thing we know about life. We want them to share our values so that they will grow up to be good people, hopefully contributing to the world in their own unique way. We must protect them from the bullies on the playground. We must start saving for college and for that perfect wedding he will have some day. We know deep within ourselves that we could dive in front of a moving train or into shark infested waters to save this child from danger. We glance at him again and realize that he is already a month old. He is growing up way too fast.

September 14th

Go where the love is.

Speaking of love on a higher level, it is of utmost importance to *go where the love is*. This does not mean to completely cash in our chips on challenging individuals. It does not mean to give up trying or not to make an effort, as there are times when there is great pay-off in reaching out. There are certainly times when we can and should love people past their pain.

We are all a mixed bag as they say and most of us are worth giving it that last college try. There are, however, certain individuals who are *toxic* for our spirits and will remain that way for the rest of their days on this earth. It is important to recognize toxic individuals regardless of their place in our families or their roles in our lives, and to stay far away from them. Toxic people are like turpentine running through our spirits. They poison our very essence. They take away from who we are. They weaken us. It is of utmost importance to recognize these people and stay as far away from them as possible.

The flip side of this, of course, is to go where the love is. My husband and I have often been told after a gathering that we have such nice friends. It's true. We do. This is because nice people tend to hang around other nice people.

When we passively allow toxic individuals to enter our inner circle we feel violated. The reason we feel violated is because we *are* being violated. It would be no different than letting a terrorist purchase a ticket for a tour of the White House. We need to give ourselves permission to protect our spirits from emotional perpetrators, regardless of the pressure or manipulation coming from other family members. We may need to dig deeply into ourselves to find our menopausal strength within as well as the blissful confidence that comes with middle age.

When we follow through with such strength, we dis-empower these bullies. We send them on their way to go be hateful to someone else as we are unwilling to accept their animosity. By doing so, we are empowered. It is another deposit in our self-esteem bank. When we remind others that it is a privilege and not a right to be in our lives, we begin to believe this ourselves.

This is *fifteenth principle of the Tao of Menopause-screen your life of toxic individuals and absolve yourself of all guilt for doing so.*

September 15th

Yom Kippur.

The Jewish people really knew what they were doing when they designated September as the month in which to celebrate their new year. September feels like a beginning. For many, school is starting again with the academic calendar becoming the center of many families. The weather is perfect in most places. The sun shines and there is no humidity. Flowers are still in bloom and the nights begin to cool down making it nice for sleeping or a fire in the fire place. September is pleasant.

To begin a new year and a new start seems like a natural thing to do. September invites change. We want to be physically active in the gentle weather that September brings. We walk. We eat healthfully as things are still in season and we are still cooking on the grill. Our mood is good as the sun is shining and it is warm. Making changes or New Year's resolutions feels right in September.

For many of us, however, we prefer to wait until the cold, dark, blustery month of January to make changes when we are kept inside by Winter's powerful vengeance. For some, after indulging ourselves through the holidays we are now burdened with guilt for over-eating, not exercising, and over-spending. Some are in a bad mood due to newly acquired clutter and recent forced visits by toxic family members. It is dark and cold.

Making a change feels as forced and unwanted as Marine boot camp. Making a change also takes the will power and determination of a marine which is why most of us fail. We start a diet which causes us to feel lack and deprivation. We are stuck inside which makes us more apt to over-eat than we would be in the active summer months. Caving in on that miserable diet after only three days makes us feel like an overweight loser with absolutely no sense of self discipline. We carry on daily internal dialogue of how we are fat and will look horrible in a bathing suit. Maybe we should cancel the cruise we just booked. It would be way more productive to stay home and wrestle with our self-loathing cycle.

A Full Moon Rising…and the Tao of Menopause

September 25th

Principal on the run.

I had a nice chat with my mother-in-law last night in regards to menopause and the challenges it brings. We discussed mood swings and feeling so different at times that it is almost as if we are undergoing a complete personality change. My mother-in-law, we call her Ma, began to reflect on how she felt in her forties and told me that she didn't have too many moments of feeling down but that her quills remained high throughout most of the menopausal process.

Ma is retired now after spending nearly thirty years teaching third grade. She remembered sitting in faculty meetings with her fellow colleagues, most of whom she liked, when all of the sudden she would feel her quills rise. They would reach dangerously high levels within seconds, not giving her inner most self a chance to catch up. All she could think about was organic poison and where to get it.

The worst part, she said, was that she usually liked these people. She tried very hard to hold onto these pleasant thoughts, reminding herself of past memories and faculty Christmas parties. The quills, however, gathering their momentum at a rapid rate, quickly take over the shell which is the body and in a robot-like fashion force the legs to stand up and the hands to reach for the jacket pocket which holds the organic poison.

Her fellow faculty members, deeply absorbed in the school politics and curriculum changes, neglect to notice her glowing yellow eyes or the bristly hair gradually making its way out from under the cuff of her powder blue blouse. Her newly done French manicure slowly gives way to sharp, pointed claws. She tries not to grin as her fangs will reveal themselves and her intentions. With frustration she frantically reaches for the last drop of organic poison. They never should have hired that new principal with her issues and new ways of doing things.

September 26th

It is amazing how we write about that which we need to do ourselves as well as about where we are in life. Ma ended up making a visit to her gynecologist and asking for hormones. She said that she could not believe the difference that it made for her. Her quills immediately came down and the new principal made a narrow escape.

Controlling our quills is certainly important as the alternative may be living with a little more structure than we would like for the rest of our lives. It is also important to try very hard to pull ourselves up after feeling low. It is certainly all right to sit with our low feelings for a day or two, sobbing in a hot bubble bath, or listening to bad country songs. But sometimes we need to make a conscious, very disciplined effort to do something to pull ourselves out of it. It is the old theory of "fake it till you make it." Even if we feel like complete crap and not worthy of the ground we are walking on . . . we need to pretend. We need to get up off the floor and act the part.

In fact, my very wise grandmother used to say that is when we feel our worst that we should dress our best. When we feel like a penny waiting for change, it is then that we should dress like Jacqueline Kennedy. Only then will we begin to *feel* like we respect and value ourselves.

My grandmother was a wise lady.

September 27th

I'd swear that the Japanese know everything also. I just got back from having a Reiki treatment and I feel loads better now that my chi is once again flowing smoothly and one with the universe again. According to my Reiki healer, I had several blocks in my energy field.

I could have guessed this as I have felt blocked lately and off center. I think that most of us can relate to feeling off center and not on track at times. It kind of feels like getting off at the wrong exit. You can see the traffic moving steadily on the freeway next to you while you try to figure out just how to get back on. After making a few more wrong turns and several stops at gas stations to ask, our frustration level reaches the sky and choice words begin to leave our mouths. It is so easy to get off track and sometimes so difficult to get back on.

As I mentioned previously, I did not know what I was in for with my first Reiki treatment. I didn't even know what it was or what I should wear. I wasn't sure if it fell more into the massage type category.

For my second treatment, I was asked to sit while my Reiki healer placed his hands on my head. They always begin and end with the head. He simply places his hands on certain areas on the body and with different hand positions. I could feel the heat on my skin. Occasionally I could feel heat in more than one place. Last time it was in my right leg which made sense as I have sciatic nerve pain sometimes due to the birth of my fifth little blessing.

Today I felt heat in the stomach area and my Reiki healer told me that I was *pulling* a lot in that area. His hands were on my back at the time and I felt heat in both places. Last time, I was pulling more from my head area and he said that this represented the *Divine area*. I stopped right there in my tracks when he said this as I had been wrestling with a large amount of guilt over taking a one year break from Sunday school due to being thoroughly overwhelmed with a teenager starting high school and playing on a Division I soccer team, as well as the next one turning into a teenager, as well as three other soccer teams with our elementary and middle school kids.

A Full Moon Rising...and the Tao of Menopause

We live in a very remote area and therefore there is a lot of driving. One day alone I spent five hours in the car. The high schooler popped one of his braces off and the orthodontist is in the opposite direction from his high school which is an hour away from our house. He then had a soccer game after school that was an hour away in an entirely different direction. For years, I felt that I had it all down pretty well and that I was a champion at multi-tasking. This year, I will admit, has been a humbling experience.

After running the adult group at our church for five years and helping last year in my youngest daughter's class I decided that taking a year off from the frantic, very early, mad dash out the door on Sunday after going full speed in a million different directions all week was o.k. It had to be or I was not going to be any good to anyone. I had been operating well beyond my limits for two months since soccer tryouts had started. I was getting snappier and snappier. My ability to be a good mommy was sliding and I could feel myself beginning to get depressed from the loss. I was feeling the loss of our oldest as he was taking a big step going to such a big school and so far away. I was feeling the loss of our old life stage where all five of our children were in the same little school just down the road.

If someone forgot a lunch or sneakers for gym I could run down and drop them off within a few short minutes. This had all changed. It would never be this way again. No more familiar faces in the new school or at soccer games. I was used to screaming for everyone's children. We all did it together. Now I had to look up the number on their shirts, read the name on the program, then yell, and try to do this before the play was over. It also didn't feel the same because I didn't know these kids like I knew the kids at the elementary school. These kids had been over for birthday and Halloween parties forever. We had watched them all in the school concerts since the beginning of time. The high school kids were all new and part of a bigger world, a more adult world.

It took me a while to realize the source of my sadness and to realize that I was grieving the loss of how things used to be and of the control we once had of our small town world.

The very thought of time-slotting every Sunday right now felt to me like a lethal injection. To have the kids miss Sunday school for a whole year made me feel like a bad mother.

All of this had been sitting in my subconscious mind, smoldering like a campfire refusing to go out.

It is quite possible that I was experiencing a *menopausal guilt transfer*. This can happen when your guard is down and you forget to visualize and implement a *proper menopausal force field*.

My parents later verbalized when we were adults, their own guilt for not giving us much spiritual guidance. I then, made it a priority to make sure that our kids went through the whole process, start to finish, and this is why I had such tremendous guilt over taking a break for just one year. I had transferred their guilt to myself and this is what my Reiki healer was noticing.

In fact, my sister even got less religion than I did as I went for a while with the Italians to St. Joseph's.

September 28th

I am realizing that I am in the midst of crossing over and moving through, from one life stage to the next. Even though I still have one foot and a few toes in my previous life stage as I have a six and a nine-year old, things have changed and they have changed forever. Again I am faced with change and the choice to resist or accept.

I stand at the edge of a cliff staring out into the horizon. I am aware of my *halfway-ness* and my mortality. I am aware of being part of Life's process with no beginning and no end. I am aware of my role in the lives of these spirits who have been loaned to me. I am aware of the fluidity of roles and how they change with time. I become aware of entering the world as an infant and leaving as one also.

September 29th

Standing at the edge.

I am no longer standing at the edge of this great cliff with the ocean's waves crashing against the rocks. I am sitting here now with my feet dangling over the edge hundreds of feet up from the foam which has gathered in between the jagged rocks. I look down and realize the potential for an end to my journey at anytime and realize that my end is not up to me. I realize that control does not belong to me and that when it feels as if I have control that it is nothing more than an illusion. This is frightening and yet comfortable at the same time.

Just as young children want control but are unable to handle it. The parent steps in and takes charge.

They feel angry, but safe knowing that they are not in control. A power greater and more knowing will protect them. They close their little eyes and fall fast asleep. We come into the world this way and we leave this way also.

September 30th

Imagine that I sit here on this cliff all because of a teenager going to a large union high school, the oldest of five children beginning to start a life of his own. This is how it happens actually. It is like walking along on a beautifully wooded trail at a nice brisk pace on a cool autumn day when all is well. All of the sudden the root of a tree goes unnoticed and we trip and fall down. The tree is simply trying to grow but it caught us by surprise. It woke us up and forced us to pay attention. The tree root made us realize our footing and our place on the trail. It caused us pain.

Fall

October 1st

Tree roots.

I have never enjoyed tripping on tree roots. I am also aware that I can avoid the experience of tripping on tree roots and falling down by obsessively looking down at my feet as I run. The problem with this of course, is that when we are distracted by looking down and preventing a fall we miss what is in front and all around us. By playing it safe we lose out on the fullness and richness of what surrounds us. When we look down every few seconds to watch out for potential tree roots our attention and energy are fragmented. We know this, on some level, yet it is difficult to keep our eyes focused on what is ahead and to allow our senses to be filled up with all that is in our immediate midst. We do this because we know what pain feels like. We try to avoid what hurts.

The bigger the hurt, the more we try to avoid it.

October 2nd

Cliffs.

I believe this is also true for cliffs. We avoid the edge and looking down. We avoid looking at fierce waves crashing on the jagged rocks below even though their sound is so peaceful that it could lull the most troubled of souls into a deep sleep.

The edge brings with it awareness and many of us do not want to be aware. We don't want to expose our consciousness to where we have been or where we are going.

October 3rd

There are times, such as where I am at the present moment, when my life circumstances lead me to the edge and request that I sit. I do not fall. I sit there full of wonder and fear. I am both comfortable and uncomfortable at the same time.

The waves sooth us. The jagged rocks scare us. We do not fall but the potential for falling is there and keeps us alert and our senses acutely focused. Our fight or flight instinct kicks in. The choice to resist or accept is there, once again. This is a road that we have been down before, many times. On some level we know that in the end resistance does not work. Resistance is futile.

This is why we do our best to avoid cliffs and sitting on the edge.

October 4th

This time of year the leaves begin to change and turn into brilliant colors. I have always enjoyed the change of seasons. Especially the Autumn season seems to bring with it a desire to reflect and be contemplative. It is a season that feels deeply spiritual.

The seasons also seem to be somewhat symbolic of our existence as a whole. We are born in the Spring, then enjoy the light, carefree Summer season of our childhood where we sit barefoot in the grass and eat hamburgers and delicious veggies from the garden.

When Autumn arrives, we put on a sweater and go hiking in the woods. We are surrounded by color and rich natural beauty. We are aware of our surroundings more than ever before. We take in and savor the details of our atmosphere.

We think about how we enjoyed the summer and how it was too short. There was so much more that we had wanted to do.

We then return to the present because we realize that with all of these bold colors and the richness that is infiltrating our senses, that there is truly no where that we would rather be than right here and right now. We become aware of the *Power of Now* and embrace it. We want to slow Autumn down. In our middle life, we savor this season.

October 5th

The seasons of life.

Before long, the wind begins to pick up and the brilliant colors of the Autumn foliage fall gently to the ground. Another season and another time in our lives has now gone by. We can only revisit this time in our lives in our mind's eye. We now have only memories of the Autumn season.

Summer seems even farther away. We open a photo album and glance back on how much fun we had at the beach, the sunshine, all of the barbecues in the backyard and the friends we had over, and the simplicity of shorts and flip-flops.

Occasionally, when we allow our lives to get too complicated, we miss our flip-flops. Sometimes we miss our flip-flops very much. We want them back, but what we are left with is snow boots, lots of layers of clothing, and a heavy jacket.

When we think of flip-flops it causes us to resist snow boots. This can make us feel resentful.

October 6th

As we have now lived through three seasons, we are well aware of ourselves and of the source of resentment and spiritual discomfort. We know that this type of discontent comes from trying to live in more than one season at a time.

We know that spiritual discomfort comes from a lack of acceptance.

At this stage of the game we know better than to resist snow boots.

October 7th

Snow boots.

Not only do we know better than to resist snow boots, but we know that snow boots are valuable in their own right and they have a time and a purpose just as flip-flops have their own time and purpose. We kick ourselves as this is a life lesson that we have already learned. This is simply a review or a revisiting of a place we have already been.

Of course, once we release Autumn with a grateful heart for all it had given to us and for all it had done to enrich our lives, we return to Winter.

The wind picks up and the temperature drops. The snow falls gently to the ground and it relaxes us to watch it out the window. We think about snowflakes and how there are no two snowflakes in existence that are exactly the same.

We put on our snow boots and lace them up so they are snug and comfortable. They feel warm. Our feet feeling warm makes our whole body feel warm. We walk outside and head out for a walk in the woods. Our feet landing in the freshly fallen snow feels new. Everything around us feels new. New, yet seasoned and wise. It is white and beautiful, a winter wonderland.

We continue our walk. The woods are so peaceful during a snow fall. It feels as if you can almost hear the quiet. We are grateful for winter and for our snow boots.

October 8th

The decade of *judgment*.

Today I woke up feeling like the *Judgment Queen* of the universe. I have heard this about the forties. In fact I got a fortune cookie last weekend that said, "In the 20's humor reigns, in the 30's wit, and in the 40's judgment." Isn't that the truth . . .

I would really like to meet the fortune cookie people some day, the wisdom behind the wafer.

October 9th

Fortune cookies.

As I picture the fortune cookie people diligently working in their fortune cookie factories, I cannot help to wonder where they get their wisdom. Some of them sit there typing. Others cut the words of wisdom into little slips of paper. Others wrap them gently into the fortune cookie dough.

Then there is the actual baking staff. They make the dough, put the cookies in the oven and take them out when they are ready. They roll them into those wanton shapes. Still others wrap them up in individual plastic baggies, stuff them into boxes, and then ship them out to Chinese restaurants everywhere.

What I have always been curious about is the brains behind the wafer and who is coming up with these wise words to live by. I picture a little Asian man or woman, either Taoist or Buddhist, sitting there quietly on a floor pillow with incense and candles lit all around.

They are unaware of the chaos of the world because they have closed the door on it. They eat a nearly pure diet and allow no toxins into their bodies. Material things do not matter to them.

Some how they know to whom these fortunes are going. They have fortune cookie insight. The cookie I got this weekend was just right for me at this time in my life. This is usually how it is with fortune cookies. It is just the right cookie for the one who opens it. It is quite amazing when you stop to think about it.

October 10th

The gloves are off.

So anyway, as far as the *judgment phase* is concerned, well, it just sort of happens and it is part of the whole inner warming process. I think what the urge to judge is all about, is that during our forties we become very self aware.

There is no more pretending.

Many of us know who we are at this point along our mid-life journey and many of us think that we know who other people are also. Either that, or we are annoyed that they do not know who they are. We wonder why they continue to do the same stupid things in their relationships when it is so obvious that it isn't working for them.

Things become crystal clear to us and we get frustrated that others do not have the clarity that we do.

If only they had our wisdom.

October 11th

Last night a few of us went out to dinner. We were having the urge to judge so we went to a restaurant a couple of towns over. *Dirt and dessert* we call it . . .

It can be challenging to judge others at restaurants in your own town as there is always the risk of being over heard. Certainly no one wants that. Our own personal critiques of the lives of others need to be kept private and several towns away.

It is far too stressful to keep looking over your shoulder or to wonder if the waitress is listening.

October 12th

I rethought our discussion from last night's judgment session. As I was about to get my period, I was feeling a bit more critical and judgmental than I would be on a day during peacetime or a crescent moon. For some strange reason, my quills were at moderate levels. Hormones do not have any rhyme or reason to their madness.

Even when our quills are moderate, it is difficult to resist the urge to judge as we are in our forties. This is the judgment decade. It is actually not much different than having the urge to go out on the town in our late teens and early twenties, or to reproduce in our mid to late twenties and thirties, or to travel the world in our fifties and sixties. The forties is a decade where we become very self aware and then get irritated with those around us who resist making really obvious changes in their lives.

There are those who are self-disciplined and say nothing, not even to their *safe* people who they know are air tight and would take the information to their graves. They appear to be above judgment, but not to be fooled. These people are self aware also. These women know who they are. Their minds are full of clarity and opinions.

The girl scout leader next door who is on her third husband and yet continues to spend way too much time with her personal trainer. The other neighbor goes to *Fat Class* every Wednesday night because her husband has asked her to slim down. The delivery guy from the Italian restaurant down the street stops by her house each day at noon. She tips him big as if to stick another pin in a doll that resembles her husband. She sits on her couch enjoying her calzone with extra sauce while the bastard is at work.

There is a lot to say about the goings on in the neighborhood, yet the select few, the *menopausal elite* remain silent.

October 13th

Repressed judgment.

When thinking about the menopausal elite I almost want to think of the Buddhist monks in Tibet. They live on bugs and berries all day long while sitting in what would appear to be very unnatural and painful positions. They exist at a higher level of being, part of the world yet free from its chaos.

For Buddhist monks, however, they get to this state by prayer and meditation and a desire to be at peace with their universe.

Menopausal women who refrain from expressing their judgment are biting their lips until they bleed. They are dying to say what they think but just cannot bring themselves to do it. They listen to the conversations at dinner, collecting their opinions. Their opinions sit in a mental file, in alphabetical order for a later date when they can be discussed openly, possibly after three or four margaritas.

October 16th

I have had a very productive day thus far. I was up with the moon, a crescent moon thankfully, and the stars to drive the teenager to his bus stop. If we oversleep, the entire day is affected as his high school is an hour away, so the pressure is on.

The moon and the stars were very bright. If I didn't know better I would have thought that it was midnight. But no, it was the very ugly, heinous hour of 5:00 am.

Once I drop him off, and finish a cup of coffee which at this hour is as necessary as oxygen, I am of course awake.

This morning just seemed to start off with a bang. I woke up to several professional e-mails, one specifically catching my attention. The director of a large New York Agency was asking if I would come down and do a training for their therapists and addictions staff who treat adolescents. I was immediately flattered and excited as I am very passionate about parenting and treating teens in today's fast-paced and uncertain world.

I then reflected on this contact, as my mother also runs training programs for professionals and has established quite a good reputation for herself. It was my mother who dropped my name when she was running one of her own programs.

I was having a grateful moment. A door had been opened for me and an opportunity had been offered to me due to the efforts of someone else.

I then began to think of how we can only take so much credit for what we do, any of us, no matter how much we have accomplished in life.

The reason being, that all of us get where we are going by the help of other people. Even if we feel that we have never received help from a soul and we are self made, we still, at the very least, had to have some key moves fall into place. This help may even have come from strangers whom we will never meet, but each of us is connected to the other.

We all have our gifts, but they are only as good as the people behind us.

October 17th

I had another grateful moment. I love it when that happens. I got to thinking about what a gift it is to use our gifts.

All of us have something to offer this world, and it is such a privilege to be able to do so. When we are following our authentic path, we feel *on*. We are in sync with ourselves and with the universe around us. There is no where else we would rather be then in our own skin, experiencing a true joyful moment that can only happen from using our authentic gifts, unique only to us.

A true joyful moment is difficult to put into words. It can be felt right in the area where the hearts is and gratitude resides.

October 18th

Tabitha.

I woke up this morning and realized that the changes in the local wind patterns were nothing more than our teenage daughter whipping her wand around in her bedroom. It is definitely a bit of a *Divine joke* if you think about it. Teenagers tossed into a family with all of their hormones wildly running through their veins while simultaneously living with and being managed by a mother going through menopause with her estrogen levels plummeting each second. The timing of adolescence and menopause is almost humorous, though it certainly does not seem that way at times, or most of the time.

We can only be grateful when hand guns and all sharp objects have been removed from the immediate atmosphere.

October 19th

Well, Tabitha is back at it again today, circling on her teenage broom annoyed with both of her parents and with life in general. The heavy sighs and eye-rolls have now given way to door slams. One more slam and Miss Tabitha may come home from school to a *door-less* room . . .

This means that there will be no more sacrificing of small animals in privacy.

She will not like this and will then hopefully alter her behavior in order to *earn* her door back. This is our plan.

October 20th

I was thinking of throwing some garlic cloves around the perimeter of her doorway and maybe the entire downstairs living area just to keep the evil demons at bay until my husband and I can brainstorm some ideas to deal with our little darling.

The *bless in the mess*, as they say, is that teenaged girls force us to grow. They force us to come up with new ideas and keep us on our toes as parents.

Parental stagnancy is not possible if you have teenaged girls.

October 21st

Teen demons.

I couldn't find *exorcism* listed in the yellow pages anywhere. Tomorrow I will call around to some local churches to see if there is a priest available who specializes in expelling unwanted demon spirits from teenaged girls. I was thinking of calling some of the mothers of her friends. Maybe we can get a group rate.

October 22nd

Here we go again. It seems as if it is a teenager's job in life to challenge her parents to grow, especially her mother. Everything that used to work well no longer does. All bearings have been lost as we have now landed in the deep end of the ocean without a compass.

October 23rd

On a more positive note, at least I won't have to buy Miss Tabitha a costume for Halloween this year. She *is* her costume.

October 24th

Once again I was talked into having a Halloween party. Our middle daughter had the idea of having *her people* only as the older ones had had a good deal of attention on them recently. Our oldest two children have birthdays in September and early November, and both played soccer so we ran around to watch all of their games. The middle man also played soccer so we ran around and watched him also.

In an attempt to be good parents, and to avoid a future therapy bill, we agreed to allow child number four to have her own Halloween party as long as she agreed to allow child number five to have a hand full of her people also. With a bit of hesitation and tightly folded arms she complied and we began the planning.

October 25th

Well, we went to the drug store, which is pretty much the choice in northern Vermont, and left with arm loads of skeleton goblets, pumpkin plates, and pounds and pounds of white, refined sugar. I could land myself on Mayberry's most wanted list after these kids are returned to their parents, each under the influence and in a sugar trance. Of course the sugar trance is not nearly as bad as the sugar crash which follows shortly after the high reaches its peak.

October 26th

The list is getting longer. My patience is growing shorter.

October 27th

Tiffany.

The Halloween party hostess, currently nine years old was on the phone with Tiffany, her very closest friend. Tiffany is very sweet. She and our daughter look like Mutt and Jeff when they are together as Tiffany towers over our little Shannie. Miss Tiffany has always felt not only an allegiance to Shannie but also somewhat of an *ownership*. Shannie having a Halloween party meant that Tiffany was a co-host of the event, automatically and without discussion.

Little did I know that Tiffany's gears had been turning and her creative energy flowing. I was not aware of this until I looked up from a project I was working on to a disgruntled nine-year old tapping her foot nervously in the doorway, again with tightly folded arms. She looked nervous and a bit indignant.

She looked to the right, then to the left, followed by a *not sure if I should confess this to my mother sigh*. Then she spilled it. "You are not going to *believe* what Tiffany did," she sighed, again with an indignant tone.

I was afraid to ask. Shannie continued, "Tiffany sent out *her own* invitations to the Halloween party . . ."

October 28th

I woke up hoping that the saga from my last night's memory was nothing more than a bad dream, that Tiffany had indeed sent out her own batch of invitations to additional children under the age of ten as if the list was not lengthy enough. I was also wondering how she knew the date and time as we had just decided this.

As it turns out, Tiffany did not know the date or the time. I know this because I called her mother in an attempt to do damage control and prevent Miss Tiffany from inviting any more children, endearing though she was. Otherwise, we may have needed to move the Halloween party to the elementary school gym.

Tiffany's mother was not home, so I talked with the party planner herself. She had put on her invitations that the party was on Sunday and with an open ended time. The party, was in fact to take place on Saturday night from 5:00 until 7:00 pm. Now may be a good time to start calling parents to clear up the confusion.

Before I got a chance to reach for the phone it started ringing. This would be parent number one. She called because her daughter had received two invitations to the same party. Tiffany's invitation also mentioned that there would be a variety show and that prizes would be awarded for the best act.

Some day this will be a funny story.

October 29th

The *Brooks Lady*.

Back to *Brooks Pharmacy* I went, hoping that they had not completely run out of skeleton goblets and cauldrons. As it turned out,

Shannie and I got really lucky. The cauldrons were all gone, but they had mummies and they were the same size and capable of holding the same amount of candy corn. They would work just fine. Not only that, but everything was on clearance now that Halloween was three seconds away.

I noticed the *Brooks Lady* watching us inquisitively. She stared as we walked up and down the isle frantically grabbing what was left of the scarcely stocked shelves.

As we approached the counter, the *Brooks Lady* couldn't help herself and mentioned that she had just seen us last week with arm loads of pumpkin plates and skeleton cups, and wondered why we were back. Only in rural, northern Vermont is one quizzed about one's purchases. People notice things up here.

So, we went on to explain the whole story about Tiffany, the extra invitations, the wrong date and time, the variety show, and the prizes. As I looked up, the *Brooks Lady* had made herself quite comfortable behind the counter and was entrenched in our Halloween saga.

She looked up over her glasses, staring in partial disbelief as she eyed my arm load of purchases. As she began to scan each item, slowly and thoroughly, she began to offer tips as far as how to survive it all. She also let me know that each and every item was now on clearance and exactly how much I was saving on each one.

I could tell that she would be looking forward to the story's happy ending the next time we came to *Brook's Pharmacy*. I will have to make sure to allot myself that extra time, so that I can tell the conclusion of our Halloween saga to the *Brooks Lady* with great expression and special effect.

October 30th

Well, today is the day, the moment we have all been waiting for . . . and it is a monsoon outside. The wind is gusting at 70 miles per hour. The trees are waving back and forth frantically and the rain is coming down at a forty-five degree angle. Maybe some kind hearted soul will slip me a mickie . . .

In northern Vermont, when the power goes out there is no telling when it will come back on, if ever. Occasionally, there may be a bit of a tease when the lights flicker or they even come on entirely only to go out minutes later and immerse us in darkness once again.

Just as with anything else, it is the not knowing part that drives us northerners crazy and of course the timing of the power going out is always impeccable. If we had nothing planned, with only our five children and a good Italian take-out place near by, we could sit and enjoy each other by candlelight, sharing stories and bonding in an *eighteen hundreds sort of way*.

When the threat, however, of the power going out happens when we are expecting twenty-two children under the age of ten to show up dressed as witches and goblins we do not greet the opportunity with the same kind of excitement or enthusiasm. We instead light a candle for serenity and the strength to get through the next few hours.

The next step, is to pour a really tall glass of wine and to search the junk door for a straw.

October 31st

Happy Halloween! And it is a happy Halloween indeed as there is no such thing as a small miracle. The power managed to stay on thank God.

November 1st

Outside of the whole party thing, I do so enjoy the actual day of Halloween itself. Some people get really deep about it and boycott the whole thing as they believe that it is worshipping the *dark side* or something. How unfortunate. For us, it is all about candy and costumes. It is so fun to be someone else for one day, and to let your inner child out to play.

In our town, people really get into decorating. The carved pumpkins are works of art. The yards and houses are very inviting, in a sort of haunted way. Some of the *candy-giver-outers* get all dressed up to play the role. There are sound effect machines on many of the porches just to add to the overall experience. Some have mist that slowly leeks out as you dare to walk up their sidewalk. You see, in our town you have to earn your candy.

No guts, no treats.

Each Halloween I can't help but to think of Pony Boy and the Rosenbergs. Those memories will be with me forever.

November 2nd

It seems like after Halloween a gun goes off and the race to Christmas begins. It starts off as a sprint, gaining speed with each day. We then round the corner of Thanksgiving and take off for the home stretch. I am tired already.

November 3rd

Today I am off to the big city. This is just a little rural humor. Burlington is about one hour away from our tiny little town with an approximate population of a thousand. In fact, it is quite possible that we have more cows than people.

Of course, there are days when my quills are somewhat high and I prefer cows to people. Lately I have been having more and more days like this.

I love Vermont, but sometimes I crave the anonymity of Manhattan. It is so enjoyable to sit on a bench and watch people all day long and guess what their lives are. I crave great bagels made with bad water. Then I come home to our wooded heaven and I am glad to do so.

We went into Manhattan a lot as kids. We used to go to Yankee games in the summer. In fact, my little sister was sure that she would be the first female Yankee. She had pictures all over her bedroom walls of the 1978 Yankee line-up. When Thurman Munson died she did not come out of her room for three whole days. No joke. We were all worried about her.

What was great about the Yankee games was that our organic mother stayed home which was good, as much as we loved her, because this way Dad could be *Fun Guy* and buy us all of the hot dogs and crap that we could eat in one day. I am not sure we even knew who won at the end of the game. We were so zoned out on junk that we were in a trance.

The stadium vendors would yell, "Getcha ice cold be-ah he-ah . . ." We looked forward to this every summer.

In fact, one day as we were leaving the stadium we saw a crowd gathered out in front. Of course we were curious as it was New York after all and this could be *somebody*. It was. It was former President Nixon shortly after he had resigned. What a huge head he had. People were surrounding him on all sides and it was exciting.

Another time we saw Joan Jett in the box seats. We were always in the low rent district of the stadium which our dad had labeled *the nose bleed section* as we were so high up. Birds and helicopters flew below us. Then, after the third inning we would move closer. He taught us to walk down the stairs with confidence and then enter the box seat area without making eye contact. This way people would know that we were season pass holders so it didn't matter if we came in after the third inning. When you are a season pass holder you can be on your own schedule and people look up to you with admiration and reverence.

This is true unless the real owners of the box seats arrive right after you. Then they very politely go and get a stadium usher who then asks to see your tickets in front of all who can hear them. Rather than show him our bleacher tickets in the high altitude section, we simply get up and proceed back to our own neighborhood making no eye contact of course. No eye contact is the key to avoiding complete humiliation, especially with our fellow Yankee fans yelling *busted* at the top of their lungs.

You have got to love Yankee fans. They are who they are. They don't care about what they say and they don't care who's listening.

In our section of the bleachers they smoked joints. This is probably because the beer guys didn't want to climb that high carrying those heavy coolers.

I also used to look forward to Billy Martin getting fired. This was a fairly regular occurrence and was very entertaining. He would storm out onto the field and kick dirt on the umpires. He would get right in their faces and say choice words and then get thrown out of the game. The crowd would go crazy as they loved the drama of it all. They even had a *Billy's Back Day* where everyone in the stadium got a *Billy's Back* t-shirt. I wish I still had that shirt. It would be worth a fortune.

This is how it is with Yankee fans. They are loyal to their rogue, actively alcoholic coaches. They smoke joints around small children in the bleachers, and they hate the Red Sox. This, of course, is the primary requirement of a Yankee fan. You must hate the Red Sox with all of your heart and soul.

The hatred for the Red Sox is thrown into our bodies with our spirits. It comes from a place of which we are unaware, but has always been and always will be. It all started the day the Bambino crossed over from the *dark side*.

We also went to the Bronx Zoo. One day we went and the Polar Bears were having sex. I love New York.

November 4th

Now I have to make a trek to the grocery store. The teenager is going to have his birthday party this weekend. He will be fifteen. Monday he goes for his driver's permit test. It is hard to believe that our oldest will be driving in less than a week. Time seems to be flying by.

Time seems to be flying by because it *is* flying by.

It seems like we just had our first child. Now he is in high school and about to get his driver's permit. Next week he will go to college, and a week from next Tuesday we will be grandparents. This is how it feels. It feels fast.

It seemed like it was just yesterday that my friend and I were stealing our parents' cars. I even had my own set of keys made. This is because my parents were in the middle of a really ugly, nasty divorce and I was pissed off. I had parties every time they left the house and I took the car. I did this because I didn't like them.

One day, we *borrowed* my friend's dad's car. It was a Toyota Celica and it was a stick shift. We did pretty well considering neither one of us had a license yet. We drove all the way over to the race track in

Monticello. We didn't have to worry because her dad was at work and didn't get home until later in the evening so we had plenty of time.

We did manage to hit a couple of meridians and a drive-thru but thankfully there was no lasting damage. We stopped and got some chips and soda and blasted the radio with the windows open. My friend was pissed off at her parents also. This made it all right to borrow their car because they were rotten parents also and they should be punished.

We pulled in after our little adventure with plenty of time to spare, or so we thought. Her dad, Big Franco, was waiting for us in the doorway. He had come home early from work for a dentist appointment and parked the other car on the side of the house to fool us into thinking the coast was clear.

This would be the end of our summer together as my friend was grounded for three months, possibly the rest of her life and not allowed to hang out with me ever again, possibly longer. She whispered in my ear as she entered the house that I could have her *Fry boots*.

She knew how much I liked those boots. It was her living will.

November 5th

Happy Birthday Ryan!

I love birthdays and have always made a huge deal out of each and every one our kids' birthdays. This is because birthdays are not achievement oriented. Instead, they are a celebration of who we are as well as another year of health. This is also because I do not want our five children to be in therapy later in life because they are from a large family and feel that they did not get enough attention.

November 6th

Awakened by extraordinarily high quills.

Here I am in the middle of the night with extraordinarily high quills. The experience of high quills is enough for almost any mid-lifer to handle, however, high quills occurring during the middle of the night is all that much worse. They have an intensity that is far stronger than that of even the highest of day time quills.

The reason for this intensity is due to the subconscious mind. Whenever the subconscious mind is involved with quills the reaction is far more intense as the subconscious stores and builds. Storing and building are dangerous things, especially when it comes to anger molecules and quills.

Add to the recipe that the holidays are around the corner and there is sure to be a disaster.

In addition, and of far more menopausal significance is the fact that the full moon will be entering into the fire sign of Sagittarius. Anyone who knows a Sagittarian, knows that they are complex individuals. They are born leaders, highly creative, and have an innate zest for life. They are also strong, passionate, and have a tendency to have complicated lives. Nothing is easy with a Sagittarius, though they are also the types of friends you would want to have as they will fight to the death for anyone considered to be *their people*.

Knowing a Sagittarius can be of great benefit or tremendous detriment depending on which side of their circle you fall into.

They also have an insatiable *wander lust*.

As I am a Sagittarius, it would make sense that I was awakened by extraordinarily high quills and without warning. I think I will plan a trip somewhere, anywhere.

If the trip idea doesn't work out, maybe I'll torment a few P.T.O. members. P.T.O. members are like catnip for the Sagittarian.

Aunt Marla is not only completely oblivious to the moon's schedule but she also has a tendency to reside in my subconscious. In fact, not only is she residing there, but she has her own cot and extra set of clean sheets. She occasionally has her mail forwarded there when she stays for long periods of time.

The thing is that Aunt Marla goes through phases where she behaves herself and all is somewhat peaceful. I have always tried to enjoy these times of peace. The only problem is when things have been too easy for too long that I get out of *Aunt Marla shape* and my guard is down.

It is when my guard is down that I am vulnerable to Aunt Marla maneuvers.

This is what had made my quills high to begin with. Then, when the moon entered into Sagittarius, I began to feel the anger molecules racing through my veins as the power emerged from deep within. We feel the energy within like hot lava on the verge of erupting. We bubble and spit behind our glowing yellow eyes.

To be a menopausal Sagittarian when the full moon enters your sign is to be omnipotent. No one is safe, especially not telemarketers, P.T.O. people, and politicians. If they are smart they will run, hide, and wait for the moon to enter the next phase.

With Aunt Marla, I always know that it is just a matter of time. I always know that it will rain eventually. I just don't know how much or when.

It has rained and it is a down pour.

November 7th

Boy does she tick me off. I honestly do not understand people like Aunt Marla. Things are so much easier when people play nice. She is a woman of many issues. In fact, I think that she is an *issue junky*. Aunt Marla can only go so long without issues and things being smooth and peaceful within the family.

If things do not go her way, she will need to find a way to force it. She will pull out all stops to get what she wants. I do not like people like this, but they do cause a person to grow as we are challenged to figure out a way to deal with their behavior.

Sometimes I grow tired of life lessons, especially during the holidays.

November 8th

My quills continue to be high and this is not good as it is difficult to remain out of the public at this time of year. I will have to make a concentrated effort to attempt to control my quills, at least long enough to purchase a turkey.

November 9th

I have decided not to get into what Aunt Marla did to tick me off as it was just another Aunt Marla maneuver, and discussing it will only give it further energy. As my grandmother used to say *less said soonest mended* . . .

My grandmother was a wise lady.

November 10th

I now need to focus my efforts on enjoying the very small window before Thanksgiving, and it is a small window. Soon things will begin to pick up. There are only a few more days remaining where I will be able to cast the impending stress out of my mind as the week before the big day is when it all begins.

It will start with a grocery list. There are two times a year when I make a grocery list, now and Christmas.

November 11th

Little weenies. I woke up thinking about little weenies, a sure sign that the impending holiday stress is creeping its way into my subconscious. People love *piggies in a blanket* which is why I make them every year as an appetizer.

Little weenies have become my holiday signature trademark.

November 12th

The lesson.

The teenager flunked his driver's permit test so we are off for his second attempt today. The lady at the DMV said that it is the *honor roll curse* as they see this all the time with straight A kids. They get used to coasting with minimal effort and then assume that the driver's permit will be the same, and of course, it is not.

I tried to explain this to the teenager, but the very nature of a teenager prevents him from internalizing and validating this useful information. At least I did not have to say *I told you so*, as this message was intrinsic to the results.

I am bringing along a couple of friends for emotional support and lunch. If by some chance we end up making a third trip over the mountain to the DMV, the teenager will be responsible for all testing fees, lunch, and travel expenses, including mileage.

November 13th

He passed it. Actually he aced it. It was like he was on a mission or something after the very humbling first experience.

We all enjoyed lunch also. Any excuse to go out for lunch works for me. It is certainly cheaper than therapy.

November 14th

Sneak attack.

Panic has set in. Apparently I have had not a hint of *calendar awareness*. I was thinking that I had two and a half weeks until the fleet of relatives descend upon us. Then my husband said something the other night about a week from Thursday, and I felt a chill race down my spine. This had to be a mistake, or horrible untruth.

I haven't even had a chance to make it to *TJ Maxx* to get napkin holders or plates with little turkeys on them. I wonder if they will have any left or if I will be at the mercy of the clearance table.

November 15th

Strange thing, calendar awareness . . . With it, one has the world by the ass and without it there is stress and chaos. I will make a note for next year.

November 16th

Tomorrow I will head to the big city to immerse myself in porcelain pilgrims and cornucopias filled with plastic fruit.

I love Thanksgiving.

November 17th

The only porcelain pilgrims left unfortunately had a couple of chips in various places, though the good news is that the *TJ Maxx Lady* took off an additional ten percent, a basic win-win situation.

November 18th

Take your mark. Get set. Go!

Well, here we are again . . . ready to enter the holiday race. It goes like this . . . "Moms, please approach the starting gate. Be careful not to push or shove the opponent next to you. You must navigate the obstacles along the track with grace, speed, and agility. This includes the cookie baking challenge, turkey basting, gourmet appetizer sweepstakes, the how to create a new and exciting recipe for your veggies contest, and last but not least, managing challenging family members during the stressful holiday season.

Each contestant will be judged on how they manage each of these obstacles and will be awarded points based on their degrees of grace and dignity, as well as their overall ability to multi-task. Now, mothers, take your mark, get set, go . . ."

And we're off . . . This is where we begin to practice the art of Chinese expulsion on a daily basis. Women across the country can be seen pressing their fingers firmly between their thumb and forefinger on the opposite hand. Some of them may even be whispering incantations simultaneously as they focus on relieving themselves of these stressful individuals.

This method is way better than Tai Chi or Yoga or any of the other forms or techniques of relaxation. This is because Chinese expulsion yields tangible results. Of course, there can be no malice on the part of the expeller. We do not want to reduce ourselves to that, unless of course, we are having a day where our quills are particularly high or if the moon is full, in which case we are often unable to help ourselves.

If this is the case, then we are to give ourselves a *menopausal pardon*, as we know not what we do. The reason that we are given a *menopausal pardon* is simply that people should be aware of high quills and full moons and keep a distance, just like people should know enough to stay out of the woods during hunting season. If you take walks in the woods during hunting season then it is your own fault if you get shot. The logic is the same for approaching menopausal club members with high quills.

Using the art of Chinese expulsion is also a lot better than sticking pins in dolls that resemble our irritating family members. It is far more discreet. Not only that, but for those of us who don't know how to sew, it is much easier. We simply press the area between our thumb and forefinger while focusing on the challenging individual disappearing from existence, not painfully, as disappearing is enough. All we are after is mental health and freedom from these fire-breathers.

Advanced expellers will often receive a phone call from the unwanted individual the day before Thanksgiving. They will say that they received an unexpected invitation from an old friend and will be going there instead. The unwanted individual will delight in rejecting your invitation. Meanwhile, the expeller is doing a victory dance in the kitchen while singing cheerfully into the *turkey-baster-gone-microphone*. The best part of the whole process is that the challenging family member truly believes that *they chose this*, that they actually had control over their own destiny. They are not aware in any way that they are merely another victim of menopausal voodoo . . . one of many . . .

November 19th

Top secret recipe.

I don't know what happened. Yesterday I felt just fine and dandy and today I woke up with high quills. They are quite high actually, so I have once again tried to remain out of the public eye.

I have already received e-mails about who is bringing what to Thanksgiving. Aunt Marla always seems to want to bring beets. No one ever eats them, especially after they traveled all the way from Teaneck, New Jersey. The beet is quite a horrid vegetable when it is fresh, so an eight-hour car ride only brings out the worst as far as I am concerned.

Aunt Marla, however, will go on and on about tradition, her secret spices, and the importance of keeping things the same year after year. After all, Squanto introduced the beet to the Pilgrims. If it wasn't for the beet the Pilgrims never would have survived. Beets were at the very first Thanksgiving and they will be at every Thanksgiving until the end of time. Beets are a large part of our heritage.

Not only that, but Aunt Marla believes they have medicinal purposes. Maybe they do.

Whether beets can cure cancer or not, no one has ever been able to tolerate Aunt Marla's top secret beet recipe, so each and every year we have to get even more creative as far as how we get rid of the beets without leaving a trace. Last year, we almost got busted, but thankfully we had a very altruistic Golden Retriever who helped out. Although, just a few short moments after he lapped up the beet purée, the poor thing was whimpering by the door to go outside. He was fine after he chewed on a little grass, but I still felt bad for him. No wonder dogs are a woman's best friend. They are loyal straight to the end, even if it means eating Aunt Marla's beets. Of course, none of us have ever had enough guts to let Aunt Marla know that it was corn that Squanto introduced to the Pilgrims, but then again, it really isn't all that important.

November 20th

Red wine and reverence.

Exactly five days from today the relatives will descend upon us, some carrying mysterious beet recipes and some with wine. Wine is always welcome in our home. In fact, I do not believe that wine gets the proper attention it deserves either. We should have a *Wine Appreciation Day* and it should be celebrated somewhere in mid-

November prior to the holiday madness, the cleaning, the shopping, the baking, the cooking, and the challenging dinner guests.

Wine warms us up from the inside out, and right in the chest area. It's kind of like Vicks Vapo-rub only better. It also helps those of us who are mere beginners at the art of Chinese expulsion. After eagerly walking around town pinching the area between our thumb and forefinger hoping that the Aunt Marlas of the world get some kind of unexpected dinner invitation to anywhere, many of us resort to a couple of very tall glasses of *juice*. We are immediately warmed from within and much better able to deal with challenging dinner guests. If we get really lucky, the challenging dinner guests will slug down a glass or two themselves, making things easier for everyone around them.

Of course, from a health standpoint, the benefits of red wine are tremendous, especially for women. Red wine is the reason that the French live so long, even though they exist on artery-clogging diets of buttery crescents, cheeses and creamy everything. The French live long and they don't get fat, and they have red wine to thank for it.

It is said that two glasses of wine each day will keep the cardiologist away. It will flush out all unwanted cholesterol leaving one's arteries smooth and free-flowing for circulation. If this is true, than a small bus would not have an ounce of difficulty navigating its way through my arteries, especially during the holiday season. It is also said that more than two glasses can diminish these benefits and actually have the reverse effect. I think I'll get a bigger glass.

November 21st

The Pilgrims.

I have just uncovered a horrible truth. Our nine-year-old's book order came in yesterday chock full of Thanksgiving books as well as books on four different Native American tribes. She just could not wait to plunge into the one about the pilgrims as they had spent all week studying all that these brave people had endured over four hundred years ago. It is truly amazing when we stop to think about it. According to this book, one of the things that the Pilgrims were most thankful for was water, as the water was so contaminated over in England.

In fact, the children were the most thankful for their newfound land and natural springs because they no longer had to drink beer for breakfast. Apparently beer was considered more healthy back then, primarily because it was free of the dysentery causing bacteria that frequently took lives.

I also learned by reading to my fourth-grader, that Squanto's real name was really Tisquantum and that he had spent a large portion of his life in England. He was kidnapped as a young boy and it was years before he was able to escape his captors and make it back to his tribe. At this point, he was able to speak English fairly well and help the Pilgrims.

At the back of the book there were two pages with food on them, one with pictures of everything the Pilgrims ate more than four hundred years ago and the other of what we eat now on Thanksgiving Day. It is amazing how much we have all changed things. The only similarity I could see was the turkey. They had bread also, but they didn't roll those neat little triangular pieces created by the Pillsbury Dough Boy and stick them into their preheated, digital ovens. It probably took them a day or two just to grind the flour and churn the butter.

For me, it takes exactly eight minutes at 350 degrees.

As we may guess, the Pilgrims ate lots of seafood including clams, seas bass, and cod. They ate deer meat.

They ate cornmeal made out of Indian corn, much different than the perky little yellow kernels that we are so used to today. They also ate some kind of pumpkin hash, the forerunner to Mrs. Smith's frozen pumpkin pies available in your grocer's freezer everywhere. And here is the worst part . . . on the page of foods eaten at the very first Thanksgiving . . . right before my very eyes . . . was the beet. And just when I thought I knew my veggie history.

Aunt Marla was right all along even if her mysterious beet recipe could be used as a secret weapon against the terrorists. The Taliban could be wiped out in one shot if they were forced to consume Aunt Marla's infamous beet purée. This should be worth considering.

November 22nd

November.

Good Morning God! I just got back from the most brilliant early morning walk. The sun was just barely climbing up and over the mountains casting its rusty glow upon the silver November trees. The bare trees shimmered as the sun awakened them from their late Fall slumber, even if only for a moment. I have always loved the color of November.

Some people may not have noticed that November has a *color*, but it does. It definitely does. It is a color that is sort of rust-ish and sort of glow-ish, but difficult to put into words. It is a color that is contemplative and spiritual. More than likely, Land's End or L.L. Bean will figure it out and it will become a staple color in their holiday catalog, kind of like the color *sea foam* was in their summer edition. I think that the color should simply be called *November*. Personally, I wear earth tones quite well, and would gladly order a sweater or jacket in *November*. The color *November* would also blend well with ivory and olive green. Maybe I should start a company.

Of course the whole reason that I escaped for an early morning walk other than the gorgeous sunrise, was that I was beginning to feel an *ADD wave* coming on. I was the lucky winner in the Attention-Deficit Disorder lottery at a very young age, and now thankfully, as an adult, have learned to manage it quite well. Just as with diabetes, those of us with ADD cannot be *cured* from the racing thoughts that fly through our minds all day long without ceasing. We can only learn to manage our condition so that we are able to live more joyfully and function with greater ease.

The ADD wave was of course triggered by the impending mental doom of juggling thirty guests for Thanksgiving as well as the obvious advanced multi-tasking involved. And here is the kicker . . . I enjoy having a house full and very much enjoy cooking. Unfortunately, the fact that I enjoy hosting holidays for large numbers of people is very much incompatible with how I am wired. So . . . since the Good Lord chose to give me gifts other than the ability to focus, I have to be a bit more planned and organized to take it all on. I need to come up with a holiday strategy and stick to it.

Not only is it essential for me to stay on top of my game and to do as much as possible before people actually arrive, but I also have learned to give myself permission to make the break when the whole thing is done and go for a walk or a ski . . . alone. The whole key is the *alone* part.

Once an individual with ADD gets over-stimulated and the momentum gets going, an explosion is inevitable. This is a good thing to avoid when you have a house full of people. Thankfully, they understand at this point that I am not being rude, but doing something healthy and *in all of our best interest* by managing my ADD. After a walk or a ski, I will enter our home full of people brand new and recharged. This is why I went on a walk this morning.

November 23rd

It is entirely possible that I have graduated to the level of intermediate in my skills of Chinese Expulsion. According to the weather report, there is a nor'easter headed right through the center of Teaneck, home of Aunt Marla and her beets. If, by some outside chance she is actually unable to make it up here in her Saturn to be with all of us, then I will have satisfied the requirements of a novice expeller, as well as some of the initial requirements of the intermediate level. You see, whenever the weather is involved in someone's plans changing due to the concentrated application to pressure points, this is considered at least intermediate, and in some cases advanced, depending on the severity of the storm.

It is about the ability to maintain even and consistent pressure to the area between the thumb and forefinger while simultaneously focusing on that individual's empty seat at your table in your mind's eye. This is very difficult to do for any length of time, as thoughts tend to intrude upon your expulsory meditation. This is even more so with those of us who have an attentional deficit to begin with. It is very, very difficult to maintain a focused mind's eye on Aunt Marla's chair in the middle of our beautifully decorated harvest table without our dear Aunt Marla in it or her beet purée in the center right next to the very delectable turkey.

It would be easier to run a marathon in high heels.

This is why it is considered an advanced move to be able to focus enough to have a nor'easter roll right through Teaneck. It is not that we have the power or ability to create a storm, but the ability to channel the energy that is so exceptional. Add the fact that Aunt Marla has not had her snow tires put on yet and we are good to go. Of course we should not get excited just yet as anything can happen with the weather. We certainly don't want to jinx anything.

November 24th

I may as well accept that Aunt Marla will be coming tomorrow. As we have discussed, acceptance is the key to most problems . . . even Aunt Marla.

I will probably never live down the whole beet thing. Who would have guessed that Squanto and the Pilgrims could have indulged themselves in that horrid vegetable. Then again, it was a real life

Survivor situation. Imagine if the Pilgrims were on reality television. Now that would be something to watch.

November 25th

Happy Thanksgiving! Today is the day that people across the country think about all they are grateful for. It is a shame that out of 365 days in a year that many of us wait until today to count our blessings. It is quite sad, actually, as counting one's blessings is one very simple way to experience the true feeling of joy that sits right inside the rib cage and makes us feel warm and cozy and desiring to do for others.

This is one nice thing about the menopausal club members. We are quite a grateful group. We gather not only to judge others, but to be truly grateful for what we have.

November 26th

I have a secret. I woke up at 4:30 this morning and snuck out to join the crowds of eager bargain hunters for *Black Friday*. I am ashamed of myself, though I got a computer for just two hundred dollars. Secrets are self-sabotaging as well as the deep feeling of shame they bring. I feel dirty.

No one was awake when I got back. The dark circles under my eyes will give me away. I just know it. I think I'll go put on some make up.

I feel like a teenager who has been drinking, slipping into the bathroom with Visine and some Wrigley's gum.

I was bad and I know it.

I hid everything in the garage. Everyone is acting normal so I act normal also. It is only 9:00am and I am exhausted. I am ready for lunch and everyone else is having their coffee. I contemplate a support group. Maybe I should get a sponsor.

November 27th

Diving off the wagon.

Well, one thing good about hitting rock bottom is that you can always point your toes and bounce right back up.

After the majority of the relatives pulled out of the driveway, I slipped into the garage to stare at my treasured bargains. I began to get excited about wrapping them, though this would have to wait as we still had a few stragglers, hanging on for that last bite of left over apple pie. Time to go home. Thank you for coming.

November 29th

Well, the last of the relatives cleared out on Saturday. A good time was had by all, all except Aunt Marla that is. So what else is new. She showed up with her mysterious beet purée right on schedule. Baby food without the jar. No one ate it for the fortieth consecutive year. That has got to be some kind of record.

The three-day impending blizzard completely missed Aunt Marla, however, which has made me realize that I need to spend a bit more time practicing the Chinese arts. The blizzard hit Teaneck with full force, leaving many holiday travelers alongside the interstate and many others without power.

One of those travelers, however, got so nervous about the impending storm that she drove up a day early and stayed in a hotel just a half an hour away. That's right. Aunt Marla was less than an hour away the night before Thanksgiving, wrapped up in her bathrobe and fuzzy pink slippers and watching *Sex In the City* reruns at the Holiday Inn. She probably left her beet purée in the trunk in order to keep it cold. This explains the cold draft I felt that night. It kind of drifted in and around the dining room table until the little hairs on my neck stood up. Maybe Aunt Marla did a counter-curse . . .

After I adjusted to Aunt Marla's ingenious escape of menopausal magic, I moved on to the more likable and lower maintenance family members in the room. It was actually nice to have a house full, a real old-fashioned Thanksgiving. What was also nice was that some of our friends dropped by later in the evening, once the challenging family members had left. We let our hair down, so to speak, and laughed out loud. We drank wine and put our feet up. The candles stayed lit all evening until they were mere nubs adhered to the coffee table, a true sign of a good use of valuable life space.

This, of course, is another benefit to the menopausal life stage. One can branch out beyond the challenging family members and choose one's own family. Once we truly realize that we have the ability to choose our own inner circle of people we begin to feel empowered. We can stay up as late as we want to with our friends and talk about our challenging family members until the wee hours of the night. We can say whatever we want to about them until we feel really good inside. We won't even care if we can't get the wax off the table. We had fun, safe people to process our holiday frustrations with and for this we are eternally grateful.

November 30th

By now, it is safe to say that most of America is sick of cooking, even if you normally enjoy it. In fact, I would be willing to bet that the night following Thanksgiving is one of the most lucrative for the pizza industry, at least for those of us who invite thirty people to Thanksgiving dinner. For those less fortunate souls, who have smaller, more manageable, and therefore far less chaotic holiday dinners, there are left-overs.

Small, boring, *toast* families dine on left-over turkey as well as on dishes that left-over turkey can morph into such as turkey tettrazini, turkey enchiladas, and hot, open turkey sandwiches with gravy. Those of us who truly live *My Big Fat Greek Wedding* during the holidays and pick the bird clean, have pizza. We do this because we are *eaters* and we are *left-over-less*. We are the ones placing large orders at area pizza places. I know that for me, I usually order a salad also, as even this feels like too much effort.

Oompa!

December 1st

It is December which means that it's official. The gun has gone off and the race has officially begun. There is not a free weekend minute between now and the second weekend of January. It feels too fast.

There are school concerts and recitals, parties, parties, and more parties.

I want to slow it down but I do not know how.

December 2nd

I am now feeling the holiday momentum picking up as we zoom full speed into December. The snow is gently falling from the sky and landing on our deck like confectioner's sugar on a brownie. It is delightful. Of course, as we live in northern Vermont, much closer to Santa than most people, we move quickly from *delightful* to *completely sick of it* by April.

For right now, however, it is beautiful and somewhat exciting as ski season has officially arrived. It is now time to drag out the clunky snow boots, ski pants, hats, and all of the miss-matched gloves and mittens from last year. People often speak of socks getting eaten in the dryer, but in this house it is mittens and gloves. This is also partly due to the volumes of children we have in our house at any given time. They rifle through the big plastic hat and mitten bin with as much comfort as our own. By April, they are struggling to find right handed gloves to go with the scads of left handed ones.

Another thing that the first snowfall brings with it, is the urge to wrap. Most mothers by this time, or at least those who are determined to avoid the anxiety of shopping with all of the husbands the last day or two before Christmas, have mounds of boxes and bags tossed in the closet waiting to be wrapped for the big day. For those of us who purchase things as they find them or when they are on sale throughout the year, are once again pleasantly surprised as by now we have completely forgotten what we bought.

For me, as I have five blissful children and two godsons, I feel the need to spread everything out on the couch so I can see what it is that I purchased for whom, as well as what I need to buy in order to even it all up. Putting on Christmas music helps the evening up process. My inner material girl comes right to the surface with the happiest of glows as she wraps and re-experiences the original *shopping high* that she had only a few short weeks ago. In fact, it is not just a shopping fix, but an actual *shopping orgasm*, and it gets more intense with age.

The shopping orgasm normally begins during the teenage years, and is most definitely carried on the X chromosome. Later on, however, as we progress to the stage of mid-life, we feel the shopping orgasm with far more intensity. Not only that, but the buyer's remorse and overwhelming shame that we often feel as we put our packages in the trunk begins to dissipate. Menopausal women, especially when shopping together, learn to embrace their inner material girl and to work each other through their shame. Not only this, but menopausal women actually *encourage* each other to indulge themselves, to buy the soft pink leather pants, the ivory cashmere sweater, or that new Tina Turner CD. Menopausal shopping is guilt free, and it should be. Girls, we have most definitely earned it.

December 3rd

A weekend away with the girls.

Speaking of shopping, this morning I received a call from one of my best women friends in regards to a little Christmas overnight, complete with power shopping, dinner, wine, and late night girl talk.

I am packing as I type, with one hand on the keyboard and the other in my dresser drawer. As much as I love my little darlings, a break from responsibility does wonders for one's spirit and recharges one's maternal batteries. In fact, twenty-four hours spent the right way can feel like a week long vacation.

I can't wait. I think I'll go start the car.

December 4th

Weekend *junkie*.

I am on a roll. All of the sudden I am having a revelation that short little breaks from responsibility are a really good thing. With five children, we can certainly never be away for long as we are devoted to our cubs and bring them with us wherever we go. As we enter mid-life, however, I have been thinking that it would be good to plan a long weekend with my honey in order to recharge our batteries as a couple.

This is important, I think, as *we* were there before the kids and *we* will be there after they leave the nest. In other words, there was a *we* before here was an *us*. It is so easy for *coupleness* to get lost in *familyness* because the momentum of family life is fast and all encompassing. This is never more true than during the wonderful month of December when there are what feels like thousands of concerts, recitals, parties, and visits with Santa. Add in the basketball games and ski meets and we actually may consider borrowing a few hours here and there from a next life.

It can all become too fast and overwhelming. This is when it is a good idea to take a step back and plan a brief escape from adulthood and responsibility, as much as is possible of course, as our little darlings are always with us in our hearts and minds. It is simply the day to day running around and emotional involvement with all of the goings on of the day that one needs a break from.

So I planned a trip to Boston.

For us, Boston is only about four hours away. I have made arrangements for the kids and the dog. We will leave right after the school bus pulls away from the driveway, stay overnight at the

Marriott Long Wharf, walk around, eat a fancy dinner, have a sex-a-thon, and then return after lunch the next day. Short and sweet.

I love having something to look forward to. Now I have two somethings. I will go over night with the girls, be home for two days, and then go overnight with my Beloved.

Life is good.

§

I had another thought.

This could become an addiction. I could become a long weekend *get-a-way-a-holic*. I am now having yet another brilliant idea. As Christmas rapidly approaches, I ponder what to get my darling husband. He certainly does not need any more stuff. We are too old for that. We are more into the smaller, more thoughtful things in life at this point. For me, I like *Basic Instinct* perfume from Victoria's Secret. It is one of those simple pleasures in life that I really enjoy, and it makes me smell nice.

Anyway, I was surfing around on one of those travel sites and what jumped out at me but a deal to *Sin City* . . . My husband has always wanted to go to Vegas. Why, I am not quite sure, but it is a dream none the less. We all have something about us that is a little off center and the desire to go to Vegas is his.

The plane tickets were practically nothing. I decided to splurge on the hotel since we were only going to be there for three nights. We will be staying at the Venetian Hotel which is just like Italy. In fact, this is my compromise even though he knows nothing of what I am up to. It is a dream of mine to visit Italy so now we can both get excited, that is, after he knows about it.

Staying at the Venetian Hotel in Las Vegas will be almost like Italy. They even have a river that runs right through the lobby and they offer gondola rides to the guests. I can't wait.

This is one thing that is very cool about short get-a-ways. You can splurge a little and it doesn't kill you because you aren't staying long enough to spend a ton of money. In fact, I got tickets to the show called *O*. It is supposed to be outstanding and the best show that Las Vegas has to offer.

The rest of the time we will do lots of free stuff. Our friends Roger and Jonathan will be watching the kids. They have been to Vegas loads of times and said that there are lots of really great shows at the theme hotels that are free. The Bellagio apparently has a musical light show that is supposed to be really pretty. This is all so exciting. I am becoming addicted to planning long weekends.

The sneaking around part is fun also. I already bought my darling a pair of silk boxer shorts with dice on them. I will give them to him on Christmas Eve and this is how I will surprise him. I can't wait to see his reaction. He will be so happy.

December 5th

The *Conspiracy*.

Today I had to temporarily leave my day dream world of Sin City and become reality-based once again. I went out to the garage and dragged in the big card board boxes full of Christmas decorations. The lights, as usual, were tangled up in a rather large knot. Oh well. Not my job. The Christmas tree lights would be de-tangled by my husband when it is time to decorate the tree, complete with heavy sighing followed by loads of choice words.

He looks forward to this every year.

We will get our tree on Sunday evening. I will make a pot roast and put on some Christmas music. I love tradition. Change is certainly good also, however, I think that there is a feeling of security wrapped up in keeping some things the same. We all look forward to my husband having his tirade each year over the Christmas tree lights. Every year, it is as if it is some unforeseen problem that the lights are wrapped up in a tangled ball.

He takes the lights out of the ripped, battered box, blows some dust off the ornaments lying on top, then shakes his head in disgust at the wad of lights in his hands. He then announces to the kids that they may as well go down stairs while he untangles the huge knot as we cannot put any ornaments on the tree until he puts the lights on first.

The kids then sigh also, as if disappointed for the first time, and head downstairs. My husband proceeds to swear in every direction as if the whole thing was a conspiracy, and that some devious individual deliberately snuck into the garage, probably sometime during July and sat there, weaving the Christmas tree lights into a brilliant, complex knot.

Such criminals are rarely caught.

December 6th

I have been informed that our family Christmas tree experience will now be combined with the *Amazing Race finale* which happens to land on the same day. My darling husband has invited the guys over and I am now making two roast chickens and scalloped potatoes. It's all about redefining tradition and thinking outside the box. Our children are becoming *Amazing Race addicts* also, so it will work for everyone.

December 7th

We woke up to a beautiful snow fall. The ground, up until this morning was as bare as a new born baby's ass, which is strange in northern Vermont. Santa would have had to exchange the runners on his sled for wheels just to land on a roof. I do believe we are victims of global warming. It is definitely real.

The snow is so beautiful. The mountains and the trees look as if they have been sprinkled with confectioner's sugar. This is the ideal day to get a Christmas tree.

December 8th

A change.

O.K. This is weird as well as somewhat symbolic. As it turned out yesterday, four out of our five children ended up skiing, which would have been tough for us to say no to as it was the first real snow storm. Our youngest got a last minute invitation from her godmother to attend a Christmas concert at a nearby high school to watch her daughter dance as the sugar plum fairy.

Long story short, we ended up getting the tree ourselves, just the two of us.

It felt strange, yet familiar at the same time. We picked it out and had it tied to the roof, just as we had done sixteen years ago before we had kids. That was the last time it had been just us. A year later our oldest was born.

We put the tree in its stand. It was unusually easy this year. There was no swearing or cursing of the Christmas tree lights corporation or its incompetent workers. This made me sad in a way.

There it stood, waiting to be decorated. We promised the kids that we would wait until everyone was home to put the ornaments on. With the exception of our youngest, I'm not sure they cared that much.

It is the beginning or a new era for us.

December 9th

It is hard to believe that *Sin City* is only 7 weeks away and my very unsuspecting husband has no idea. I am getting excited even though this is not a destination that I would have chosen for myself. I have Tuscany on the forefront of my mind, though staying at the Venetian Hotel will satisfy that itch somewhat, in a tacky sort of way.

I have heard that the suites in the Venetian Tower are gorgeous and quite large. I believe they are 650 square feet which is plenty of room for a mid-life lady to be playful with her boy toy of sixteen years.

A Full Moon Rising…and the Tao of Menopause

This is all very exciting.

December 10th

This morning when I was taking the teenager to the bus stop in the dark the song came on *Mary did you know*. What an incredible song that it is and so beautiful. I get chills up my back every time I hear it.

Anyway, the part at the end where it says the *Great I Am* really made me think. It made me think about how all we really have is now, yet most of us don't reside here, at least not very often, and especially not during the month of December. It is philosophically deep, yet simple at the same time.

At this time of year, when there is so much focus on material-ness this can be very difficult to do. It is not merely commercialism either, but the anticipation of what is to come. It is the not only the buying and wrapping, but the planning and the thinking. For an entire month at least we reside on December 25th.

As last we knew, there are only twelve months in a year, this is quite a chunk of the year to sacrifice.

Where is *Mr. Power of Now*, Mr. Eckhart Tolle when we really need him . . .

December 11th

I am trying very hard to remain in the *I Am* state of being, though it is very difficult with the numerous activities surrounding us and pulling on our family. In the midst of the Christmas goings-on, we also have the regular basketball season. This should be against the law.

All regular sports, as much as we enjoy them, should be temporarily brought to a halt for the two weeks before Christmas as it is plain and simply too much.

On top of basketball season, we have Aunt Marla threatening to come up with her beet purée again. Normally this is strictly a Thanksgiving threat, but her niece down in Teaneck has chosen not to host Christmas this year. I have never even met Aunt Marla's niece but I don't like her.

She should give some thought to others before she goes and cancels major holidays in Teaneck, New Jersey that affect those of us in peaceful northern Vermont. Now I will have to focus on not getting stressed about something that may not even happen, though it quite possibly could.

Just to be safe, I will practice the art of Chinese expulsion with some extra focus and creative visualization of a three day blizzard.

Aunt Marla is terribly afraid to drive her Saturn in the snow so this could be the way out. If I devote just a few minutes each day to firmly pressing the area between my thumb and forefinger, while visualizing an enormous snow storm we could be home free.

I just hope it doesn't backfire and snow for three days once she is already here. This would be my nightmare.

December 12th

As my birthday season approaches, I remember birthdays of the past. I didn't have the *season* back then that I indulge myself in now as a mid-lifer. It was just a day and I would go skiing.

In fact, I remember having only one birthday party and it was a sleepover. I was ten years old.

The girls all brought their sleeping bags and sprawled them out on my bedroom floor. We had pizza and lemonade and played *truth or dare*. My little sister was allowed to hang around for way too long and then my parents finally put her to bed. She snuck out a few times and by the third time I lost my patience and told her that if I saw those red pig-tails just once more that I would put bubble gum in them when she was sleeping and then she would have to get her hair shaved off the next day.

She stopped bothering us after that.

Later when it got dark, Dad came in and told the story of *The Hook*. He first turned off all of the lights and then put a flashlight under his chin which made him look very scary. He proceeded to explain that *The Hook* was a murderer who roamed the streets at night on the run from the cops. They had been trying to catch him for many years but *The Hook* was too clever to get caught. He hung around campgrounds mostly and houses that had birthday sleepovers.

One night, *The Hook* was lingering around a campground by a lake *nearby*. There were two teenagers in a car kissing and listening to the radio. The radio said something about a *Hook sighting* nearby and they got nervous. Then they started kissing again and forgot about being nervous. All of the sudden they heard a sort of metal sound make a noise against the car. The girl screamed and the boy started the car and drove off.

When the boy dropped his date off at her house he went around to her side to let her out and there was a hook dangling from the door handle.

All the girls screamed and ran into the living room.

December 13th

I always loved that story. I didn't scream because I had heard it before, but it was fun to see everyone else get scared.

After we got a snack and the girls settled down we played the *Ouji* game. It was not a game exactly because you didn't win or lose. You called the dead back to life. We tried a bunch of people that we knew such as great-grand parents and other ancient ancestors. Then one of the girls came up with Abe Lincoln though I am not sure why exactly. She was a smart kid, the kind that always raised her hand and never got in trouble. I wanted to call on Elvis but I let her choose since it was my birthday party and she was a guest. Besides, Elvis was newly dead and maybe he hadn't settled into the spirit world just yet.

We all placed our fingers gently on that little piece with the glass in the middle and asked for a visit from Abe. Apparently he was in a deep slumber because nothing happened, then the piece began to move. Two of the girls pulled their fingers off the little wooden piece. The rest of us kept at it as we proceeded to ask Abe some questions about his current existence in the afterlife. The more I think about it, that girl was strange.

We stayed with our questions as well as the answers, as we suspiciously glanced at each other wondering if one of us was moving the little wooden piece with the glass in the middle or if Abe was indeed talking with us from the great beyond.

All of the sudden there was a rap, rap, rap on the window followed by a low pitched ghost noise. Everyone screamed, including me this time as we looked up at the window and saw a shadow of a bearded man in the twilight. It was Abe. Arms and legs were flying as we wrestled our way out of the sleeping bags and blankets. One of the girls caught a knee in the face and got a bloody nose. She dripped all over the new nightgown that her mother had bought her just for my birthday sleepover. She dripped all the way down the hallway of our pre-fab and into the kitchen where she dripped on the linoleum. It is all right to drip blood from your nose on linoleum because you can wipe it off with a paper towel.

When you drip on a new nightgown, however, it stays forever even if your hippy mother uses special organic herbs and oils on it to get the stain out.

I had to give that girl a pair of my pajamas and we all had to move out to the living room because everyone was too worked up after *The Hook* and the visit from Abe. One of girls called her mother to come get her.

Then Dad walked in from outside with his un-kept 70's beard and introduced himself as Abe Lincoln. He said he was back from the deh ... eh ... eh ... ad ...

Maybe this is why I only had one birthday party.

December 14th

One of the girls gave me a piggy-bank for a present. It was in the shape of a *Holly Hobby* doll which was so not me as I was never into dolls. My inner tomboy resisted dolls from the very beginning and would have much preferred a new baseball mitt, however, I had never had a bank before and I was enjoying saving money. It felt good to save money. I had shoveled some sidewalks and done some odd jobs and I had saved about twenty dollars in a week. This was a lot in the 70's.

Then one night I was awakened by someone prowling around in my room. There was some banging and stuff was falling off of my dresser because the intruder was fumbling around in the dark. Then I heard my new bank break open. I picked up my head from my pillow squinting in the dark to see who was in my room and what had happened to my new Holly Hobby doll bank with my shoveling money in it.

Fall

It was Dad. It was Friday night and the guys were over to play poker. He whispered something about being down a few hands and that he promised to give it all back to me. Then he pulled the covers up over me real snuggly and kissed me goodnight on the forehead.

Holly's head was missing. He had smashed it against the dresser to get the money out. Maybe he didn't know that there was a little plug on the bottom. He filled his pockets with my stash and promised me that he would give it all back tomorrow.

The next morning Dad slept in for a long time and when he woke up he was very crabby. He did eventually give me the money back but I had to tape Holly's head back on with masking tape and there were still a few holes here and there.

It was all right because I really didn't like that bank very much anyway. That smart girl gave it to me and I didn't like her very much either.

I was glad that I was able to help Dad in his hour of need.

December 15th

The only other *almost* birthday party I had was when I was sixteen. I had a few girls over and we drank in my room without my parents having any idea. I had accumulated a stash of Kalua in my dresser drawers so all we needed from the kitchen was milk and snacks. This could be why they didn't question anything as we were only asking for milk and snacks.

What wholesome teenagers. This is a contradiction in terms, *wholesome* and *teenagers*.

The next day when we were totally hung-over, I thought of having my own teenagers someday and how difficult it would be for them to get away with anything.

December 16th

Though I didn't have actual birthday parties, I did have parties each and every time my parents left town because I was a rebellious teenager and I didn't like my parents. I liked the freedom of having the house to myself. I felt grown up and in charge, plus I did not have to do the dishes or my homework.

One night in particular I had a huge bash. Nearly every kid in the high school was there because word travels quickly when someone's parents are gone. It was August and the weather was perfect for a *parent-free* party. The football team was there. I loved the football team. They were my friends.

Very early on in my high school experience, I learned that boys were nicer than girls and so I chose to hang out with them instead. There was no caddy behavior or rumor starting kind of stuff. Boys are direct and honest. They are who they are and I liked this about boys. After a while my parents got used to eleven guys showing up on a Friday night to go to the movies. They were nice kids and we had lots of fun together. I definitely felt safe hanging out with the football team. That was for sure.

The party rapidly spun out of control because people had heard about it all over town and soon there were way too many people in our pre-fab. They were also in our yard and in the street. The police called because a neighbor had complained about the noise. I pretended that I was my mother and let the police know that things were now under control and that *Kimberly had been grounded for a month.* I assured them that this would never happen again.

Then we climbed up on the roof and set off some fireworks that I had bought off a kid in the smoking lounge at school.

From the roof, I could see one of the seniors dealing cocaine from the picnic table in our backyard. This was bad. I was all right with the kegs of beer rolling in and out of the yard, but not coke. Coke was serious and this made me nervous. I told my football friends and they took care of him for me.

Then my uncle showed up. He had walked over in his boxer shorts because it was late. By the time I entered high school, we had moved across the street to a different pre-fab and my hippy mother's sister had moved into our old one. Our new pre-fab was a little bigger and it had a basement. We had achieved upward social mobility.

My uncle's *cool level* was quite high as he promised not to tell my parents about my underage drinking extravaganza, but he suggested we cease to set off any more illegal fireworks as his phone was ringing off the hook with irritated neighbors and he was trying to sleep.

I agreed.

The next day when I woke up surrounded by bottles, cans, and empty bags of chips, I noticed that the hands on the clock in the living room had been broken. They were still hanging on but they were limp. I called my uncle and he suggested that I try peanut butter.

It worked. This guy was the best. I owed him big time.

Another little problem we needed to deal with was that we had left some bottles on the roof that we had used to set off the fireworks. They looked like the Statue of Liberty perched up there on top of the chimney for all to see, announcing that the teenagers of New Paltz High School and the greater surrounding area were up to no good the night previous. We had to get them down and we had only a short time left before my parents got home.

I hoped they got stuck in traffic.

We got a ladder out of the garage and set it against the pre-fab. The pre-fab was sort of built into a small hill so the back was two stories. This was the entrance to the basement and the garage. My hippy mother had gone through a short gardening phase that last year and the remnants of her attempt lined the back perimeter of the house. There were bricks set in the dirt at an angle surrounding what would be a flower bed had she planted anything.

Anyway, we elected our friend Tanya to climb up and retrieve the bottles. Up, up, up she went. She made it to the chimney and then held the bottles up high as if to signify the victory of rebellious teenagers against their parental persecutors.

We signaled her to hurry up as we were running out of time and we still had to do a last minute sweep of the yard for any miscellaneous bottle caps, cigarette butts, or anything else that would get us busted. Down she came, one foot after the other.

Then the ladder gave out. We had forgotten to secure the hitch and it slid all the way down. It seemed like it happened in slow motion. Tanya fell on the bricks that my hippy mother had decorated the weed bed with. She was lying there on the ground holding her leg. She was bleeding.

We had to think fast. We would all be in severe trouble as our friends all told their parents something different as far as where they were last night, not to mention the unsupervised, underage drinking issue.

I came up with an idea. We gathered around Tanya and gently lifted her into my hippy mother's Oldsmobile. We made her comfortable in the back seat with a blanket and a pillow beneath her leg. I got the keys to my hippy mother's car that I had made for myself even though I did not have a license as of yet. I did have a learner's permit though, and this made everything all right as this was a true emergency on many levels.

We drove to the Town Pool. All of us gently carried Tanya to the bottom of the parking lot by the big hill which was somewhat out of the way, and rubbed dirt on her other leg. Then one of us ran to get a lifeguard.

We told him that we were going on a walk and that Tanya had slipped. The lifeguard ran and got two more lifeguards. They called an ambulance and Tanya was taken to Vassar Hospital in Poughkeepsie where they took very good care of her injured leg.

Tanya was a hero. She saved us all. Not only that, but the Town Pool had to pay for the whole thing being as it happened on town property.

To this day, none of our parents knows this story.

December 17th

A few weeks passed and I was feeling pretty confident that I had pulled off the largest bash in New Paltz High School history without getting caught, not to mention some minor insurance fraud which saved our asses. I was practically famous, at least in my world. Kids were still talking about how great the party was.

Then it happened. I was watching football with my Dad. It was half-time and he was just about to get up from his recliner chair to get another beer and some more pretzels when it happened. The hand on the clock drooped and then fell straight down, pointing to the six. Dad looked up and stared as if to question what his eyes had seen. I made a move to get up and head outside, possibly to go visit my friend or hitch hike to Colorado for a new start in life.

I was told to sit down. I was told this with a firm, authoritarian voice, the kind that judges sentence people to life in prison with.

I sat down and Dad got up from his recliner. The game was about to start again and this only made him angrier. He touched the hands on the clock and then smelled his fingers. "Peanut butter," he said. I looked down in shame. Then I looked up in fear.

He asked me what happened and this was the end of my life as I knew it.

December 18th

I think that this happens to most of us in our mid-life years when yet another birthday is approaching. We look back on birthdays of the past and reflect on how our lives have changed as well as the people in our lives. This is because at any one point in time, those specific friends, or combination of friends are only with us for a short while.

They are passing through and we are passing through, creating memories. These moments, with these exact friends will never happen in the same way again though it does not seem like this at the time, especially during our younger years.

December 19th

Tomorrow is my birthday and all I want is snow. This is all I ever want and I pray for it each year. My prayers are also answered each year as I cannot remember a birthday without snow. This is my present from God and I accept my snow with a grateful heart.

December 20th

Heaven.

Today is my birthday and what a grand day it is. It snowed lightly last night and then again this morning. The sun is now shining brightly and it looks sparkly all over. It looks like heaven really, or at least what I picture heaven might be like.

The mountains were beckoning, so off I went on my yearly pilgrimage to Jay Peak to ski and pay homage to myself and another blissful year of a healthy and happy life. When we get right down to it, if we have our health then we have it all. Anything else is a big, fat bonus, icing on life's cake.

There I stood at the top of the mountain, staring out at the gorgeous view in front of me. How anyone could view this sight and not believe in our wonderful Creator is a complete mystery to me. There had to be so much involved in making this wonderful world so beautiful.

In the very far off distance there is a lake. It is called Lake Memphramagog and it touches both the United States and Canada. Just a hair past this beautiful lake and beyond its surrounding foothills is the North Pole.

On very clear, icy nights, the northern lights can be seen. If it is an exceptionally clear and starry night, then it is possible to see the smoke coming from Santa's Village.

I love Santa.

Anyway, as I stood there gazing out into a vast winter wonderland I gave thanks. I am healthy and happy, as is my family which means that I have it all.

For this I am grateful.

December 21st

Show me the *cake love*.

I continue to celebrate my birthday season with a rather large slab of cake for breakfast. There is not much better than birthday cake with coffee very early in the morning before anyone else in the house is awake. The sweet taste of moist cake with the creamy frosting combined with hot coffee is just one of life's simple pleasures. Add to the recipe that the cake was baked with love and I realize that there is no better way to start the day.

I will share with you the story of my cake. We moved to northern Vermont nine years ago, this month actually. Right away, we started our now fifteen-year-old in kindergarten. There were eight kids in his class. He made nine, and he was another boy which the kids were thrilled about as his class leaned *girl*.

The move was tough on all of us. The first day of school was the toughest, meeting new kids in a new place with new teachers. Of course it was hardest on our son, but it was hard for us, too, mainly myself as my husband had moved a few months ahead of us to get his business going so he at least had his bearings.

The second day turned out to be much easier. Our little boy had made a friend and the tears that had rolled down his cheeks outside the classroom the day before had now dried up. He had been invited over to play after school. Even now, as freshmen in high school they remain close friends.

Kindergarten was half day, so each day we mothers waited outside the door at 11:30 for our little ones to be dismissed. It was all mothers and one dad. He seemed to be a little shy, but anxious to meet people I started talking in an attempt to strike up a conversation. He was in construction and had to use his lunch hour to bring his son from school to daycare which was up the mountain road. It was a good half hour to go up there and back.

He told me that his wife had just left and that it was just the two of them now. I told him that I wouldn't mind bringing his son to daycare for him if he wanted me to. The single dad took me up on my offer even though he had just met me.

Two weeks went by and our sons became fast friends. He had a construction job across the road from us so his boy would walk across the street to play while his dad worked. Then, on my birthday, just a couple of weeks after we had met, I heard a knock on the door. It was my new friend and he had a cake in his hands. He had baked it himself. It was white with little mandarin oranges all along the edge. It was so good that I do not have words.

In fact, it is the best cake I have ever had.

Nine years have gone by now, and each and every year I look forward to that knock on the door and my white birthday cake with the little oranges.

December 22nd

I am still basking in the love from my cake and my birthday season. I looked at my funny birthday cards over and over. It seems to mean even more that people take time out for my birthday because of where it lands on the calendar. It is the busiest time of year for most people, especially people with kids.

And speaking of kids, it is now back to the reality that Christmas Eve is the day after tomorrow. I am all done wrapping. The cards have long since been mailed. The tree is up and decorated with working lights. Now all that is left to do is the grocery shopping. This will be huge. I will more than likely need two carts.

Christmas Eve is the best at our house.

December 23rd

Stamp worthiness.

I forgot to mention to you about my husband's little Christmas card fetish. Every year he stands them up along the perimeter of the living room on top of the barn board that runs along the walls.

Every year he will quiz me on who we sent them to. Every year he will threaten not to send them to those who did not send us a card. They are not *stamp worthy* he will say.

There are lots of people in the world who are not stamp worthy, sucking up the air out of the atmosphere and usually taking more than their share. They are leaches, barnacles on the ass of humanity.

December 24th

Ingrates.

Of course, my dear husband does not discuss the nine or ten cards that we received from people whom *we did not send them to*. His primary focus remains on those ingrates whom we spent a stamp on as well as the effort to go to the post office, wasting valuable life minutes on their unworthy selves.

Every year, he has his Christmas card tantrum and vows not to grace the ingrates of the world with a stamped envelope.

After we process and release this energy, we can then move into the magic that is Christmas Eve, and it is a magical evening.

December 25th

Merry Christmas!

December 26th

It is the day after. That's right, the day after. I spent nearly six weeks buying, wrapping, planning, cleaning, cooking, baking, and sending cards to ingrates. Now it is all over. Just like that. It is amazing really, when you stop to think about it.

It is all done in a morning, finito.

By 2:00 in the afternoon I am ready for the tree to come down. We don't take it down because my husband wants it up for New Year's Eve, but underneath I yearn to have my house back. I want to de-clutter so I may breathe freely once again.

Too much stuff makes me feel as if it is hard to breathe. I can't get enough air until things are put away and I can walk from the living room to the kitchen without breaking an ankle. Big black garbage bags are my friend.

December 27th

Christmas week as a mother of five with a very challenging great Aunt Marla has given a new definition to the word exhausted. We escaped her for Christmas, but she is threatening to drive up from Teaneck, New Jersey to ring in the New Year. I will pray for an ice storm.

December 28th

It looks like my wish may come true. This is menopausal magic at its best. Our neighbor is a meteorologist and he says that there is a storm coming the day after New Year's Day. This would prevent our dear Aunt Marla, the party animal, from making the trek up here from

Teaneck, New Jersey, as she could not get home. This would be my nightmare.

December 29th

I am grateful that I do not live in Teaneck, New Jersey. That's it for today.

December 30th

I am grateful that Aunt Marla does not have an identical twin as this could result in my being found on the bottom of Lake Champlain wearing size 6 ½ cement shoes.

December 31st

The addiction substitution.

Happy New Year's Eve! I am beginning to realize that I have a problem. I am an *entertaining addict*. I am no longer entranced by the clearance sales at *The Gap*, but I cannot stop myself from making stuffed mushrooms and little weenies.

I have invited all of our friends over to ring in the New Year this evening. I have bought purple and gold hats with fringe and noise makers. I made a crock of chili. They are all bringing an exotic drink to share. I will stick to my red wine in order not be found dancing naked on the coffee table with sequined tassels. It is a good decision I think.

We will watch the ball drop at midnight.

I am not quite sure what all the hype is about the ball dropping. Everybody counts down then we all toast and hug each other when the new year has arrived. I like the hugging part the best. I feel grateful to have such nice friends. They are fun, too, an added bonus.

As I am originally from New York, I felt it necessary to buy *Time Square*. It is really good. It cost $5.99 at a party store in Burlington. It is a seven foot mural complete with the ball ready to drop on top. We will have to take lots of pictures in front of it. I don't think people will know the difference.

January 1st

The *egg roll omen.*

Happy New Year! I just know that this is going to be a good year, very prosperous. I know this because I had a really good omen happen last night as people were arriving. I went to dump a box of frozen egg rolls on to a cookie sheet. It said on the box that there were twelve egg rolls and when I dumped them out there were fourteen.

It will be a year of prosperity for sure.

January 2nd

I was serious about the egg roll omen. We got two extra egg rolls out of that box and this means something. I am feeling very good about this year so far.

January 3rd

It is still difficult to believe that Christmas is over. All that work. When it is all said and done, the whole process is good for about six weeks. I cannot help but to ponder why we continue to do this each year.

As the good doctor *Phil* would say . . . because there must be payoff in it. That's why, or we would not do it.

It must be self punishment, as punishing one's self continues to be number one as far as reinforcement for behaviors. We must, on some level, enjoy the hustle and bustle, as well as the complete lack of free time and inner peace. We are gluttons for it and it goes against all that we are trying to embrace in our middle life. The insane holiday momentum and chaos most definitely go against the Tao and even the most basic principles of menopause.

It seems that even when we are doing well along the menopausal path and listening to our inner most voice, that many of us still tend to slide back into a worldly tail spin around the holidays. It seems very difficult to help and I believe that this is because we are surrounded by it. Holiday everything infiltrates our senses.

Now, during the darkest and coldest month of the year it is time to regroup and get centered once again. We need to take a long, deep breath as we breathe in the positive energy of a brand new year and breathe out the stress and holiday craziness that we were hanging on to so desperately only a week ago.

In with the good and out with the bad . . .

As mentioned previously, I prefer September as the month to make changes, however, changes to improve one's self and increase spiritual awareness are *always* a good thing. The fact that January is so dark and cold can be a blessing and beneficial to the spirit as it is all in the perspective. If this is the perspective that you choose then good for you. Whatever works.

This is a month that can bring with it the desire to make changes. January has a certain element of newness to it, a blank slate. Add to that the fact that it is so dark and cold and we are set up to look inward. January can also be a month to start over and to sit next to a warm fire with a book.

A Full Moon Rising…and the Tao of Menopause

January 4th

Well, that all sounded good, creating time for reflection and the whole reading a book by the warm fire thing . . . now I have to get to work trying to plan my darling husband's surprise 40th birthday party. This will be no easy task as there is not a nosier person in the universe, at least not in *my* universe anyway. I will have to concentrate very hard each day to remain centered and focused on the principles of the Tao as I will need them to get me through the potentially overwhelming stress of a surprise party and a severely nosy beloved.

I am having the party at a restaurant called *The Blue Moose* which is a nice place, casual and comfortable which is what he likes. They have a downstairs part that is used for weddings and such. I have hired the band that I heard over the summer when I helped out at our friends' new wedding facility. This band is rockin'. They reminded me a bit of the band we had at our wedding. No one sat down all night. That is the trademark of a great band in my opinion. The band makes the party and my honey's party is going to be a bash, the biggest social event of the season in our tiny little town.

I have already told everyone that I have invited thus far to make sure to bring their *eating pants* and their *dancing shoes*. There will be a buffet and an open bar for the first hour. One hour is enough. After that it will be a cash bar as this is what I can afford. The open bar part, however, needs to remain a secret from Aunt Marla as she is no fan of open bars. She says that there is a lot of waste and that people take advantage. I am sure that there is some truth to that, however, in my fairly large nutty Irish family, people are treated with tremendous hospitality, especially when they travel. Being frugal with family who have made such an effort to come all that way is a huge *no no*.

So . . . an open bar it is and I think that Aunt Marla will have to find that out for herself when she goes up to order her first Manhattan.

After a few martinis, maybe Aunt Marla will lighten up . . . at least for the night anyway. I am certain that I will hear about it the next day. She has already involved herself in planning the whole thing. In fact, I think that I deserve to be free of any further character building experiences throughout my middle life simply because of Aunt Marla. She is a walking, breathing, life challenge, and she is all I need to maintain steady personal growth.

January 8th

People with ADD should really not try to take on planning surprise parties. It is completely overwhelming and against the Tao. It is all I can think about. I think about who is coming, who is saying that they are coming now but who will more than likely not show up. Then there are the long distance wild cards. As the party is in February in northern Vermont there is a better than 95 percent chance that there will be a blizzard that day. Even the most determined, good-hearted family members may not opt to trudge through a blizzard.

As I am not one to attempt to control the uncontrollable, this is tough, as the restaurant will need a solid number a week prior to the event. That part is a game I think. If you are quite sure that you will have about sixty people then you tell the restaurant fifty. This way, if a few do not show up at the last minute then you don't get stuck paying for them. The restaurant probably knows this, and tacks on at least another five or so people to the number that you give them. This way they make sure that they have enough food. I don't mind playing the restaurant game, actually. It is kind of fun. I just hope I can give them a fairly accurate estimate. What if I tell them fifty and then eighty show up . . . That wouldn't be so good.

I have had a self aware moment of realizing that I have taken on way more than I can handle and still maintain some degree of mental health. It is now time to explore what my need to do this is. It all goes back to self-punishment. In fact, I left out an additional part of this scenario that will have at least one foot and three big toes in the grave after the weekend is over. Our daughter's birthday is the next day . . . so I have hired a baby-sitter team to stay in the suite they are in to watch the kids during the party. This way the grown-ups can do our thing on Saturday night, and then our daughter can have her sledding party with all of her cousins the next day. It is an ideal situation, exhausting, but ideal . . .

There must be a life lesson in here somewhere.

Maybe my next book should be *How to Throw a Great Surprise Birthday Bash While Still Maintaining Your Sanity* . . . or . . . *The Quickest Path to a Straight Jacket* . . . depending on how the whole thing goes of course.

On top of the birthday party stress, I have the nosy husband factor. Very few people have a nosy husband like I do. He is very cute, certainly, but has a need to get into people's business. He likes to know *the dirt* as he says. So . . . I have had to be extra mindful and sensitive to that gut feeling that someone is looking over my shoulder because nine times out of ten my gut is telling me the truth. I wonder if anyone has ever done a study on gut feelings. It is a bit strange how someone can be standing behind us, even at a distance, and we can sense it on some level without hearing, seeing, or smelling anything. I know one thing for sure. When my gut tells me something and I ignore it, I almost always regret it.

My gut can warn me about my nosy birthday boy husband peering over my shoulder as I type on the computer, and my gut can warn me when something is not in my best interest, and even when I am in danger. It is not just that dark alley kind of danger either. My gut is quite adept at warning me about impending emotional danger, and I must say that in the wisdom of my mid-life years, I have learned to listen.

My inner voice is tuned in not only to my spirit, but also the energy and intentions of anyone connected with me. My inner voice serves as spiritual radar to guide me through what I am unable, and sometimes unwilling to see.

I am aware that only by becoming skilled at listening to and following this inner voice can I grow and reach a higher level of living.

This is the essence of the Tao on which all principles are based.

As I think of my gut and how I have learned to listen to it, what I remember is that this instinct of gut listening is natural and effortless. *Learning* to listen to our gut is really *learning not to let other worldly voices distract us* and pull our attention away from the Divine within us.

I have a memory of having a conversation about this with my friend when we were very young. We had deep conversations about real issues, usually on the roof, or in my club house, sometimes up in the tree in the front yard of my pre-fab. It was a really good tree with branches in all of the right places.

One day Mari came over to look for us and needed us really quick. She looked nervous, or maybe excited. I am not sure which. We yelled down to her and climbed out of the tree. She told us that we had to follow her over to the *hide-out*. The *hide-out* was an old abandoned house on the other side of the highway beyond the New York State Conservation Department and future sight of our marijuana crop. It was a small, two story, gray shack with broken windows. It is possible that it may have been used as a hunting camp before the area became developed. I am not quite sure.

Mari told us to run and to be quiet. I was not sure how you were supposed to run and be quiet at the same time as breathing was involved.

When we arrived at the *hide-out*, there was a campfire still smoldering and stuff that belonged to people lying on the ground. There were liquor bottles under the bench. We thought no one knew about this place but us. It was deep in the woods on the other side of the highway. No one ever came back here. At least we did not think so.

This was our secret place and someone had found it.

We slowly walked into the old house with Mari leading the way. Whoever was here was gone for the moment, but not forever. They had jackets and things hanging on nails on the wall. All of the sudden I crossed over from feeling like Nancy Drew to full blown terrified. We needed to get out of here.

Mari pointed to some bags over in the corner. We walked over and looked inside.

They were filled with money. There was one whole bag filled with quarter rolls and four others stuffed with bills. There had to be over eight thousand dollars in these bags. We grabbed the bags and ran to Mari's house as it was the closest, plus no one was ever home.

Completely out of breath, we ran into Mari's garage, dumped the bags on the floor and closed the door. None of us said a word. We counted the money. There was just short of ten thousand dollars in these paper bags in Mari's garage.

We thought about what to do.

Calling the police seemed like the best thing to do as we were scared to death at this point. We flipped a coin for who had to be the one to call and tell the whole story. Mari won which was good as she was less nervous than the two of us. The police arrived quickly and asked us about a million questions. Then they took the money.

They headed over to our *hide-out* but with different cars, the kind that looked like teachers or insurance people drive. No sirens, just regular cars.

The next day the story about Mari finding all of that money was in the newspaper. I guess Shop-rite had been robbed by three armed, masked men the night before and the police had been combing the lanes of New Paltz looking for them. Now they were caught. When we read this I felt my heart begin to race. Mari was a hero and we helped, but we also could have been killed had the three armed bears come back from wherever they went.

I was glad that Mari's gut had brought her to the *hide-out* and glad that mine had gotten us out. Now we had an exciting story to tell. My whole childhood was like this, one adventure after another.

I am grateful that video games and the Internet had not been invented yet.

I am grateful that our mothers made us play outside all day.

January 9th

My temporary visit back in time has brought me joy as well as relieved some stress as it was a break from party planning, phone calls, and e-mails.

I think it is safe to say that the long range weather forecast will be a three day blizzard. It is also fairly safe to say that the long range Aunt

Marla forecast will be that she will be there regardless of whether it is a snow storm or a meteor shower. I have to prepare for this.

I also have to get ready to help Aunt Marla help me as this is how it works. As you know, she has a need to control everyone and everything in her immediate atmosphere regardless of whether it actually has a thing to do with her or not. Aunt Marla will roll into town like gangbusters wanting to be the brick foundation upon which the surprise party was built. I have also learned over the years to let her help, which takes an enormous amount of energy but still less energy than it would be to resist her efforts. Aunt Marla has never accepted *no* as an answer very well.

January 10th

Yesterday I received a phone call from my favorite cousin, actually three phone calls regarding her dog chasing deer in some guy's yard. They rented a cottage nearby to come up for a ski weekend with her family as well as to visit with us. So now, in addition to the stress of Aunt Marla's impending arrival we have deer stress. This guy owns a dairy farm on the other side of town and he was very upset as he saw her dog chasing deer through his backyard several times and is concerned that someone could shoot her, not the deer, but the dog.

In Vermont, deer are held with only the highest of regard. Numerous pictures of light brown stags can be seen on the covers of magazines in every convenient store and gas station. They are worshipped and discussed all year long, that is, until mid-November when people shoot them. It is a bit of a strange dynamic if you ask me.

Anyway, this very nice dairy farmer is upset so now we have to figure out how to get my cousin's dog to not do what most would consider to be very normal animal behavior, especially as she is a border collie who was born to run circles around large animals.

Stress can take all forms.

January 11th

Here is a plan. When Aunt Marla arrives, we will have her chase the dog back to the cottage. This way she will feel useful and the dog will have a safe return. It is a win-win. Just for an added bonus, Aunt Marla will be out of our hair for at least an hour which will be just long enough to come up with some creative way to dispose of her beet purée. Brilliant.

January 12th

Angels watching over me.

I cannot think about Aunt Marla because tomorrow is my grandmother's birthday. She is the one that I am always telling you

A Full Moon Rising…and the Tao of Menopause

about as she has so many wise things to say. The day she died a piece of me left with her.

I have to tell you the strangest thing. My grandmother had been sick for almost a year, primarily from old age. We were in New Hampshire, just myself and the kids as my husband was in New York for ten months for training with his company. We had four kids under the age of five at the time.

This was the worst ten moths of my adult life.

There was no refrigerator. Well, there was, but it didn't work so I had to shop each and every day in order to have milk and fresh fruit for the kids. I had four kids five and under everywhere I went. It was a neighborhood that was mainly seasonal as we were on a lake, Lake Ossipee.

There was a mix of people there. There was a group who donned numerous tattoos with their pit bulls and holding cans of Budweiser. There were a few young mothers though not many. Actually there was one. We got to know each other through the older woman across the street. Her name was Marilyn. She was an angel sent from heaven. There was another older couple next to her who used to bring things over for the kids and I, cereal and muffins, things like that. They must have known we were struggling. Then there was a hunter guy next to them, also an angel.

Fall

In fact, one day, in our rustic little cabin with four kids five and under, I came home from taking the kids on a walk. We had only been there for a month. I could hear a strange sound coming from inside. As I climbed the stairs and approached the door the sound got louder. I opened the door.

All I could hear was water. It sounded like Niagara Falls coming from the basement. As we were planning to move to Vermont in October, we had only unpacked the necessary things to survive the interim months. Everything we owned was down there, all of our furniture, my husband's history books, everything.

I walked in and opened the door to the basement. It was so loud. I could see water gushing out of the pipe. I stood there paralyzed. I had a two month old baby in my arms and I didn't know what to do. The other three were behind me. I had to stay calm. I had to focus. I didn't know anyone. The closest family was down in Massachusetts. My husband was seven hours away. There I stood, stuck for a moment.

Then came the moment of clarity and strength. I closed the door to the basement and locked it. I sat my oldest, then only five years old but very responsible, with his siblings and instructed him to watch them and not let them move while I ran across the street. I had to go fast and find anyone.

With my two-month old in my arms I ran across the street. I chose the cabin to the right. There was a truck parked outside. I knocked on the door. A hunter guy answered. I was so glad he was home as it was not yet summer and most people had not yet opened up for the season. He looked a bit rugged but he had a nice smile. Besides that, I needed him, anyone. I felt so vulnerable.

I got my story out as fast as I could. He threw his boots on, grabbed his tool box and darted across the street. Within seconds he turned off the water. I sat on the couch with my four kids, tears welled up in my eyes. They had not moved just as they were instructed.

Thank God for this nice stranger. He was an angel. In fact, an hour later he came back and knocked on the door with his tool box in hand and some part from a hardware store. He went down to the basement and welded something back on. Our furniture was under water. All of our nice things were 20,000 leagues under the basement sea and I didn't care. Maybe I would care later as we didn't own that much to begin with, but for right now I was glad that it was over.

I was grateful for my angel.

January 13th

Happy Birthday Gramma!

I really miss you.

Now I have to finish my story about the whole New Hampshire episode of my life. We moved there just six weeks after our fourth child was born and I had had a c-section due to child number three breaking my pelvis. As it turned out, she was a petite 7 lbs and 2 oz. They would have needed a catcher's mitt to grab her as she flew out of my well-oiled baby-making machine. The docs, however, were erring on the side of careful which I appreciate. Of course, my abdomen was a tad on fire and stayed that way for roughly six weeks. Tylenol with codeine was my new best friend.

I had to pack up our condo by myself as my husband was away again for his pre-training training at the time. I am beginning to get resentful just thinking about this time in my life. Breathe. O.K., continue.

Anyway, my grandmother was my very special person in the world. I had imprinted on her at a very young age. She was mine. Whenever I was upset or disappointed, she said exactly the right words. Her words entered my heart and warmed me up on the inside. She made me feel light and free of burden.

A Full Moon Rising…and the Tao of Menopause

She made me feel loved and important.

I was so far away when she started to get sick and I had four young kids and a husband who was seven hours away. She was in a hospital in Indiana and I was in East Slabovia, New Hampshire, miles away with no way to be with her. I could only talk to her on the phone, and at the end, all I could do was tell her that I loved her because she wasn't able to talk back.

I cried myself to sleep the nights before she left. I knew that I would I miss her deeply. I knew that my life would never be the same again and that I would never be quite the same again.

Then, one night, I awoke at 4:21 am. I have a very clear memory of this time as I had a clock radio next to my bed with bid red digital numbers. I was having a dream that my grandmother was talking to me. She was very calm and peaceful. She wanted to know if I would be all right. She told me how much she loved me and how special I was to her. She told me how proud she was. Then, she asked me again if I would be all right. She was asking my permission to let her go.

I assured her that I would be fine. I told her that I loved her, too, so, so very much.

I wasn't able to go back to sleep, so I got up and made some hot tea. When morning came I called the hospital to check on her as I did every morning. There was an awkward silence on the other end of the phone. My grandmother had died.

I took a deep breath, holding back the tears. I asked them what time she had gone. It was 4:21 am.

January 14th

It is amazing how certain times of year or certain dates can trigger us into memories and feelings. I have been *thoughty* of my grandmother all week, every day actually.

Thoughty is a word straight from Gramma's dictionary and is defined by an inner cognitive awareness of someone. It is more than thoughtfulness. It is a more intense character trait as it involves the spirit on a much deeper level. When I am *thoughty* of someone, they are not only on my mind, but in my heart, and connected to and felt by my spirit. This is what it means to be *thoughty*.

I have also been focused on angels and their importance in my life. I know that my grandmother would never leave me alone. The fact that the hunter guy happened to be home at just the right moment on a rainy April morning a solid two months before any of the summer residents returned was no coincidence.

In fact, I don't believe in coincidences, only angels.

January 15th

And speaking of angels, I am going to say numerous novenas so that we do not have any unforeseen difficulties on the plane flight to *Sin City*. As we have five children, we are very much in need of a safe arrival and return.

I am now getting somewhat excited. I have a seminar to teach down in Rhode Island first and then I can pack. I will first pack my evening wear, primarily *dental floss* from Victoria's Secret, assorted colors. I am still in need of a new dress and shoes as we will be seeing a show called "O". I have heard that it is the best show that Vegas has to offer.

I am happy about this whole thing. As difficult as it is to have the kids growing up, it is nice to finally have some quality time with my love muffin. I feel very blessed that we actually like each other as there are so many couples out there who do not, as well as those who may not know if they do or not due to crazy and hectic lives.

January 16th

Still on the subject of love and my impending plane flight, I am grateful to have made it this far, and I have to say that I am looking forward to growing old. I am looking forward to growing into who I am and who I am fully meant to be.

To run the whole course is nothing short of a miraculous gift.

January 17th

Fully present.

I am fully present in my thoughts at the moment. To be fully present where one is and calmly be able to journey inward is a gift of this particular life stage. This gift then grows and matures along with us as we enter a more seasoned stage of life.

With each wrinkle comes more clarity as we have more to look back on. With a shorter distance in front of us, there is less to be concerned about and therefore less to burden our spirits.

We have the confidence of what is behind us. As we look over our shoulder, we can look at the path that we have already traveled with confidence. We have already been there and we have done the best we can with what we experienced and with any surprises that may have jumped out at us.

Images of the faces of those we have loved smile at us. There is a feeling of warmth. The journey so far has been a good one. We turn our heads back around and look straight ahead at the path in front of us. Our posture is straight and sure of itself. We have touched many lives. Without this one spirit that the Creator tossed into this body the world would be a different place. The lives of each and every spirit we knew and loved on this earth would not be the same.

We become aware of and treasure our uniqueness, and realize that the love we have inside is part of us and will remain with us wherever we go.

Breathing deeply, we step forward.

Epilogue

I thought you may want to know how everything turned out and where everyone sort of landed with their lives. The *Rosenbergs* continue to be racist and wear polyester, though they currently reside in a retirement community somewhere in Arizona. *Asumpta* still lives in the New Paltz area though I am not sure what he does. *Mrs. Kowalski*, of course, was a hundred years old back then and has obviously gone to her *great reward*.

My *mother* continues to be organic and my father continues to be a Republican, only now he lives in Florida with his wife. They are retired and play golf a lot. Dad still has his beard though it is neatly trimmed now. Often when he calls, we talk about the Yankees and relish in stories of *the league*.

As far as my organic mother's career, she facilitates workshops on *stress reduction and preventing its toxic effects* and *creating the life you choose to live* and has become quite well known in the greater New York area. As she practices what she preaches, she continues to sun bathe and meditate at every given opportunity and will not eat anything with additives or preservatives. More than likely, she will outlive us all.

Ma, my mother-in-law and a retired elementary school teacher, is quite busy reinventing herself each and every day. She is currently at the helm of the *Hero's Project* for the area's elementary school children and volunteers for the local battered women's shelter and the

Literary Festival, an annual event in the area. Ma currently resides with her husband of forty-two years in northern Massachusetts. They travel together to many places fun and interesting and several of those trips have been to Italy. This, of course, makes me happy for them and jealous for me.

Ma can be found strolling along the streets of Boston donning a pink *Red Sox* hat. For this, she receives a menopausal pardon . . .

My *little sister* resides in New Paltz and is a successful journalist and author. In fact, she was recently published in the New York Times. She is married with three children and spends her summer days at the Town Pool. The town has recently added a playground and rock climbing wall. It is newly landscaped.

Mari resides in the New Paltz area and has three children. She works as an EMT and is in a good mood almost all of the time.

My friend lives in the New Paltz area also and is married to her husband of twenty-two years. She has purple hair though she changes this according to her mood and the lunar schedule. She is currently working as a tattoo artist and rides to work each day on her Harley.

Pony Boy is currently working for the New York State Department of Corrections as a parole officer and I am not making this up. In fact, I recently heard that he was promoted to Assistant Warden. He has a wife and three children.

Mr. Schwartz is retired after working for years with at-risk youth in the area and continues to be a well respected member of the community.

As far as *Vince* and *Mr. Chase*, their inappropriate kissing and fondling eventually caught up with them and unfortunately brought shame to their families and all involved. As these stories are true, this is all I can say.

Floyd Patterson, as most are aware, died within the last couple of years. In addition to being a world renowned athlete, he was a kind person and a source of pride for the town of New Paltz. His presence is greatly missed.

Dan O'Shea continues to live in the area and works with at-risk youth making a big difference in a small corner of the world.

Clancy lived deep into his old age and continued to roam the lanes of New Paltz for quite some time, biting small children on bicycles, Jehovah's Witnesses, and people with bad energy. The day he died was a sad day for all of us and the end of an era.

What ended up happening with Aunt Marla was quite incredible actually. She received a phone call one day from a case worker at a clinic for eating disorders somewhere in New Mexico. Apparently Angela was struggling with anorexia and her condition was severe. No one knew this because it had been so long since anyone had seen or spoken with her. I guess her husband had left her also.

Anyway, Aunt Marla had her house sold within a month. She traded in her Saturn for a cream colored Mercedes convertible and last anyone knew, she was headed to New Mexico to be with Angela. Unfortunately this delayed her visit to an Indian Ashram which had been planned for quite some time, as part of the application process involved being free of personal or family trauma for six months. Once Aunt Marla gains *crisis clearance* she will reschedule her trip. Not only that, but she has given up her martinis and cigarettes and has started painting. She started out with water colors and is now working with oils also.

David, unfortunately continues to be actively alcoholic, numbing his pain and his shame. Hopefully, with all of the recovery and renewal going on with his mother and sister, he will also find his way.

The stories from my childhood are all true, though the names have been changed to protect the guilty. The only exception to this would be our beloved Beagle-Basset. His real name was Clancy and he will be remembered forever.

Principles of the Tao of Menopause

1. *Practice thought control*
2. *Let the little stuff go*
3. *Have a lot of sex*
4. *Embrace spontaneous moments of solitude*
5. *Keep fresh cut flowers in your bathroom at all times*
6. *Take lots of bubble baths*
7. *Turn up the volume and tear up your living room . . . dance, dance, dance . . .*
8. *Protect your minutes by visualizing your day*
9. *Make peace with your past*
10. *Appreciate moments of horizontal quills*
11. *Appreciate skunks*
12. *Embrace the sun*
13. *Get rid of everything that you have not used, worn, or appreciated within the last year*
14. *Acknowledge junctions of choice*
15. *Screen your life of toxic individuals and absolve yourself of all guilt for doing so*

An Attitude of Gratitude
And
A Family Affair

I would like to thank Anne Quinn, my organic mother, for being my editor-in-chief. I am also grateful to the rest of my editing staff, Nancy Smith, Erin Quinn, Lori Boehm, and Dennise Delaney Smith. Thank you to our oldest son, Ryan, for his brilliant cover design as well as to our youngest daughter, Delaney, for her interior illustrations. Thank you once again to my brother-in-law, Kevin Smith, for his help with the publishing process. Thank you to Roger Torres and Jonathan Griffin for their computer wizardry and putting it all together. Thank you also to Dr. David Landers and Neila Anderson Decelles, M.A., for taking the time to review my manuscript and for their kind words of advanced praise for the book.

As it truly does take a village to write a book, I would like to express the most sincere gratitude to the above mentioned individuals. Thank you.

Kimberly

www.ingramcontent.com/pod-product-compliance
Lightning Source LLC
Chambersburg PA
CBHW020939230426
43666CB00005B/88

Resources

The Power of Now *by Eckhart Tolle*
> Copyright 1999 and 2004 by Eckhart Tolle
> Namaste Publishing and New World Library

Thresholds-Navigating The Difficult Transitions in Life*-a talk by poet David Whyte*
> Copyright (2003) by David Whyte and Many Rivers Company

The Secret *by Rhonda Byrne*
> Copyright (2006) by TS Production Limited Liability Company
> Atria Books and Beyond Words Publishing, divisions of Simon & Schuster, Inc.

The Energy of Money *(How Regaining Our Financial Health Reduces Stress, Anxiety, and Depression)*
> By Anne Quinn, M.S., CASAC
> www.anneliz.com

*I did not actually quote any of the above listed resources directly, however, I was inspired by them and wanted to give credit where credit is due.